ORIGINS OF CRIME

THIS IS A PAPERBOUND EDITION OF
PUBLICATION NO. 49 IN THE
PATTERSON SMITH REPRINT SERIES IN
CRIMINOLOGY, LAW ENFORCEMENT, AND SOCIAL PROBLEMS

A listing of publications in the SERIES *will be found at rear of volume*

ORIGINS OF CRIME

A New Evaluation of the Cambridge-Somerville Youth Study

WILLIAM McCORD *and* JOAN McCORD

With IRVING KENNETH ZOLA

Montclair, New Jersey
PATTERSON SMITH

Copyright 1959 by Columbia University Press
Reprinted 1969, with permission, by
Patterson Smith Publishing Corporation
Montclair, New Jersey

Paperback edition 1972

ISBN 0–87585–908–9

Library of Congress Catalog Card Number: 69-14939

*To our parents, who, "After All These Years,"
still allow us "Room for Argument"*

PREFACE

THIS BOOK IS A FURTHER EXAMINATION OF THE CAMBRIDGE-SOMERville Youth Study—a project, begun in the 1930's, which attempted to prevent delinquency and develop character by means of friendly guidance. Our research based on this experiment leads, unfortunately, to some very discouraging conclusions. They are discouraging in that our investigation of the origins of criminality reveals that the roots of crime lie deep in early familial experiences —so deep that only the most intensive measures, applied very early in life, can offer hope of eradicating them.

The research is discouraging, too, for we are forced to admit that the treatment administered by the Cambridge-Somerville program, probably the most extensive and costly experiment in the prevention of delinquency, largely failed to accomplish its goals. It failed primarily because it did not affect the basic psychological and familial causes of crime.

But these are not our only conclusions. Happily, we can also report some positive findings about the causes and course of deviant behavior. For the first time, to our knowledge, it has been possible to study criminality in a developmental manner. Rather than reconstruct causes retrospectively, after men have become criminal, we have had access to a vast fund of information concerning a relatively large number of individuals, gathered before the onset of criminality. From this data we have been able to isolate some of the more crucial sources of crime.

The most important section of this book is, we feel, that part which concerns causation. For as we increase our knowledge of causation, our ability to conquer social problems may also increase. As one consequence of this investigation, we have begun to understand the specific determinants of those crimes which the community regards as the most dangerous.

The subjects of this study are several hundred young men who, as boys in the 1930's, were selected as participants in the Cambridge-Somerville plan. As children, many of them lived in the most blighted, depression-burdened areas of these two Northeastern towns. A number of boys were considered by their teachers and other officials as maladjusted, disordered, pre-delinquent children. But an almost equal proportion were regarded as average, well-adjusted boys. To establish a control group, half of the "normal" boys and half of the maladjusted boys received treatment; the others did not.

Forty percent of all the boys eventually developed criminal records. The two major tasks of this study were: first, to discover what part the Cambridge-Somerville project played in deflecting a boy from a life of crime, and second, to ascertain what forces turned some of the boys into criminals.

The early chapters explain the background of this research; the third describes the effects of treatment; the next chapters delineate the origins of criminality; and the last section contains our speculations concerning the relevance of this research to the community and to the study of human nature.

Many people contributed to the research. Professor Gordon Allport of Harvard suggested the project and originated many of the plans for carrying it out. His advice, encouragement, and criticism of the manuscript were invaluable.

Irving Zola, a Robert Treat Paine Fellow at Harvard, devoted his inexhaustible energy to the task of reading case records, categorizing the backgrounds of the children, and making statistical comparisons. The honors thesis which resulted from his labors exhibited his intelligence and originality. We owe him thanks for many insights.

Edwin Powers, one of the directors of the Cambridge-Somerville program and now Deputy Commissioner of Correction in Massachusetts, always stood ready with practical help and suggestions. Miss Carolyn Briggs and Miss Cecile Meara, as research assistants, gave unstintingly of their time and energy. Mr. Albert Carter, the directors, and the staff of the Massachusetts Board of Probation made possible the compilation of the boys' criminal records.

PREFACE

We are very grateful to the Ella Lyman Cabot Foundation, whose generous financial grant supported the research and to the staff of the Cambridge-Somerville experiment itself. At various points in this book we criticize some of the practices of the project's staff. We do not intend these criticisms to be taken as an attack upon the devotion, sincerity, or intelligence of the people who carried out the difficult program. In reviewing the history of the experiment and the case records where that history was recorded, we have been continually impressed with the quality of the counselors as kind and thoughtful human beings. While they may have failed in attaining the immediate goals of the program, they succeeded in uncovering a mass of knowledge which, in the long run, will advance our understanding of criminality and of human nature. Although we would agree with Gordon Allport that social science has more often focused upon "disease rather than health, upon bad citizenship rather than good, and upon prejudice rather than tolerance and charity," we believe that the discoveries made about the abnormal human being will ultimately contribute to our knowledge of the normal, healthy state of man.

WILLIAM McCORD
JOAN McCORD

Stanford, California
July, 1958

CONTENTS

I.	An Attempt to Prevent Delinquency	1
II.	Aims and Methods of Our Study	9
III.	The Effects of Treatment	19
IV.	The Origins of Crime	62
V.	Family Structure and Crime	104
VI.	The Choice of the Criminal Act	124
VII.	The Age of Criminality	157
VIII.	A Summary of the Causes of Crime	166
IX.	Implications for the Future	173
	Appendixes	
A.	Juvenile Delinquency in the Treatment Group	201
B.	Origins of Crime in the Control Group	203
	Works Cited	209
	Index	211

TABLES

1.	Number of Convictions	20
2.	Number of Boys Convicted for Various Crimes, 1938–1955	20
3.	Number of Convictions for Various Crimes, 1938–1955	21
4.	Age and Number of Boys Convicted for Crimes Other Than Traffic Violations	21
5.	Number of Convictions in Various Age Groups for Crimes Other Than Traffic Violations	21
6.	Traffic-Crime Convictions in Various Age Groups	22
7.	Convictions for Crimes after Release from Reform School	23
8.	Relation of Length of Treatment to Crime Rate	26
9.	Relation of Number of Counselors to Crime Rate	26
10.	Relation of Length of Treatment by First Counselor to Crime Rate	27
11.	Relation of Individual Counselors to Crime Rate	28
12.	Relation of Counselors of Predicted Delinquents to Crime Rate	28
13.	Relation of Age at Start of Treatment of All Predicted Delinquents to Crime Rate	29
14.	Relation of Age at Start of Treatment of Boys Predicted on Borderline of Delinquency to Crime Rate	29
15.	Relation of Age of Boy and Sex of Counselor to Crime Rate	30
16.	Relation of Treatment Intensity to Crime Rate and Incarceration Rate	32
17.	Relationship between Treatment Intensity and Boy's Personality	33
18.	Relationship between Treatment Intensity and Mother's Personality	34

TABLES

19.	Relation of Treatment Intensity and Boy's Personality to Crime Rate	35
20.	Relation of Treatment Intensity and Mother's Personality to Crime Rate	36
21.	Relation of Intelligence Levels to Crime Rate and Incarceration Rate	66
22.	Relation of Type of Neighborhood to Crime Rate and Incarceration Rate	71
23.	Relation of Mother's Religion to Crime Rate	73
24.	Relation of Father's Religion to Crime Rate	73
25.	Relation of Parental Discipline to Crime Rate and Incarceration Rate	77
26.	Relation of Home Atmosphere to Crime Rate and Incarceration Rate	83
27.	Relation of Home Atmosphere and Parental Discipline to Crime Rate	84
28.	Percent of Each Type of Home within Each Type of Neighborhood	85
29.	Relation of Home Atmosphere and Type of Neighborhood to Crime Rate	86
30.	Relation of Father's Personality to Crime Rate and Incarceration Rate	90
31.	Relation of Parental Discipline and Father's Personality to Crime Rate	92
32.	Relation of Father's Personality and Role Model to Crime Rate	93
33.	Relation of Parental Discipline and Father's Role Model to Crime Rate	94
34.	Relation of Mother's Personality to Crime Rate and Incarceration Rate	99
35.	Relation of Parental Discipline and Mother's Personality to Crime Rate	101
36.	Relation of Mother's Role Model to Crime Rate	102
37.	Relation of Mother's Personality and Role Model to Crime Rate	102
38.	Relation of Parental Discipline and Mother's Role Model to Crime Rate	103

39.	Percent of Mothers of Each Personality Type Married to Fathers of Each Personality Type	105
40.	Percent of Fathers of Each Personality Type Married to Mothers of Each Personality Type	105
41.	Relation of Parental Passivity to Crime Rate When Neither Parent Was Loving	106
42.	Relation of Father's Personality and Maternal Passivity to Crime Rate	107
43.	Relation of Mother's Personality and Paternal Passsivity to Crime Rate	107
44.	Relation of Parental Affection to Crime Rate	108
45.	Relation of Father's and Mother's Personality to Crime Rate	109
46.	Relation of Mother's and Father's Personality to Crime Rate	110
47.	Relation of Parental Role Models to Crime Rate	111
48.	Relation of Parental Discipline and Role Models to Crime Rate	111
49.	Relation of Mother's Personality and Father's Role Model to Crime Rate	112
50.	Relation of Father's Personality and Mother's Role Model to Crime Rate	113
51.	Relation of Parents' Personalities and Role Models to Crime Rate	114
52.	Relation of Parental Deviance and Absence of Love to Crime Rate	115
53.	Relation of Son's Role in the Family to Crime Rate	117
54.	Relation of Birth Order to Crime Rate	118
55.	Relation of Mother's Personality to Property Crimes	128
56.	Relation of Father's Personality to Property Crimes	128
57.	Relation of Parental Discipline to Property Crimes	129
58.	Relation of Home Atmosphere to Property Crimes	130
59.	Relation of Mother's Personality to Crimes Against the Person	133
60.	Relation of Father's Role Model to Crimes Against the Person	134
61.	Relation of Parental Discipline to Crimes Against the Person	134

APPENDIX TABLES

62.	Relation of Home Atmosphere to Crimes Against the Person	135
63.	Relation of Mother's Personality to Sex Crimes	138
64.	Relation of Father's Personality to Sex Crimes	138
65.	Relation of Parental Discipline to Sex Crimes	139
66.	Relation of Home Atmosphere to Sex Crimes	140
67.	Relation of Mother's Personality to Drunkenness	142
68.	Relation of Father's Personality to Drunkenness	143
69.	Relation of Parental Discipline to Drunkenness	143
70.	Relation of Home Atmosphere to Drunkenness	144
71.	Relation of Mother's Personality to Traffic Violations	147
72.	Relation of Home Atmosphere to Traffic Violations	147
73.	Relation of Parental Discipline to Traffic Violations	148
74.	Summary of Causal Syndromes	150
75.	Percent of Sons of Each Type of Mother Convicted of Each Type of Crime	153
76.	Percent of Sons of Each Type of Father Convicted of Each Type of Crime	154
77.	Percent of Boys Disciplined in Each Manner Convicted of Each Type of Crime	155
78.	Percent of Boys from Each Type of Home Convicted of Each Type of Crime	156
79.	Age of Criminals at First Conviction	157
80.	Relation of Father's Role Model to Rate of Juvenile Delinquency	164
81.	Relation of Home Atmosphere to Rate of Juvenile Delinquency	164
82.	Relationship between Certain Variables of Criminality and Mother's Personality	171
83.	Predictions of Criminal Behavior and Actual Results	175

APPENDIX TABLES

1.	Relation of Mother's Personality to Rate of Juvenile Delinquency	201
2.	Relation of Father's Personality to Rate of Juvenile Delinquency	201

3.	Relation of Parental Discipline to Rate of Juvenile Delinquency	202
4.	Relation of Intelligence Levels to Rate of Juvenile Delinquency	202
5.	Relation of Intelligence Levels to Crime in the Control Group	203
6.	Relation of Type of Neighborhood to Crime in the Control Group	204
7.	Relation of Home Atmosphere to Crime in the Control Group	204
8.	Relation of Home Atmosphere and Type of Neighborhood to Crime in the Control Group	205
9.	Relation of Father's Personality to Crime in the Control Group	205
10.	Relation of Father's Personality to Crime in the Treatment Group	206
11.	Relation of Mother's Personality to Crime in the Control Group	206
12.	Relation of Parental Affection to Crime in the Control Group	206
13.	Relation of Father's Role Model to Crime in the Control Group	207
14.	Relation of Mother's Role Model to Crime in the Control Group	207

ORIGINS OF CRIME

CHAPTER I

AN ATTEMPT TO PREVENT DELINQUENCY

THE PERIOD OF THE THIRTIES WAS A DISCOURAGING ONE FOR CRIMInologists. This decade opened with an explosive series of prison riots and ended with Cassandras noting an alarming rise in the rate of juvenile delinquency. Its years marked the publication of an important but highly disillusioning piece of research by Sheldon and Eleanor Glueck. After meticulously tracing the lives of several hundred ex-convicts, the Gluecks reached the dismal conclusion that less than 20 percent had reformed.

The year 1935, however, marked the beginning of what many hoped would be the most progressive experiment in many years—the Cambridge-Somerville Youth Study. The project had originated in the fertile mind of Dr. Richard Clarke Cabot, a distinguished physician and social philosopher. Reared in a New England atmosphere which combined reforming zeal with industrious practicality, Cabot had developed the opinion that delinquency could be deflected early in life if only the potentially maladjusted child had an opportunity to form a friendly, understanding relation with another person.

Reviewing reformations he had witnessed, Cabot believed "there [had] been at least one necessary condition: that someone should come to know and to understand the man in so intimate and friendly a way that he comes to a better understanding of himself and a truer comprehension of the world he lives in." [1] Friendship, example, understanding—these were the elements which, in his opinion, led to social living.

Under the leadership of Dr. Cabot, the purpose of the Cam-

[1] Cited by Gordon Allport in his Foreword to Edwin Powers and Helen Witmer, *An Experiment in the Prevention of Delinquency.*

bridge-Somerville Youth Study was to prevent delinquency and to develop stable elements in the characters of the children. Believing that friendship with an adult counselor might prevent criminality, Cabot provided generous funds and formulated extensive plans for the treatment of hundreds of boys over a ten-year period. He selected two industrialized cities in Massachusetts as the setting for the project. Densely populated, dominated by factories, and economically deteriorated, Cambridge and Somerville possessed those social conditions most fertile to delinquency.

The program actually commenced in 1937. Approximately one thousand boys were referred by the city schools, churches, social agencies, and the police department to the Cambridge-Somerville Youth Study. The staff of the project carefully evaluated the boys, selecting a core whom they believed would benefit from individual counseling and social work. To this group of maladjusted children, an equal number of average or "normal" boys were added to counteract a reputation which the project might have developed as a refuge for "bad boys." A total of 650 children was ultimately selected to be subjects of the experiment.

Since Cabot wanted to test the results of treatment, his plans provided for a control group so that the efficacy of his approach could be established as objectively as possible. The treatment group was to receive the counseling offered by the project; the control group would receive only such services as were proffered by the community. Thus, if children treated under the program seemed to be benefited, one could ascertain whether adjustment was a factor of maturation—and therefore not attributable to the Cambridge-Somerville program—or a factor of the treatment itself.

Of course, the control group had to be as nearly similar to the experimental group as possible. Laboriously, the 650 boys were divided into 325 matched pairs. They were equated in terms of physical health, intelligence, emotional adjustment (judged by their teachers), home background (evaluated by a social worker), neighborhood, and "delinquency prognosis." For the "delinquency prognosis" each boy was rated on an eleven-point scale by a committee of judges as to his chances for developing into a criminal. This rating was based on a combination of variables ranging from teachers' ratings of social aggressiveness to social workers' judgments of home conditions.[2]

When each of the boys had been matched to another child, the pair was split: one boy was placed in the treatment group and the other was left to the control group. A flip of the coin left the allotment to chance.

By May, 1939, the assignments had been completed and 325 boys were prepared for treatment. Their average age was eleven—not so young as Cabot had wished, but still, the staff hoped, sufficiently malleable.

Stricken with a heart attack in 1939, Dr. Cabot died before he could witness fruition of the idea he had conceived four years before. Although deprived of his leadership, the Cambridge-Somerville project continued, first under the direction of Dr. P. Sidney de Q. Cabot, later under Mr. Edwin Powers.

Since the children in the project had not requested treatment, counselors on their first visits to the homes were suspected of everything from peddling Fuller brushes (no counselor carried a brief case for fear of being taken as a salesman) to sexual perversion. Surprisingly, however, once the purposes of the study had been explained, very few parents or children refused their cooperation.

What did the treatment involve? In some cases, as Cabot had hoped, it meant a close, intimate friendship between boy and counselor. In most cases, however, treatment consisted of talks between the family and counselor, trips for the children, and medical, dental, or welfare aid whenever it was required. Some counselors, emphasizing educational assistance, tutored the boys in reading and arithmetic. Others acted primarily as coordinators for welfare and family agencies, the Y.M.C.A., and summer camps. Religion formed an important part of the treatment: boys and their families were encouraged to attend church, priests and min-

[2] In making the delinquency prognoses, the following factors were considered: teachers' judgments of the boy's mental health, social adjustment, social aggressiveness, and acceptance of authority; a social worker's opinion of the discipline used in the family, the degree of disruption in the home, and the incidence of delinquency among the child's relatives. The boys received a numerical rating ranging from plus five (least likely to become delinquent) to minus five (most likely to become delinquent). See Chapter IX for information concerning the accuracy of the predictions.

isters were alerted to their problems. Police departments, particularly the juvenile bureaus, kept in close touch with the project.

Counselors avoided making structural changes within the community. That is, they did not form new clubs, neighborhood gangs, or play groups; they did not originate new community projects or seek the building of additional recreational and social facilities. In addition, they shunned initiating radical family changes. Only as a last resort did the counselors remove a child from his home and place him with foster parents.

Although the experiment sought out its "clients" (and continued treatment over a longer period), its methods were similar to those used by the Big Brother Association, progressive probation officers, family welfare agencies, and some mental health clinics. Thus, the Cambridge-Somerville project can illuminate the effectiveness of treatment used by many social agencies concerned with the problem of crime.

The treatment fell short of testing Dr. Richard Clarke Cabot's original hypothesis that a sustained, friendly relation would prevent delinquency. A necessary condition for close relationship is frequent contact; yet counselor turnover and heavy case loads prevented the establishment of close bonds.

The times placed numerous handicaps in the path of treatment. The Second World War necessitated many changes in the counseling staff (a minority of whom were women), and few children had the same counselor throughout their treatment. Gasoline and tire shortages curtailed the counselors' mobility. Also, before the ten-year period had ended, a number of boys had joined the armed forces.

As the years passed, counselors found themselves overloaded with cases. In 1941, their burden was eased by dropping 65 children from the treatment group—boys with good backgrounds who showed no signs of needing further special assistance. Because of a change in neighborhood, military service, or death, another large group of children was dropped. Only 75 boys remained in the "active" file at its closing date, December, 1945.

Although the project had not fulfilled Dr. Cabot's plans either in intensity or in duration of treatment, the staff could look back with satisfaction at their record. A very large number of children

AN ATTEMPT TO PREVENT DELINQUENCY

had received social aid and some individual counseling averaging close to five years per boy. Furthermore, careful records had been kept. Thus, the Cambridge-Somerville project provided an opportunity for evaluation of treatment—analogous to many similar treatment practices—and it stands as a unique event in the battle against delinquency.

The first evaluation of effectiveness was attempted before the program had ended. A variety of psychological tests, a check on school adjustment, and a review of court records failed to turn up any significant differences between the treatment group and the control group.

In 1948, Edwin Powers and Dr. Helen Witmer began a more careful analysis of the experiment. In 1951 *An Experiment in the Prevention of Delinquency*,[3] their report on the outcome of the project, was published. The results proved discouraging.

Despite the fact that many boys with no official court records were known by their counselors to have been delinquent, Powers recognized that official police records offered the best objective measure for assessing the extent to which delinquency had been prevented. So, three years after termination of all treatment, Powers secured official police and court records of all 650 boys. As many treatment as control boys had run afoul of the law.

Powers searched for a more "sensitive" measure of the usefulness of treatment. Hoping to take account of the nature of the delinquencies, he asked a board of judges to rate crimes according to their "seriousness." Although the judges agreed completely in only 59 percent of the ratings, Powers used the "seriousness standard" as a way of differentiating the most delinquent from the least delinquent children. He found that a few more control than treated boys had committed "serious" crimes.

For subjective evaluation, the boys themselves were asked their opinions of the project. Powers' staff interviewed about one third of the treated boys. Of this sample, approximately half said that treatment had been valuable to them in one way or another. Powers presented this conclusion with "a grain of salt." One boy, for example, responded that his counselor had been of great serv-

[3] Edwin Powers and Helen Witmer, *An Experiment in the Prevention of Delinquency* (New York, Columbia University Press, 1951).

6 AN ATTEMPT TO PREVENT DELINQUENCY

ice to him: "He told me what to do—what's right and wrong—not to fool around with girls. It gives a boy a good feeling to have an older person outside the family to tell you what's right and wrong—someone to take an interest in you." [4] Although this boy may have been helped in some intangible way, a few years later he was serving a five-year sentence for a serious sexual offense.

Dr. Witmer, a distinguished social researcher with an entirely different orientation, believed that only a case-by-case analysis could uncover the effects of treatment. In her opinion, conclusions based on comparison of a control group with a treatment group could not "satisfy the clinical worker, who, by the nature of his task, has little interest in averages. What such a person wants to know is whether there are any cases—even if only a few—in which the introduction of the new factor tipped the balance in the boy's favor." [5]

After discarding the boys who had been retired early from the treated group and the boys matched with them from the control group, Dr. Witmer rated each boy on his "terminal adjustment"—primarily his social behavior at the time when treatment ceased—and compared the treatment boys with the control group. She found no significant differences in terminal adjustment between the two groups.

Dr. Witmer next analyzed each of the treatment cases and categorized the boys as having benefited or not benefited from the treatment. (Unfortunately, no check was made on the reliability of these judgments.) Fifty-one of the boys, she concluded, "clearly benefited" from the treatment.

Yet if so many boys did benefit, why had not the treatment group a lower crime rate than the control group? Dr. Witmer answered that we must assume a corresponding number of boys in the control group also improved, or alternatively, we could assume that treatment actually harmed some boys. (She believed that eight of the treated cases may have been harmed by their counselors' methods.)

Dr. Witmer found the greatest improvement among children who were not seriously maladjusted and were not active delinquents. She partly attributed the apparent failure of the general program to inadequate methods on the counselors' part. One counselor, however, was tabbed as being outstandingly effective.

[4] *Ibid.*, p. 159.   [5] *Ibid.*, p. 342.

AN ATTEMPT TO PREVENT DELINQUENCY

Unlike Dr. Witmer, the current authors believe that a statistical comparison of the crime rates of both the treated and the control groups can better lead to conclusions which will aid in the prevention of delinquency. Use of a control group is more likely to determine in an objective fashion whether treatment really "tipped the balance in the boy's favor."

Dr. Witmer questioned, in addition, the possibility of evaluating treatment in the Cambridge-Somerville program in view of the fact that no single theoretical orientation guided the counselors:

> To give a great variety of service to a great variety of boys, each practitioner doing what he thinks best without reference to any commonly held body of theory, seems—control group or no control group—no more a scientific experiment than a medical one would be in which different kinds of medicine were given to patients suffering from different kinds of disorders by doctors who held different theories as to the causes of the illness.[6]

We cannot agree, however, that uniformity is necessary for either effective treatment or for an evaluation of effectiveness. The Cambridge-Somerville project's attempt to match two groups of boys in terms of personality and background approaches the scientific procedure of holding constant all but the treatment factor in question. Although treatment varied from counselor to counselor and from boy to boy, this variation can itself be studied by the investigator. If differences had appeared between treatment and control groups, this would be an indication that some forms of treatment were effective. The task for the evaluator would then be to isolate those forms of treatment which did secure the beneficial results.

In summary, the analyses conducted by Powers and Witmer, three years after termination of the project, seemed almost totally discouraging. Dr. Witmer commented: "Dr. Cabot's hypothesis . . . appears to be disproved."[7] Edwin Powers wrote: "The special work of the counselor was no more effective than the usual forces in the community in preventing boys from committing delinquent acts."[8] About 40 percent of the children in each group developed official criminal records. If the Cambridge-Somerville program truly failed, its results cast serious doubts upon the effectiveness of other community services.

[6] *Ibid.*, p. 343.   [7] *Ibid.*, p. 573.   [8] *Ibid.*, p. 337.

Aside from the subjective testimony of the boys, only one indication of a positive result from treatment appeared in these early evaluations: fewer boys from the treatment group were sentenced to institutions for adult criminals. Fifteen control boys as compared to 8 treatment boys served time in Massachusetts prisons.

Professor Gordon Allport, in his introduction to the first report on the Cambridge-Somerville Youth Study, turned this finding into a hypothesis: "The counselor's efforts may take effect after the boy has been burned. The boy must learn, in part, from hard experience. He then learns more surely if he has had the benefit of friendly precept and example." [9]

Edwin Powers, too, projected a hope for the future: "Our belief (admittedly based on slight evidence) that in the next decade there will be a preponderance of adult criminals in our control group as compared to our treatment group must, of course, be checked at some later date." [10]

In 1955, the present study took up the task of following the Cambridge-Somerville boys. Originally we wished to check only the effectiveness of treatment ten years after its termination. We wanted to know whether the control group had committed more crimes or could more often be found in prison. As the study progressed, however, we became concerned with the comparative effects of different types of treatment, with the relationship of certain varieties of crime to other factors, and especially with the detection of causal syndromes. The largely untapped files of this giant project afforded a unique opportunity for checking many hypotheses.

This book is the record of our findings. Perhaps, if they pave the way to projects as important as that conceived by Dr. Cabot, the Cambridge-Somerville study will have proved its place as a pioneering enterprise, justifying the praise given it by Gordon Allport: "Here is a bold and significant conception of social research, faithfully executed in spite of many obstacles, rich in conclusions, and foreshadowing future developments of greater importance both for social science and for social policy." [11]

[9] *Ibid.*, p. xx.   [10] *Ibid.*, p. 338.   [11] *Ibid.*, p. xxx.

CHAPTER II

AIMS AND METHODS OF OUR STUDY

IN 1955, TEN YEARS HAD ELAPSED SINCE THE TERMINATION OF THE project. It had been sixteen years since the beginning of treatment. Thus, enough time had passed to warrant a long-term evaluation of the project.

As has been suggested, Dr. Cabot's foresight laid the groundwork for two forms of research. On the one hand, the effectiveness of treatment could be measured against a control group for whom no treatment provisions had been made. On the other hand, if treatment failed to induce marked differences, new light could be shed on the genesis of criminal behavior. In fact, the causes of crime came to be our major focus of attention.

Our first serious problem, as Helen Witmer and Edwin Powers had already emphasized, was to decide upon definitions of "crime" and "successful treatment." Powers and Witmer had concentrated on the effectiveness of treatment at the time of its termination. We hoped to follow the lead suggested by their material: perhaps treatment had had a delayed beneficial effect. To answer this question we could either attempt a full-scale investigation of the total "adjustment" of the boys or we might select a single area of adjustment, assuming it to be a central one.

We rejected the first alternative primarily because of the immense difficulty and prohibitive expense involved in tracing the boys, now men, after more than a decade of broken contact. Even had we been able to find them, there would have been the further problem of gathering accurate information about their jobs, marriages, and personalities. (Powers, as we have already remarked, had secured the opinions of the subjects on the beneficiality of treatment from their own point of view. With the passage of seven years since his study there seemed even less likelihood that this technique would be valuable.)

At least as a first evaluation, we felt that some objective measure would be necessary. Because the purpose of the project was to prevent criminality, we decided that court records were the most practical measure of success. Official records have the virtue of relative reliability as well as accessibility. Furthermore, they seemed to be the most pertinent standard by which to assess the success of a project aimed at prevention of delinquency.

Though official records are admittedly incomplete, they probably chronicle a significant portion of the acts which society most condemns. Sheldon and Eleanor Glueck, in their numerous studies, have found from interviews with former convicts that about 10 percent of the men discuss undetected crimes. How many of these revelations are brags and how many men do not discuss undetected crimes càn never be accurately ascertained. In our opinion, it is doubtful that a confirmed criminal can pass through the first thirty years of his life without being apprehended at least once.

There is another criticism often leveled against use of criminal records as a measure of criminality. Some sociologists argue that the records represent only the bias of society against the underprivileged classes. The police, they argue, are more alert for crimes in the slums. Poor families cannot afford to "cover" the crimes of their children, and some officially "criminal" activity does not run counter to lower-class mores. In the Cambridge-Somerville project, however, treatment and control boys came from similar areas and were closely matched according to sociological factors—thus vitiating this particular criticism.

Currently, some sociologists are experimenting with "self-report" techniques as a measure of crime. Unfortunately, the validity of this approach can be established only by intimate and constant observation of the subject or by reference to court convictions. Yet court convictions are the very standard which these sociologists wish to avoid.

To the objection that court records offer but one of the many possible checks on adjustment, we would answer that any distinction between "adjustment" and "maladjustment" is necessarily

AIMS AND METHODS

arbitrary. This experiment, aimed at delinquency prevention, can best be evaluated against the standard it set for itself.

We believe that court convictions offer the best opportunity for unbiased identification of criminals. Whereas records for arrests may be subject to the bias of police, and sentences to correctional institutions to the bias of judges, convictions are a result of the operation of the legal system in its most objective form.

For these reasons, we consider official court records as an adequate, although not perfect, reflection of delinquency and a suitable measure for the assessment of the treatment program.

Through the cooperation of the Massachusetts Board of Probation we secured lifetime court records of the boys. These records noted court actions (not merely arrests) and the disposition of each case. Financial limitations and governmental complications prevented us from gathering such records from other states. However, a check made in 1948 revealed that only 10 percent of the boys were living outside greater Boston. Since this was the period when the boys were eligible for the draft and most likely to have left their home city, it seems fair to assume that Massachusetts records alone would be a valid standard for at least 90 percent of the sample. A few men undoubtedly committed crimes outside Massachusetts, but probably only a small proportion of these men had no record in Massachusetts. Out-of-state crimes were reported in the records if they resulted in conviction for a major felony and if the criminal had, in addition, a Massachusetts record.

All of the treated boys, except those who had died and those who had been dropped in 1941 (we, of course, dropped their matched mates from the control group), were included in the 1955 study. The dropped cases had been judged as not requiring the services of the study and had received very little treatment. Like Dr. Witmer, we believed that these men were not fair samples of the treatment's effects.

Naturally, one of the foremost goals of our study was to ascertain whether the treatment group produced fewer criminals than the control group. Had the treated boys committed a smaller number of crimes? Had they committed different types, perhaps less serious kinds, of crime? Had fewer of them served sentences in penal institutions?

Hoping to uncover differences which might be obscured in an over all comparison, we held various factors constant. Each of these factors, we thought, might alter the effects of treatment. We posed a series of questions.

1. Did the treatment's effectiveness in preventing crime vary with the age of the boys? Although many of those connected with the Cambridge-Somerville experiment were disappointed with the 1948 findings, they hoped that the treatment might have a "latent effect." As the boys grew older, they hypothesized, the treatment group might contain comparatively fewer criminals.

2. Did the method used in treatment affect the outcome? Dr. Witmer, among others, maintained that certain types of treatment led to successful adjustment. We wanted to test this hypothesis—not in relation to general adjustment, but in terms of the boys' criminal behavior.

3. Did the value of treatment vary with intelligence? Perhaps more intelligent children were better able to respond to the treatment.

4. Did the duration of therapy have any effect? Some of the boys were under the project's supervision for three years; some for as long as seven years. Did longer treatment result in less criminality?

5. How important was the part played by the personality of the counselor? Dr. Witmer found that certain counselors were of "more value" to their children than others. We wished to test this finding in relation to criminal acts.

6. What was the relation between the personality of the child and the outcome of treatment? Dr. Witmer judged the program to be more valuable to the child unhampered by serious emotional maladjustment. We wanted to know whether this assertion was borne out by the children's long-range criminal records and, in addition, whether a particular *kind* of boy treated with a certain *type* of method was less apt to commit crimes than was a different sort of boy treated with the same method or than was a similar type of boy under a different method of treatment.

7. Did the personality of the child's mother, of his father, or his general home atmosphere make a difference in the treatment's success? One might hypothesize that treatment would have been

most effective if the mother had been loving. Such a mother should be cooperative and probably eager to help the counselor. Equally, however, one could hypothesize that if the mother was neglecting or rejecting, treatment might be most effective: the counselor would then fill an important need for the child. We wanted to test both of these hypotheses and to extend them to other familial relationships.

8. Did the child's neighborhood make a significant difference in the treatment's effect? Did children from the worst slum areas respond to treatment less favorably than those from relatively good neighborhoods? It could be argued that to the degree neighborhood conditions counteracted treatment, the effect of counseling would be weakened.

To answer these questions we compared the treatment and the control group, holding constant the variables to be tested (and using the two-tailed Chi-square test of significance). In answering the last question, for example, we compared the number of criminals among the treatment boys who had lived in the poorest neighborhoods with the number of criminals among the control boys from similar neighborhoods; we then followed this procedure in comparing treatment and control boys reared in other types of neighborhoods.[1] In later pages we describe with more detail how the selections and comparisons were made.

One central issue in the 1955 study was the effectiveness of treatment and how that effectiveness was governed by other factors. But we were also vitally interested in the problem of causation. Reliable information about causation, we believe, is a necessary prerequisite to effective prevention of crime.

The Cambridge-Somerville experiment primarily attempted to prevent delinquency. It sought to obtain, through a controlled test of treatment, possible cures. Yet due to the foresight of its directors, a mass of evidence concerning the etiology of crime was accumulated. The project's workers played with, interviewed, counseled, and advised hundreds of children. Social workers investigated the neighborhoods and recorded the school progress of

---

[1] At the beginning of the experiment, the boys had been matched on the basis of many factors. In making our 1955 comparisons, we had more complete information about the boys and therefore felt justified in using our own information as the basis for equating the control group and the treatment group.

each boy. Perceptive investigators visited their homes, talked with their parents, and observed their families. Psychologists and psychiatrists measured intelligence and analyzed the personalities of the children. From all this came thousands of pages of records.

Seldom has so large a group of children been so carefully studied over such a long period of time. The social and psychological observations, dating back to 1937, told about their boyhood homes, their families, their neighborhoods, and their personalities. We knew which boys had been convicted of crimes. The results of matching these pieces of information would, we believed, yield valuable insights.

During the treatment years, the staff had observed certain conditions which seemed to lead to crime. In their 1948 evaluation, Powers and Witmer reported some of these impressions. Their conclusions have been summarized by Gordon Allport:

> It is the home emotionally broken in an irreparable manner that predisposes to crime. This finding fortifies social psychologists in their claim that all sources of moral ideals pale in comparison wtih parental influence. Children absorb both their ethical and their religious ideals from parents where—if this basis for identification is lacking, or if the parents himself is an antisocial model—the child rarely becomes a good citizen.[2]

In 1955, we wished to test these etiological conclusions and to examine certain additional causative factors which had not been analyzed. As in our investigation of the effects of treatment, we asked a variety of questions.

1. Does the child's intelligence, or other "biological" factors, affect whether or not he becomes criminal? At various periods in the history of criminology, theories have linked health, intelligence, glandular disorders, and other physical variables with crime.

2. What influence do gang membership and cultural conflict have in the causation of crime? Is it correct, as many sociologists assert, that the roots of crime lie primarily, if not entirely, in the delinquent sub-culture?

3. What effect does parental discipline have on the origina-

---

[2] Gordon Allport, in his Foreword to Edwin Powers and Helen Witmer, *An Experiment in the Prevention of Delinquency.*

tion of crime? Does firm, punitive discipline or discipline which depends primarily on the withdrawal of love have more success in preventing delinquency?

4. We wanted to see what relation the personality of the child's parents and his general home atmosphere have to criminality. Did the material gathered seven years later, we asked, support Allport's summarization? This query gave rise to several new questions. If, as might be expected, familial patterns influence delinquency, is there a perceptible difference between the influence of the mother and that of the father? Is one particular factor of the parent-child relationship—parental affection, disciplinary techniques used by the parents, or the actual behavior of the parents as role models—of greater importance than others? Is it possible that home influence is subordinate to other social influences?

5. Is there a relationship between early environment and specific types of crimes?

We wanted to discover not only the discrete effects of each of these factors on crime, but, as far as possible, their combined effects. If the child, for example, had a loving mother and a rejecting father, was he more likely to become a criminal than the child who had a rejecting mother but a loving father? Does discipline have a direct effect on criminality or does its influence depend on other conditions in the family? By finding answers to these types of questions we hoped to separate the primary from the secondary causative factors of criminality.

In a supplementary way, we wished to ascertain the accuracy of delinquency prediction.[3] Had the prognoses assigned to the children at the beginning of the study proven accurate? Were there single factors which might yield reliable predictions? Is there a possibility of predicting types of criminality as well as criminality itself?

Before we could begin to answer these questions, the thousands of pages of records needed to be systematized. For several months we read reports written by counselors, home visitors, psychologists, and social workers. As we read, we noted the descriptions they

---

[3] See Sheldon and Eleanor T. Glueck, *Unraveling Juvenile Delinquency*, for information about the prediction of delinquency.

made of the factors which interested us. We then established general categories for each variable. These categories and their definitions are described in detail as we discuss each of the findings. After six months of reading cases, five workers had codified almost every case within each of the variables.

The reliability of this approach turned out to be satisfactory. In a random selection of 10 percent of the cases from the treatment group, three judges agreed in their ratings 88 percent on discipline, 88 percent on mother's personality, 80 percent on over-all home atmosphere, 80 percent on father's personality, 80 percent on type of treatment, and 75 percent on boy's personality.

The records on the control-group cases were less complete. Not unexpectedly, therefore, we found that classification could not be as precise as with the treatment group. Thus, we made less fine distinctions within the variables for the control cases. Three judges, in their ratings of control boys, agreed 65 percent on mother's personality, 70 percent on home atmosphere, 70 percent on father's personality, and 65 percent on boy's personality.

In addition to the difference in reliability of our judgments in categorizing the treatment cases and the control cases, we felt there was also a difference in the validity of the records themselves. Case records of the treatment boys contained reports of several counselors, social workers, teachers, and at least one psychologist, one doctor, and one nurse, plus many community officials who had known the child. Not only did the records represent many points of view, but they extended over about five years. Changes in the boys, in their families, and in their environments could be followed.

The control boys, on the other hand, had been seen only during a brief time. Interviews with their families, intelligence tests, and a few other reports comprised the Cambridge-Somerville records on the control group. Within these limits, the investigation had been as thorough as possible. Though the information about these boys was less complete, we believed the records of the control group could be used sparingly.

In summary, we extracted and categorized a number of variables from the voluminous case histories. We used the same method for treatment and for control boys, although with the control group we attempted fewer analyses.

AIMS AND METHODS

Before describing our results, one crucial point should be emphasized. In categorizing the cases under each variable—in deciding, for example, which child had been rejected, which loved, which neglected—*we had no prior knowledge of their criminal records*. We did not first select the delinquents and then look back to see factors which correlated with criminality; nor did we first find out which men had become criminals and then attempt to ascertain why treatment failed. Rather, we first made judgments about the various factors in their background and therapy, and only then looked to see how these variables related to crime.

In other words, though we may have been subtly biased in making our judgments, though our standard of crime may have certain defects, and though the records themselves might not have been entirely accurate, *we could not have been influenced by knowledge of later delinquency*. This is important to emphasize, for unfortunately some inaccurate conclusions can be drawn from retrospective analyses of the lives of criminals. If an investigator knows which of his subjects are criminal, his judgments about causes may be unconsciously influenced.

From the two sources of information regarding the Cambridge-Somerville boys—files providing data on childhood and court records indicating criminality—we could compare a non-criminal to a criminal population. In discussing the effect of broken homes, for example, we could compare the incidence of criminality among boys from broken homes to that among boys from cohesive homes.

The methodological virtues and faults of our study of causation can be summarized in the following fashion.

The deficiencies of our approach are that (1) some criminals may have escaped detection and a court conviction, for our definition of crime is "operational"; (2) some men may have been convicted of official crimes, not noted in our records; and (3) some variables which might influence crime (such as the child's experiences during the very first years of life) were not directly observed by the staff.

The virtues of our approach are that (1) "retrospective bias" was eliminated because the study was made prior to the onset of criminality; (2) judgments about the environmental conditions of the boys' early lives were based on direct observation of behavior, made in a variety of situations, over an extended period of time, by a number of different observers; and (3) the "halo effect" in rating was kept to a minimum by strict definition of categories and a continuing check on the contamination of one factor by another.[4]

This brief outline of the aims and methodology of our study will be expanded as we examine each of the results. Now we are ready to discuss the two major issues posed by the Cambridge-Somerville Youth Study: Did treatment help to prevent criminality? What factors in this group of five hundred human beings tended to produce criminal activity?

[4] A recent book by F. Ivan Nye, *Family Relationships and Delinquent Behavior* (New York, John Wiley and Sons, 1958), has been published since the authors finished writing theirs. Nye's research (on a group of high school students) investigated many of the same causal variables as does this project. In most cases, the results of our work and Nye's lead to the same conclusions. At certain points, however, the findings conflict (e.g., Nye places less emphasis on parental rejection of the child, more emphasis on the child's "rejection" of his parents). These disagreements stem from three differences between the studies. One, Nye's study dealt primarily with minor violators of the law; we included major criminals as well. Two, Nye's study was retrospective; ours was longitudinal (thus, Nye argues that parental rejection of the child may follow the child's crime while our study shows that rejection preceeds the crime). Three, Nye leveled many justified criticisms against the use of incarceration or "official" convictions as a standard of crime. For his standard he substituted a questionnaire about illegal behavior. This approach is open to a number of criticisms—for example, the investigator does not know the honesty of these self-reports. It is interesting to note that Nye's only measure of the validity of the questionnaire was that it successfully differentiated between incarcerated delinquents and a high school population (although 13 percent of the incarcerated delinquents were not spotted by the questionnaire). Indirectly, therefore, Nye was forced to recognize that community definitions of crime (arrest and detention) represent the basic criterion. In our study, as we have explained, official conviction for a crime served as the definition of criminality.

CHAPTER III

THE EFFECTS OF TREATMENT

IN 1948, BOTH HELEN WITMER AND EDWIN POWERS CONCLUDED THAT the Cambridge-Somerville Youth Study had not fulfilled its major goal of preventing crime; they found no substantial difference in crime rate or personality between the boys who had undergone treatment and those who had not.

Critics pointed out many defects in the treatment program. By 1955—and even while the program was in progress—the Cambridge-Somerville study did not represent the social worker's ideal of casework. Yet it resembled in practice, if not in theory, many current procedures which are still in use today. More than half the treated boys had received academic tutoring. Over a hundred had been given medical attention. Most of the group had been brought into contact with the Y.M.C.A., Boy Scout activities, or other community programs. Approximately one third of the boys received direct counseling about their personal problems; a number of these were offered limited psychotherapy. In addition, the counselors offered advice and help to almost all the boys' families.

Each of the boys was encouraged to look to his counselor for assistance of any kind. Yet the counselors, because of heavy case loads, saw only a small proportion of the boys with any degree of regularity. Frequently, too, such meetings were casual; several boys would be taken on trips around the neighborhood or would meet for athletic activities.

Although we do not claim that an evaluation of the Cambridge-Somerville Youth Study can be generalized to programs which employ other methods, we hope that information resulting from this extended attempt to prevent crime will be of help to organizations whose aims and methods are similar to those of the study.

A General Evaluation of Treatment

By 1955, of the 253 boys who received treatment,[1] 27 had records only for traffic convictions and 104 had committed at least one other type of crime which led to a court conviction. From the control group, 35 boys had been convicted for traffic violations and 93 had committed at least one other crime. Thus, 41 percent of the boys who underwent treatment committed non-traffic crimes, compared to 37 percent of the control boys. The two groups also committed approximately the same number of crimes (Table 1). The criminals who had received treatment committed an average of three non-traffic crimes apiece and the control criminals committed an average of 3.2 non-traffic crimes.

TABLE 1. NUMBER OF CONVICTIONS

Type of Crime	Treatment Group	Control Group
Non-traffic	315	344
Traffic	171	127
	486	471

Not only did both groups commit about the same number of crimes, but they also did not differ in the type of crimes committed. We categorized the men's criminal records into five basic types: crimes against property, crimes against the person (e.g., armed robbery, manslaughter, attempted homicide), sex crimes, drunkenness, and traffic violations. There was no significant difference [2] between the two groups in the number of boys convicted for each type of crime (Table 2); nor did the treated boys commit significantly fewer crimes of each type (Table 3).

TABLE 2. NUMBER OF BOYS CONVICTED FOR VARIOUS CRIMES, 1938–1955

Type of Crime	Treatment Group	Control Group
Property	86	77
Person	14	15
Sex	12	15
Drunkenness	46	37
Traffic	70	67

[1] We eliminated from our study the 65 boys in the treatment group who had been retired early and the 7 boys who had died. The boys with whom they had been matched were dropped from the control group.

[2] Throughout the study, we used the Chi-square test of significance, two-tailed.

EFFECTS OF TREATMENT

TABLE 3. NUMBER OF CONVICTIONS FOR VARIOUS CRIMES, 1938–1955

Type of Crime	Treatment Group	Control Group
Property	212	224
Person	17	20
Sex	14	17
Drunkenness	72	83
Traffic	171	127

In 1948, Gordon Allport and Edwin Powers, hopeful that there would be a "latent effect" of treatment, hypothesized that as the boys reached maturity those who had received treatment might be more stable and thus less apt to become criminal.

We did, indeed, find that with maturity there was a tendency toward decreasing criminality. Yet comparison of the treatment and the control groups shows clearly that this decrease was not a function of the treatment. No significant differences between the treated group and the untreated group appeared for any type of crime (other than traffic violations) in any age category (Table 4). Nor did the number of crimes of each type, broken down by age, differ significantly (Table 5). Contrary to our expectations,

TABLE 4. AGE AND NUMBER OF BOYS CONVICTED FOR CRIMES OTHER THAN TRAFFIC VIOLATIONS

	TYPE OF CRIME							
	PROPERTY		PERSON		SEX		DRUNKENNESS	
Age	T	C	T	C	T	C	T	C
Under 13	18	16	1	1	0	1	0	0
13–18	55	51	5	3	4	3	5	5
19–22	37	27	6	7	6	7	29	24
Over 22	17	17	4	5	2	3	18	18

Note: "T" refers to the treatment group; "C" to the control group.

TABLE 5. NUMBER OF CONVICTIONS IN VARIOUS AGE GROUPS FOR CRIMES OTHER THAN TRAFFIC VIOLATIONS

	TYPE OF CRIME							
	PROPERTY		PERSON		SEX		DRUNKENNESS	
Age	T	C	T	C	T	C	T	C
Under 13	23	21	1	1	0	1	0	0
13–18	112	120	6	3	4	3	6	8
19–22	56	58	6	10	7	9	36	52
Over 22	21	25	4	6	3	3	30	23

Note: "T" refers to the treatment group; "C" to the control group.

however, records for traffic convictions showed that a significantly higher proportion of the treated boys were convicted for traffic violations between the ages of twenty-three and thirty (P < .05)[3] (Table 6).

TABLE 6. TRAFFIC-CRIME CONVICTIONS IN VARIOUS AGE GROUPS

Age	NUMBER OF BOYS CONVICTED		NUMBER OF CONVICTIONS	
	T	C	T	C
Under 13	0	1	0	1
13–18	8	12	11	15
19–22	45	42	96	71
Over 22	40	24	64	40

Note: "T" refers to the treatment group; "C" to the control group.

In both groups, the greatest number of property crimes were committed during adolescence; the number of sex crimes, attacks against people, drunkenness, and traffic violations reached a crest between the ages of nineteen and twenty-two. Thereafter criminality decreased both for the treatment and for the control group. Without realizing that a general reduction in criminality occurs with increasing age, one might mistakenly credit the Cambridge-Somerville experiment—or other types of treatment programs—with these "reformations."

Why this decrease in criminality occurs is something of a mystery; some investigators credit it to maturation. We incline to the belief that changes in the social roles of the individual account for the decline. Later in the book, we will examine the issue in greater detail. We do know, however, that the decrease is not due to the fact that many serious criminals are in prison during their twenties. On the contrary, more boys were in reform school during the period of greatest crime, adolescence, than there were men in prison during adulthood.

Twenty-three treatment boys and 18 control boys served time in reform school.[4] Yet less than half as many treated boys as control boys were sentenced to adult institutions (jails and prisons).

[3] X^2 4.6; d.f. 1. Traffic violations were of a relatively serious nature since they were offenses which appeared on the dockets of higher courts.

[4] The discrepancy in the figures presented here concerning commitment to reform school and those presented in the Powers and Witmer report is due to the fact that 4 control boys who went to reform school were eliminated because they had originally been matched to 4 of the 65 cases dropped from the treated group.

EFFECTS OF TREATMENT

Twenty-nine control boys and only 14 treatment boys were incarcerated in penal institutions for adults ($P < .02$).[5]

The figures are puzzling since an almost equal number of boys in both groups were convicted by the courts for similar types of crimes at the same age in most instances (Table 4). The procedure of adding together jail and prison sentences seems questionable. Men are sentenced to prison for the more serious offenses, and the difference between the two groups is not statistically significant for prison sentences alone.

There are two other findings that run counter to the assumption that treatment had a delayed effect. The first has already been discussed: as many boys in the treatment group as in the control group were convicted for crimes committed in their twenties. The second appears from an analysis of the boys in both groups who spent time in reform school. After release, equal proportions were convicted for major crimes (Table 7).

TABLE 7. CONVICTIONS FOR CRIMES AFTER RELEASE FROM REFORM SCHOOL

	Treatment Group	Control Group
Boys convicted of major crimes	17	15
Boys convicted only of drunkenness or traffic crimes	2	1
Boys convicted of no crimes	4	2

If a combination of treatment and "a painful experience" had curtailed criminality, one would expect the treatment boys to have a significantly better record than the control group after their release. Yet 74 percent of the boys who received treatment and 83 percent of those who did not commited major crimes after release; 3 boys from the treatment group went to prison after reform school, as did 6 from the control group. In both groups, the majority continued their criminal activities—a sad commentary on the reformative influence of the public juvenile system.

After completion of the over-all analysis, we had uncovered only one (questionably) positive result of treatment: perhaps the Cambridge-Somerville treatment had curtailed the seriousness of adult crimes (if we presume that incarceration in jail is a measure of seriousness), since less than half as many treated boys as control

[5] X^2 5.70; d.f. 1.

boys were thus incarcerated. In any case, the program failed to reduce either the number of criminals or the number of crimes.

Cautioned by this disillusioning finding, we wondered whether the original matching of the treatment and control groups might have hidden some important clues concerning the effects of therapy. Despite the care which had gone into the matching, much had been learned during the intervening years about the causes of crime. We decided to use this research, including our own findings pertaining to causation, as a means for testing more fully the results of treatment. By holding constant various factors in making a comparison between the treatment and the control groups, we could—in effect—correct errors in the initial matching.[6] Again, our results were discouraging. When we held the mothers' personalities constant, the treated boys had no lower crime rate than their counterparts in the control group. There were no significant differences between the control group and the treatment group, regardless of whether the boy's mother had been loving, non-loving, or absent during his childhood. Nor did holding constant the personality of the boy's father uncover positive effects of treatment. There were no significant differences between the control group and the treatment group, regardless of whether the boy's father had been loving, non-loving, or absent.

When we held constant the personalities of both parents, no positive effects of treatment appeared.[7] Whether both parents had been loving, only one loving, or both non-loving, treatment seemed not to lower the crime rate.

Disciplinary techniques used by the parents had no influence on the effects of treatment. No significant differences appeared between the control group and the treatment group, regardless of whether the boys had been disciplined by the withdrawal of love, by physical punishment, or had been left relatively undisciplined.

When we held constant the neighborhood in which the child had lived, no differences appeared between the two groups. It did not matter whether the child's neighborhood had deteriorated

---

[6] Our categorization of the factors held constant is given in Chapter IV.

[7] Treatment boys as compared to control boys reared by totally rejecting parents had a significantly higher crime rate ($P < .05$, X^2 4.0; d.f. 1).

and had a high delinquency rate, was well organized and had little delinquency, or fell between these extremes.

When we held constant the child's general home atmosphere, in no category did treatment result in a lower crime rate. There were no significant differences between the control group and the treatment group for boys from either cohesive, quarrelsome but affectionate, or broken homes. Treatment boys from another type of home—quarrelsome and neglecting homes—had a higher crime rate than control boys from similar types of homes.[8]

Holding constant both neighborhood and home atmospheres, we found no significant differences. Comparing, for example, boys from cohesive homes located in poor neighborhoods, or from non-cohesive homes in good neighborhoods, crime rates of treatment and control groups were similar.

No crime-rate differences appeared between the control group and the treatment group irrespective of whether the child was aggressive, socially conformist, or withdrawn.

There were also no significant differences between the treatment and control groups when we held constant the boys' intelligence scores. Thus it could not be said that boys of high intelligence responded more favorably to treatment.[9]

These findings conflict with Helen Witmer's conclusions. The contradiction can, however, be partly explained. Dr. Witmer found that many of these variables, particularly the child's personality, affected his response to treatment; but Witmer analyzed the treatment boys without comparing them to the control group. Further, she used the children's "terminal adjustment," and not their crime rates, for her assessment. Perhaps emotionally secure children ended treatment with a better personality adjustment, even though their criminal rates did not differ significantly from children who had not received treatment.

We conjectured that longer treatment might have resulted in decreased crime. The figures, however, do not support this view [10] (Table 8). The trend would lead one to the strange conclusion

[8] $P < .01$, X^2 6.7; d.f. 1.
[9] Treated boys with average intelligence had an almost significantly higher rate of crime than control boys.
[10] In tabulations of many "traits," information was lacking for at least a few of the boys. Thus the total number of boys in some tables is less than 253.

TABLE 8. RELATION OF LENGTH OF TREATMENT TO CRIME RATE

Duration of Treatment		Percent of Boys Convicted of Crimes
Less than four years	(N: 82)	35
Four to six years	(N: 65)	29
More than six years	(N: 106)	53

Note: "Percent of boys convicted of crimes" refers, throughout this book, to the proportion of boys who committed at least one major crime and were convicted in a state or federal court for this action. If a boy committed only traffic violations, he was considered non-criminal.

that longer treatment led to increased crime. But the length of treatment reflected, to a large degree, the counselors' opinions regarding the seriousness of a case. Boys who had few emotional problems or who presented no difficulties within their society were those dropped most quickly by the project. Often, when the staff believed that a boy's problems had been resolved, they dropped him from the experiment. The children given the longest treatment were, generally, those who had the most serious problems. Thus, the apparent increase in crime rate with increase in length of treatment is understandable. Actually, the length of treatment bore no direct relation to criminality.

One of the greatest handicaps of the program lay in the change of counselors. Dr. Cabot had hoped that each boy could become attached to one adult who would remain a constant, close friend. The intervention of war caused many counselors to leave; others drifted away into different jobs. Cabot's hopes were not fulfilled. Only a minority of the boys stayed with the same counselor throughout their time with the program.

We used two approaches in testing whether counselor turnover had been responsible for the discouraging results of the treatment program. First, we examined the crime rate in relation to the number of counselors who had been assigned to each boy (Table

TABLE 9. RELATION OF NUMBER OF COUNSELORS TO CRIME RATE

Number of Counselors		Percent of Boys Convicted of Crimes
One	(N: 72)	43
Two	(N: 88)	30
Three	(N: 47)	53
More than three	(N: 46)	48

9). Second, we examined the length of treatment by the boy's first counselor (Table 10). This, like the number of counselors assigned to each boy, did not seem to have any appreciable effect.

TABLE 10. RELATION OF LENGTH OF TREATMENT BY FIRST COUNSELOR TO CRIME RATE

Duration of Treatment		Percent of Boys Convicted of Crimes
Less than two years	(N: 38)	47
Two to three years	(N: 134)	39
More than three years	(N: 81)	42

An assumption that continuous contact should be beneficial to the child seems theoretically sound. Yet the changes in counselors do not seem to account for the failure of the program.

In summary, we found that the treatment program as it was carried out on the 253 boys failed to achieve its goal of preventing crime. Not only had equal numbers of boys from the treatment and the control groups become criminals, but we also found that equal proportions had continued in their criminal behavior. Furthermore, there were no significant differences between the two groups either in the types or in the numbers of crimes committed. The single suggestion—and it is little more than a suggestion—that the treatment boys may have been deflected from their criminal careers comes from a comparison of the men sentenced to jail and prison. This comparison does not grant conclusive evidence, however—it is possible, for example, that counselors acted as "friends in court" for some of their charges and secured lighter sentences for them.

Evaluation of Variations in Treatment

Diversity of treatment has been responsible for much of the criticism leveled against the experiment. We hoped that a shift in tack—a comparison of how different kinds of treatment affected the boys—might reveal some hopeful trends. Perhaps the character of the counselors or the nature of the boys had some relation to the effectiveness of treatment. Dr. Witmer, in her earlier evaluation, had noted that one counselor achieved rather striking results—at least, in terms of the "personal adjustment" of the boys counseled by her. In order to discover whether the counselors differed in their ability to prevent criminal behavior, we grouped the boys according to their first counselors. We then calculated the average prediction scores (the judgments made by the staff at the start of treatment) assigned to the boys at the beginning of the project and their average age. Ranked in order of the average prediction, the crime rates for boys first assigned to each of the ten original counselors are shown in Table 11.

TABLE 11. RELATION OF INDIVIDUAL COUNSELORS TO CRIME RATE

Counselor	Mean Prediction Score	Mean Age of Boys When Treatment Began	Percent of Boys Convicted of Crimes
A (N: 27)	plus .9	9.5	19
B (N: 15)	plus .7	10.0	20
C (N: 29)	plus .3	10.8	52
D (N: 22)	plus .2	11.2	41
E (N: 26)	plus .2	10.5	50
F (N: 27)	0	10.0	41
G (N: 27)	minus .5	10.1	56
H (N: 26)	minus .7	9.9	31
I (N: 27)	minus .9	10.5	41
J (N: 27)	minus 1.3	10.8	52

Looking over Table 11, one notes the general pattern of lower crime rates among boys who were predicted as "plus," or nondelinquent. Thus, counselor A, whose boys were predicted as being the least delinquent, had the lowest crime rate. Yet the boys of counselor H, who were predicted as highly delinquent, in fact, had the third-lowest crime rate. Here, therefore, was evidence that one counselor was more effective than any of the

TABLE 12. RELATION OF COUNSELORS OF PREDICTED DELINQUENTS TO CRIME RATE

Counselor	Mean Minus Prediction Score	Percent of Boys Convicted of Crimes
D (N: 13)	.9	31
B (N: 10)	1.0	30
E (N: 17)	1.2	65
F (N: 18)	1.3	44
A (N: 10)	1.3	50
H (N: 19)	1.7	32
C (N: 17)	1.8	59
G (N: 18)	1.8	72
J (N: 22)	1.9	64
I (N: 19)	2.1	58

others. This view is partly confirmed when one examines only those boys who were predicted as "potential delinquents" (Table 12). Once again, those boys assigned to counselor H had a lower crime rate than would normally be expected. (Incidentally, counselor H is not the person singled out by Witmer for praise, although this person, counselor I, also produced relatively fewer criminal boys.) Those of us who had the opportunity to read the day-by-day descriptions of counselor H and his methods could not find any unique quality in his work which distinguished him from the other counselors. Perhaps, we assumed, his success could be attributed to the younger age of his charges.

To test this proposition, we examined the relationship between age and success of treatment. The analysis in Table 13

TABLE 13. RELATION OF AGE AT START OF TREATMENT OF ALL PREDICTED DELINQUENTS TO CRIME RATE

Age of Boy		Mean Prediction Score	Percent of Boys Convicted of Crimes
5–8	(N: 39)	plus .6	26
9	(N: 35)	minus .4	29
10	(N: 47)	minus 1.1	66
11	(N: 56)	minus .3	45
12–13	(N: 76)	minus .1	37

clearly indicates that the child under ten was more responsive to treatment ($P < .001$).[11] Yet the age groups were not equivalent, for the younger children were less often predicted as future delinquents. To hold this factor constant, we analyzed only those children who were predicted as being "on the borderline" of delinquency (boys whose predicted score was either plus or minus three through five were eliminated).

TABLE 14. RELATION OF AGE AT START OF TREATMENT OF BOYS PREDICTED ON BORDERLINE OF DELINQUENCY TO CRIME RATE

Age of Boy		Mean Prediction Score	Percent of Boys Convicted of Crimes
5–9	(N: 56)	minus .2	29
10	(N: 32)	minus .5	59
11–13	(N: 99)	minus .1	37

Note: Only boys predicted from plus two to minus two were included.

[11] X^2 18.9; d.f. 4.

Again (Table 14), there was strong indication that treatment which commenced at an early age was most beneficial (and counselor H had the second-youngest group of boys). Boys who began treatment when they were less than ten years old were less likely to become criminal, even though they were approximately equivalent to the older children in personality and background ($P < .02$).[12]

We hypothesized that the sex of the counselors, too, might make a difference in the effectiveness of treatment. Because the relationship between mother and child is important in the causation of delinquency, fulfillment of the maternal role by a woman counselor might greatly assist in the prevention of delinquency. A male counselor, however, might provide the ego ideal necessary to deter crime.

Thirty-one percent of the boys who had women as their first counselors, compared to 47 percent of those who had men as their first counselors, were convicted of crimes ($P < .02$).[13] Yet the two groups cannot be equated, because the average age at beginning of treatment for boys with female counselors was younger than that for boys with male counselors. Furthermore, the original assignments placed boys with slightly less favorable predictions in the hands of male counselors (0 mean score for female counselors; minus .3, for males).

In order to discover the effect on treatment of sex of counselor, therefore, we held age constant for an additional comparison (Table 15). Surprisingly, the very young child seemed to respond

TABLE 15. RELATION OF AGE OF BOY AND SEX OF COUNSELOR TO CRIME RATE

	PERCENT OF BOYS CONVICTED OF CRIMES	
Age of Boy	Female Counselor	Male Counselor
5–9	(N: 42) 29	(N: 32) 25
10	(N: 6) 67	(N: 41) 66
11–13	(N: 48) 29	(N: 84) 46

equally to both male and female counseling. (These two groups had different predictive scores.[14]) On the other hand, boys aged

[12] X^2 8.2; d.f. 2.   [13] X^2 6.3; d.f. 1.
[14] Mean predictive scores of boys aged five to nine assigned to female counselors was plus .4; for those assigned to male counselors, 0.

eleven to thirteen who were counseled by females had a significantly lower crime rate than did those boys of the same age who were under the charge of male counselors ($P < .05$).[15] This was true despite the fact that the boys counseled by females in this age group were slightly more often regarded as potential delinquents (minus .1 as compared to 0). It appears that female guidance is at least as valuable as, if not more valuable than, male guidance for adolescent boys. This discovery would seem to suggest a reversal in those programs which leave adolescent guidance to men and discourage the treatment of young boys by males.

Although this study offers no substantial basis for concluding that certain counselors were strikingly more effective than others, the evidence suggests that treatment at an early age may lead to greater prevention of crime.

In an attempt to discover additional information which might have bearing on the results of treatment, we turned next to an analysis of the treatment process itself. All the counselors served as liaison between the schools, churches, and community agencies. In almost every treated case, the counselor devoted close attention to family problems. On one basis, however, treatment varied radically: the amount of interaction a counselor had with the boy and his family. In theory, every counselor was supposed to become a close confidant of the children; in practice, many boys seldom saw their counselor. We used this factor as the primary basis for dividing the treated boys into four categories.

1. Thirty-two children were seen at least once a week for a period of at least six months. In addition, the counselors worked intensively with the families of these boys.

2. Eighty-four children were seen at least once every two weeks over a minimum period of six months.

3. Forty-seven children were seen approximately once a month for a period of a least six months. On the average, the families of these children were visited more regularly than were the boys themselves.

4. Eighty-two children were seen less than once a month during the minimum period. Treatment consisted primarily in arranging memberships in community organizations, securing medical aid

[15] X^2 3.9; d.f. 1.

for the families, sending the boys to summer camps, or mediation between the children and community agencies.

As can be seen from this categorization, startlingly few boys (32) had frequent contact with their counselors even for a short space of time. Obviously, then, the Cambridge-Somerville experiment failed as a large-scale test of the effectiveness of intensive, intimate relationships between socialized adults and pre-delinquent children. Instead, it seems a fair test of the efficacy of the commonly utilized community agencies which emphasize recreation, brief casework, medical aid, and social welfare assistance.

Table 16 indicates a curious relationship between the closeness of therapeutic contact and the criminal rate. Treatment was most

TABLE 16. RELATION OF TREATMENT INTENSITY TO CRIME RATE AND INCARCERATION RATE

Maximum Frequency of Contact		Percent of Boys Convicted of Crimes	Percent of Boys Sentenced to Penal Institutions
Once a week	(N: 32)	25	10
Once in two weeks	(N: 84)	51	15
Once a month	(N: 47)	43	11
Very seldom	(N: 82)	33	12

Note: "Percent of boys sentenced to penal institutions" refers to the proportion of boys who were sentenced at least once to either reform school, jail, prison, or some combination of these institutions.

effective for those children seen most frequently and least effective for those seen once every two weeks. A significant difference in the proportion convicted of crimes appeared when these two groups were compared ($P < .02$).[16] The group seen once every two weeks also had a significantly higher rate of crime than those children seen less frequently ($P < .05$).[17]

Perhaps the counselors unconsciously chose less aggressive boys for their most intensive attention. Or perhaps they chose those children who came from the most favorable home backgrounds, while the boys seen less frequently might have come from less favorable backgrounds. Previous research on this problem has indicated that biased selection of cases is a natural tendency among those who work with delinquents. For example, in our recent research at the Wiltwyck School, a treatment center for delinquent

[16] X^2 6.4; d.f. 1. [17] X^2 4.5; d.f. 1.

EFFECTS OF TREATMENT

and disturbed children, we discovered that the therapists had closest relationships with the less aggressive children.[18]

In order to examine the efficacy of treatment in relation to the child's personality, we classified the children. The records on the Cambridge-Somerville boys allowed a very rough classification of three types of personality, based primarily on behavior. We classified as *withdrawn* 89 children who showed a rather high degree of anxiety, a tendency to fantasy, an introspective turn of mind, and a general manner of withdrawing from life around them. We classified 87 boys, some of whom exhibited tendencies toward cruelty and intense impulsivity, and who were frequently involved in aggressive actions, as *aggressive*. We classified 57 children who had no eccentricity of manner or behavior which set them apart from their fellows, and who showed no intense anxiety and only normal assertiveness, as *socially conformist*.[19]

We used these classifications of the boys' personalities in attempting to check the possibility that the counselors varied the degree of contact depending upon the type of child with whom they were dealing. As Table 17 demonstrates, the Cambridge-Somerville staff had more frequent contact with aggressive boys than with those who were socially conformist. The group which met with their counselors once in two weeks appears to have been disproportionately composed of withdrawn boys. Since aggressive

TABLE 17. RELATIONSHIP BETWEEN TREATMENT INTENSITY AND BOY'S PERSONALITY

Maximum Frequency of Contact	NUMBER OF BOYS, DIVIDED ACCORDING TO PERSONALITY		
	Aggressive	*Socially Conformist*	*Withdrawn*
Once a week	15	5	10
Once in two weeks	28	20	36
Once a month	21	10	13
Very seldom	25	22	28

boys more often become criminal, the superior results which frequent contact achieved cannot be attributed to a biased selection of cases; nor can the poor results with the second group be attributed to the greater aggressiveness of the boys in it.

[18] See William and Joan McCord, *Psychopathy and Delinquency*, Chapter VI.
[19] Three judges agreed on the classification of 75 percent of a random sample.

We looked in another direction for a possible bias. Perhaps one category more than the others was composed of children who came from homes which militated against criminality. If this were the case, the relationship between counselor and boy might simply be a reflection of the child's relationship with his parents. Because the mother's attitude toward her child is particularly important in the causation of crime, we chose this variable [20] to compare with intensity of treatment (Table 18).

TABLE 18. RELATIONSHIP BETWEEN TREATMENT INTENSITY AND MOTHER'S PERSONALITY

Maximum Frequency of Contact	Number of Boys with "Loving" Mothers	Number of Boys with "Non-loving" Mothers
Once a week	18	13
Once in two weeks	56	27
Once a month	33	12
Very seldom	55	20

Children who had the most frequent contact with their counselors did not have a higher proportion of loving mothers. Thus, there seems to be some actual, rather than spurious, relationship between frequency of contact with the counselor and rates of crime. The counselors did not establish close relationships because certain children either were less aggressive or came from homes where the parental attitudes might lead to greater responsiveness. Treatment seemed to have a beneficial influence upon those boys who, over a minimum of six months, saw their counselors once a week.

Another important problem involved in evaluating the effects of the various types of therapy is whether the treatment succeeded with one type of child but not with another. The Wiltwyck school research indicated that "milieu therapy" (a complete change in the child's environment), was more effective with aggressive than with withdrawn children.[21] Although classification of the Cambridge-Somerville boys was not as precise, we expected that a close counseling relationship might have a greater influence upon aggressive boys. In fact, some differences did appear, as shown in Table 19.

[20] The method for categorizing the mothers is described in Chapter IV. Three judges agreed in 88 percent of the cases in rating maternal attitudes.
[21] William and Joan McCord, *Psychopathy and Delinquency*.

EFFECTS OF TREATMENT

TABLE 19. RELATION OF TREATMENT INTENSITY AND BOY'S PERSONALITY TO CRIME RATE

Maximum Frequency of Contact	PERCENT OF BOYS CONVICTED OF CRIMES		
	Aggressive Boys	Socially Conformist Boys	Withdrawn Boys
Once a week	(N: 15) 33	(N: 5) 0	(N: 10) 20
Once in two weeks	(N: 28) 50	(N: 20) 50	(N: 36) 47
Once a month	(N: 21)· 52	(N: 10) 40	(N: 13) 15
Very seldom	(N: 25) 52	(N: 22) 36	(N: 28) 21

None of the conforming boys who had frequent contact with their counselors later committed crimes; yet 42 percent of the conforming boys who were less frequently visited had done so. Similarly, only a third of the aggressive boys who had received frequent counseling committed crimes; yet more than half of the other aggressive boys were convicted. The withdrawn children, on the other hand, did not seem to benefit from the greater degree of contact with their counselors. (Twenty percent of those who had the closest contact committed crimes, as compared with 15 percent of those who saw their counselors only once a month and 21 percent of those who seldom saw their counselors.)

Although it appears that frequent counseling is of most benefit to the conforming boys and of least benefit to the withdrawn children, the comparisons yield no statistically reliable information.

Interestingly, counseling once every two weeks appeared to have a decidedly negative effect on the withdrawn children. Such counseling may have been regular enough to be remembered by the child but too infrequent to give the child security. Of those receiving this intermittent treatment, almost half committed crimes; of those receiving other degrees of counseling, however, only one fifth became criminals ($P < .01$).[22] Apparently, if the counselor cannot maintain frequent contact, it is best to leave withdrawn children entirely alone.

Intermittent contact (that is, once very two weeks) between the counselor and his case may exert a harmful influence, perhaps because it appears to the boy as a series of betrayals. Naturally the counselor himself would not look at the process in these terms. Burdened by a heavy case load, concerned with the prob-

[22] X^2 7.6; d.f. 1.

lems of other boys, the counselors did not have the time to build an intimate bond with each of their boys. For the child, however, every long gap between interviews must have seemed like a mild, but still painful, rejection. Tantalizing tastes of friendship interspersed with periods of neglect apparently creates in some children a bitter ambivalence toward other people, particularly authority figures. That this ambivalence is often translated into crime would not be surprising. We speculate that withdrawn children are most affected by these "betrayals" because they may be the most suspicious of other people. Withdrawal, an attempt to avoid contact, is probably a result of painful past experiences. Therefore it seems reasonable to suppose that withdrawn children are most sensitive to the reactions of others and most liable to respond negatively to a "rebuff."

This study leads to the conclusion that intensive contact tends to decrease crime among conformist and aggressive boys; intermittent contact actually seems to increase criminality among withdrawn boys.

Thus, the amount of contact in the counseling relationship affected children differently according to their personalities. We wondered if some differing effects of treatment were due to familial backgrounds. Earlier, we had compared the treatment and control groups, holding constant the mother's personality: there were no differences. Yet, holding constant the mother's personality in order to determine the effects of various degrees of treatment on children with loving and those with non-loving mothers, differences did appear (Table 20). Concentrated treatment (once

TABLE 20. RELATION OF TREATMENT INTENSITY AND MOTHER'S PERSONALITY TO CRIME RATE

Maximum Frequency of Contact	PERCENT OF BOYS CONVICTED OF CRIMES	
	"Loving" Mother	"Non-loving" Mother
Once a week	(N: 18) 22	(N: 13) 31
Once in two weeks	(N: 56) 43	(N: 27) 57
Once a month	(N: 33) 42	(N: 12) 58
Very seldom	(N: 55) 33	(N: 20) 55

a week) resulted in lower criminal rates. For boys reared by non-loving mothers, the difference in conviction rates between those

EFFECTS OF TREATMENT

with frequent and those with infrequent counseling (31%:56%) was significant (P < .05).[23] Among boys with loving mothers, however, those who received frequent counseling did *not* have a significantly lower rate of crime (22%:35%).

As we will later demonstrate, a lack of maternal affection causes a high rate of crime. Of those boys who had not receive frequent counseling, significantly more boys who had been raised by non-loving mothers had committed crimes (P < .02).[24] Fifty-six percent of the unloved boys compared to 35 percent of the boys reared by loving mothers had become criminal. Yet among those boys who had undergone frequent counseling, almost equal proportions of the loved and unloved children committed crimes (22%:31%). Apparently, frequent counseling counteracted the effects of maternal rejection.

Our first form of analysis—a comparison between boys who received treatment and those who did not—indicated that treatment had, perhaps, succeeded only in decreasing the seriousness of the crimes which the boys committed. (Fewer treated boys went to prison or jail than did control boys.)

The second form of analysis, comparisons within the treated group, gave us several new leads. Those children who began treatment at an early age, who had a female counselor, and who had frequent contact with their counselors, subsequently had a lower rate of crime.

At the suggestion of Professor Gordon Allport,[25] we decided to check the effects of a close, intense counseling relationship, while holding constant as many other factors that might influence criminality as possible. In this way, we hoped to provide a better test of Dr. Cabot's hypothesis that friendly, regular guidance from an adult counselor could be an effective means of preventing crime.

Final Assessment of Treatment

In many ways, the treatment actually provided by the Cambridge-Somerville Youth Study failed to match that envisioned by Dr. Richard Clarke Cabot when he founded the project. Al-

[23] X^2 4.6; d.f. 1.   [24] X^2 6.4; d.f. 1.   [25] In a private conversation.

though we have discovered certain factors which might have been helpful in improving the results of treatment (e.g., treating children at an earlier age, using women counselors with the older boys, giving more intensive treatment), we have not yet tested the full efficacy of the experiment.

Naturally, every school of thought would differ in its standard of "good treatment." Since the experiment was initiated by Dr. Cabot, we decided to use his own criterion as a basis for the assessment of treatment. Before selecting our cases, therefore, we established the following standards for judging which boys had undergone the most intensive "therapy"—standards with which, we believe, Dr. Cabot would have agreed.

1. Some counselor had to maintain a relationship with the boy for a minimum of two years.

2. The counselor had to visit the child an average of once a week throughout the two-year period.

3. The counselor had to have a *close* relationship with the child. Only if the boy volunteered statements which seemed to indicate his regard and respect for the counselor did we judge their bond as a close one.[26]

4. The discussions between the boy and his counselor at some point had to touch on the child's basic personality problems: his relation with his parents; his sexual feelings; his attitude toward authority and his peers; his feelings of guilt, anxiety, or aggression.

5. The counselor had to work with the family as well as with the boy. Frequent interviews with the mother and father and an alertness to the needs of the family fulfilled this prerequisite.

6. The counselor had to correct any obvious material, educational, or medical handicaps of the boy; that is, if the child needed an operation, or tutoring, or new clothes, the counselor had to see that they were supplied.

After combing the case records, we found that only 12 cases satisfied these requirements. The boys in these cases were some of the most potentially delinquent; they had been subjected to a variety

---

[26] A recent article by Hans Lucas Teuber and Edwin Powers concerning the Cambridge-Somerville study indicated that the counselors seriously overrated the closeness of their relation to the boys ("Evaluating Therapy in a Delinquency Prevention Program," *Psychiatric Treatment*, Vol. 21 [1955]).

EFFECTS OF TREATMENT

of the influences which research has shown are productive of crime. In order to test the effects of treatment, we needed to hold constant those factors which might have some influence on criminality but were not directly related to treatment. Therefore each of the twelve boys who received intensive treatment was matched individually to another boy from the treatment group. (We matched treated boy to treated boy because information on this group was much more complete than on the control group.) Selection was made on the basis of eight factors: mother's personality, boy's personality, method of parental discipline, general home atmosphere, type of neighborhood, intelligence, father's personality, and the delinquency prognosis score which had been assigned at the beginning of the experiment. We were able to find boys who, on the basis of these factors, closely resembled the 12 boys who had received the Cambridge-Somerville project's most intensive care.[27] The mothers of each pair resembled one another in personality. Each pair had similar fathers. Each pair of boys was of the same general personality type. Except for one set, the pairs matched in terms of the parental discipline which they had undergone. Eleven of the 12 pairs had identical ratings of general home atmosphere. Only one set differed in neighborhood by more than a single rating point. Using the Stanford-Binet intelligence scores, we were able to match the boys within five points in 8 of the 12 pairs. Eight of the 12 pairs had been given a delinquency prognosis within one point of each other.

When we had finished this matching, two groups of remarkably similar boys could be compared with each other. One set of boys had received, for a number of years, the very best attention which the project offered; the other set had received the less intensive (and, as we have seen, largely inadequate) services of the program.

The results of the comparison are encouraging: whereas 6 of the boys who received the most intensive treatment committed at least one crime, among their matched comrades 11 of the boys committed at least one crime ($P < .05$).[28] Unfortunately, however, only

---

[27] When difficulties occurred in the matching, we used a "preference table" which gave greater importance to those factors which research has shown to be the most important in the causation of crime. The matching was done without prior knowledge of the court records of any of the boys.

[28] X^2 3.9; d.f. 1.

a handful of boys underwent the intensive treatment. The small number of cases makes generalization difficult. Nevertheless, the results seem to indicate that intimate, long-term, "supportive" counseling can prevent delinquency and adult criminality.

These varied analyses may seem to have produced rather contradictory results. Before attempting a theoretical interpretation, let us review the findings.

1. The Cambridge-Somerville youth study, on the whole, failed to prevent either delinquency or adult criminality. Neither in number of crimes committed nor in number of boys who became criminal did the 253 treated boys differ significantly from the 253 untreated boys.

2. The treated group and the control group committed the same types of crimes at about the same ages. The treatment program did not prevent crimes of violence, sexual offenses, or drunkenness.

3. Approximately equal numbers of children went to reform school and equally high proportions from both groups committed crimes after release.

4. Although more boys in the control group than in the treated group were sentenced to penal institutions during adulthood, a statistically significant relationship appeared only if we grouped together commitments to jail and to prison.

5. The treated boys failed to evidence an advantage over the control group, even when a variety of important variables was held constant. The Cambridge-Somerville treatment was, in general, as ineffective with the intelligent child as with the dull child, the loved child as with the unloved, the brutally disciplined as with the undisciplined, the child from the slums as with the child from a non-slum area.

6. Intermittent counseling seemed to increase criminality among withdrawn children.

7. Longer treatment did not decrease the percentages of boys convicted of crimes.

8. Boys who had one counselor throughout the program had no lower crime rate than boys who had several counselors.

These were our negative findings. They are, taken alone, highly discouraging. Implicitly, they cast suspicion on many of the preventive methods now used in America. When variations in treatment were considered, however, hopeful signs appeared. They are summarized in the other findings which follow.

9. The children seen by their counselors at least once a week became criminal less often than the children who saw their counselors relatively infrequently. This result probably was not a consequence of a biased selection of cases.

10. Counseling once a week seemed more beneficial when used with either conformist or aggressive children than with withdrawn boys.

11. Frequent counseling (once a week) appeared to be most effective in preventing crime among those children who had nonloving mothers. Although boys with loving mothers and frequent counseling had lower crime rates, the frequent counseling did not appear to be the crucial factor in these cases.

12. Very young boys responded more favorably to treatment (although this result may have been due to individual differences in counseling).

13. Women counselors had better results than did men counselors in treating older boys.

14. Finally, when twelve children were closely matched to another twelve, the boys who had received the most extended and most intensive counseling had significantly less criminality than boys who received only average attention. Those children who *did* receive the treatment that Richard Clarke Cabot had planned committed less crime.

Thus, while the general approach of the Cambridge-Somerville study failed, intensive therapy appears to have succeeded with a few of the boys. So, in a sense, Cabot's theory was justified.

Case Study Illustrations of Treatment

Through statistical analysis, we have shown the over-all failure of the Cambridge-Somerville experiment in preventing crime. We turn now to three cases which illustrate in an individual manner both the methods of treatment and the results. In two of these cases, the boys received intensive therapy; the third child had irregular contact with his counselors.

ROBERT O'BRIEN

"My mother says I ought to be in reform school," Robert O'Brien sadly commented. "I should, too! The devil's done got me," he added. Again and again, throughout the seven years he received treatment, this pathetic boy talked of his mother's rejection.

In 1938, when he was first interviewed, everyone who met him predicted that Robert would be a serious delinquent. His teacher, in referring him to the program, said she "could not stand him." His school principal described him as "a tough little kid, secretive, crafty, sly, and restless. He is a constant show-off and braggart. In school work, he is apathetic and dull; in behavior, he is quarrelsome, a constant fighter, a cocksure little devil, very impulsive, and defiant toward authority."

This restless, aggressive little boy seemed a perfect subject for the project's ministrations. Early in 1938, a social worker visited Robert's home. In a crowded, tiny apartment, Robert lived with nine brothers and sisters, his parents, and an aged grandfather. An odor of urine and garbage pervaded the house. Robert's father, a former singer and comedian, was a "slick, crafty, small-time politician" who had lost his job with the city machine. He talked vivaciously with the social worker about how he could "always get by" on graft. Through the WPA he earned $52 a week. He still sported very natty clothes and a battered straw hat, though he had lost all his teeth. In the home, he abdicated all control to Robert's mother.

The social worker found Robert's mother to be an "easy-going, undemanding, sloppy woman." She subscribed to the Catholic faith but combined it dexterously with a respect for spiritualism. In a seance, she had been told that Robert would soon die of a lung ailment; the little boy's persistent cough convinced her of the truth of the prediction. Harassed by her many children, broken down with illnesses, the mother abandoned herself to a spiritualistic life of withdrawal. Seldom did she discipline her brood, and even more seldom did she provide for their needs. Most of the children went without shoes; meals came only at irregular intervals; and the children's health went untended. All the children had fleas. Once in a while the mother doused the boys' hair with kerosene, attempting a mass onslaught against the bugs. On several occasions, Robert was excluded from school because of sores on his face.

Like other boys in the program, Robert went through a series of psychological and medical examinations. The psychologist described him as a "cheerful, very restless, crude child" with an I.Q. of 92. The doctor, although finding no organic disease, noted the emotionally starved character of the boy. "My mother don't do nothing for me," Robert responded to one of the doctor's questions. "She always wants me to keep out of the house." Robert had a severe lisp and impressed both examiners as a "typically feeble-minded child," even though his intelligence score belied the comment. One of the interviewers remarked that Robert was potentially a serious delinquent.

Late in 1938 a Cambridge-Somerville counselor, whom we will call Miss Randolph, took up the case. Her first contact with the family shocked her. The disarray of the home, the putrid odor, the unkemptness of the children were repelling. Robert was not around: "God knows where he is," his mother snapped. The family took quickly to Miss Randolph as she listened sympathetically to their complaints. The mother muttered about her own "political disillusionment"; after years of campaigning for Cambridge politicians, she had received no favors from them. Robert came in while Miss Randolph was talking to the family, and he shyly responded to her overtures. The boy asked Miss Randolph when she would return. Embarrassed, he added, "I am tongue-tied and can't say nothing but can I go with you somewhere?"

As the weeks passed, Miss Randolph paid other visits to the family, gradually building herself a secure place in the home. She took Robert on picnics (his first), to playgrounds and museums. Usually several of the other children in the family crowded into the car with them. Robert eagerly awaited her weekly visits: "As soon as he saw me, he ran to me with open arms. His face lit up. I hugged him."

At Robert's school, Miss Randolph talked to his principal and his teacher, both of whom complained vociferously about his wild, uncontrolled behavior. "Just yesterday," his teacher recounted, "he threw an open penknife across the room. What if it had hit someone's eye and the papers had picked it up?" Miss Randolph told them of Robert's home life and attempted to modify their attitudes.

She introduced the boy, after several months had passed, to the Children's Art Center. Often she accompanied him there and played with him as he messily used the paint and clay which the Center offered the children. On one of their first visits to the Center, Robert formed a massive figure of a man from a pile of clay. Then he began smashing it with his fist and tearing off the limbs.

"Who is that?" Miss Randolph asked.

"It's the strongest man in the world," he growled.

"And you are beating him up?"

He smiled broadly, "Yes, I am strong enough to do that."

Miss Randolph had established a friendly relation with the boy. Now she felt that she could use this relation for a deeper probing of the boy's feelings. They talked often about his misbehavior in school and about one of his characteristics which most repelled his mother, enuresis. After one of these sessions, Robert met another boy and proudly introduced Miss Randolph as his "nurse."

Miss Randolph became a mother substitute for all the children in the family. One day an older brother broke out: "I hate living like this. My clothes look awful. My mother picks on me all the time. I hate it!" Miss Randolph answered that he could depend on her, and the boy responded warmly.

Working with the parents brought few results at first. "Bobby is a terror," the mother said one day after she had been pressed by the counselor for more care of the boy. The mother's overt rejection was felt intensely by the boy.

"She feels I am the worst of the lot," he sadly said to his counselor one day.

"You feel that she doesn't love you?" the counselor responded.

After a minute of silence: "Yes."

The boy smiled when Miss Randolph replied: "You know that I care for you."

In early 1940, Miss Randolph had practically taken on Robert's brother, Tommy, as another subject. The two boys often came to her office together. Once, while roughhousing in the office, Robert tripped Tommy. The boy fell and cracked his head on a radiator. Blood gushed from his forehead. Miss Randolph rushed Tommy to the hospital where his head was stitched. Robert, very contrite for his part in it, was comforted by his counselor who told him, "It was only an accident." Later Miss Randolph thought she had missed an opportunity to build an internalized conscience.

The three continued their outings together—going on picnics, visits to the zoo, swimming in the ocean. Gradually Robert revealed his pervading sense of inferiority and fear of other children, covered by an assertion of strength. In the classroom he tried to hide his feeling of inadequacy by attacking younger children. As the year passed, he gained more control over himself. He also stopped stealing in school. Miss Randolph continually impressed him with her love and respect. Once she left her purse in the car with Robert guarding it. When she returned from an errand, he asked, "Didn't you think I might steal?"

"No," she answered, "I can trust you."

"Yes, you *can* trust me," he replied with gratitude.

Each summer the counselor arranged for Robert to go to a camp. His misbehavior in the camp and his defiant reaction to punishment caused him to be suspended several times. On each occasion, Miss Randolph came to his aid.

In late 1940, Miss Randolph arranged a foster home for the boy. The parents were glad to be rid of him and Robert looked forward to his new home in the country with happiness. Within a week, however, the foster mother called Miss Randolph and insisted that she take him back; he had wet the bed and the foster mother could not stand that. The counselor regretfully returned him to his home.

Late in the same year, Robert's school work took a turn for the worse. He had been accused several times of stealing milk from the school kitchen. (He received none at home.) His interviews with Miss Randolph were sometimes stormy but the slightest hint of disapproval on her part caused him to quiet down. Even though she had established an intimate, motherly relation,

Miss Randolph wrote, "I cannot help at this point but reflect that much of my effort to help Bobby has failed."

She decided on a new approach—remedial reading. Knowing of his tremendous anxiety at school, his sense of inferiority, and his need for a formal education (he still, at ten years, could not read or write), Miss Randolph believed that the reading sessions would offer another opportunity for helping him. She tutored him twice a week and the new attention caused an immediate change in him. His misbehavior decreased; his interest in school work improved; and he evidenced great pride whenever his counselor visited him at school. Christmas, 1940, marked the first time he gave her a gift.

In January, 1941, Robert passed successfully through a series of crises. His grandfather, who had lived with the family for years, died, and Robert was forced to view the corpse. On the same day, in school, his teacher upbraided him for wearing rubber boots instead of shoes, and the other children humiliated him for his school failings and his puny size. Robert telephoned Miss Randolph and asked to see her immediately. She skillfully reassured him about death and about his failures in school.

"You are smart. I think you are smart. Look at all the progress we have made in reading."

"No, the kids think I am dumb and my mother says I ought to go to reform school. That is where I ought to be. The devil done got me."

The counselor tried to reassure him, bringing up specific achievements he had made in reading and at school.

"I am no good," he answered. "I can't go to church because what I have done is too bad to tell."

"You can tell me."

Slowly the counselor bolstered the boy's sense of confidence and worth. When he left, he was smiling cheerfully. The next day, the counselor got some shoes for Robert.

Throughout 1941, Robert's behavior improved as did his school work. But intermittent setbacks occurred. For a period of weeks Robert talked to Miss Randolph in hostile terms: "I hate books!" "Stop talking about me—drop it!" Then, on his birthday,

EFFECTS OF TREATMENT

she sent him a card and his pleasure erased the past irritation: "This is the first time that anyone remembered me."

His family situation did not change. Robert often told his counselor about his father's drinking and both parents' neglect of him, adding: "They want me to go."

Toward the end of 1941, after an explanation to Robert, Miss Randolph left the Cambridge-Somerville project. Another counselor, whom we will call Mr. Jones, took on Robert's case.

Robert made the transition to Jones easily. Their first meeting was friendly and the boy eagerly responded to Jones's interest. The new counselor, however, failed to capitalize on the superficially friendly relation. He began counseling with a firm conviction of Robert's destiny: "This boy is well-primed for a future delinquent career."

When Jones called on the child, Robert was frequently away from the house. (He had seldom missed an appointment with Miss Randolph.) Convinced of the necessity for a medical examination of the boy, Jones tried to press the child into a hospital. Robert reacted strenuously, particularly to the idea of a blood test: "I won't let them stick me with a needle!"

Contact between Jones and the child dropped off until their interviews came only at irregular intervals. In the summer of 1942, Jones arranged for Robert to attend camp. He hated his experience there and the camp directors reported him as an extremely aggressive child. Jones commented: "It may be that this boy is in search of more authority."

At one meeting, Robert reported a dream in which a needle injection turned him into a monstrous, sadistic wolf. Then he talked of another dream in which a cut resulted in the loss of his hands. Instead of understanding these rather obvious fears, Jones retorted: "Have you wet the bed recently?"

Jones hammered away at Robert's enuresis and his medical condition. Several times, the boy asked, "When are we going to talk?" The enuresis ended—through a chance incident. Robert had been sleeping with one of his younger brothers. When his mother began blaming the younger child rather than Robert for the wet bed, Robert stopped.

By 1943, when Robert was thirteen, his association with the program had become very spasmodic. Jones occasionally attempted a form of free association with Robert, but this had little effect. Once, when Jones pressed Robert about getting a medical examination, the boy responded, "You think I am yellow, huh?" The counselor protested that he did not. "Well, I am yellow," the boy snapped.

Jones joined the Army in early 1944, without having established a close relation with Robert. The boy's family had deteriorated during this period and their financial status reached its lowest ebb. Robert's father ran for the Combridge school committee because, his mother commented, "every school committeeman gets a cut when a new teacher is hired."

In his concluding report, Jones said, "I think something has been accomplished in this case, but just what, would be difficult to say."

In quick succession in 1944 and 1945, two other male counselors took Robert's case. Neither succeeded in getting close to the boy. Like Jones, their contact with the child was severely limited. They reported a gradual deterioration in his behavior. Robert began gambling for high stakes and increased his begging in downtown areas. The medical examination which Jones had demanded finally took place. Its results showed that Robert was in good medical condition. An electroencephalographic examination of Robert revealed no sign of epilepsy or brain disorder.

The two new counselors each kept in touch with Robert's school. At fifteen he was in a special fifth-grade class. His teachers again described him as obnoxious and disturbing, just as they had seven years before. One teacher told how she had reprimanded Robert for his bad conduct: "You represent your mother and father. If you are bad, people will think your parents are. You reflect on your family." Robert replied, perhaps showing some control: "I don't care anything about my mother and she doesn't care for me."

At the final party which ended the Cambridge-Somerville project, many of the boys returned. Robert was there. His "loud and boisterous behavior," his demand for food, his "obnoxiousness"

EFFECTS OF TREATMENT

caused all of the counselors to predict a dire future for him. His last counselor concluded that the program had done little to change his personality. Robert, in the judgment of the project, was headed toward a life of severe criminality.

Yet, startling as it may seem, to the best of our knowledge Robert never committed a serious crime. At twenty-six, Robert had not compiled a criminal record.

Other boys, closely resembling Robert in all important respects, committed a variety of serious crimes later in life. Though it is difficult to say that treatment deflected Robert from delinquency, we believe that certain important elements in Miss Randolph's therapy did much to alter his life.

Through her constant material and emotional care for Robert, Miss Randolph became a mother substitute for the child. Robert called his counselor "his nurse," indicating that he consciously realized the mothering role which she filled. Miss Randolph satisfied his infantile needs and at the same time pressed him gently toward more mature satisfactions.

It appears that the counselor's permissiveness provided a channel for the expression of Robert's pent-up aggression. With her, he could rant and rave without physical punishment. Yet Miss Randolph showed her disapproval for many of his acts. Perhaps inadvertently, she signaled to Robert a threatened withdrawal of love—a love which he prized highly. The effect might well have been gradual instillation of a sense of guilt over deviant acts. To keep his counselor's affection, he strove for higher grades and tangible achievements in behavior. The counselor utilized her close bond with the child to build a rudimentary conscience.

An outlet for the expression of aggression, an instiller of guilt, a satisfier of his need for recognition, a builder of his sense of adequacy—these are the functions which his counselor served for Robert. Later counselors failed to fulfill the same needs. Whether his three years with Miss Randolph actually prevented Robert from becoming criminal can never be known. Judging from the lives of very similar boys, however, it seems reasonable to believe that she did play the critical role.

Miss Randolph's treatment of Robert is, in our opinion, an

example of the type of therapy envisioned by Dr. Cabot. Another counselor, "Miss Casey," used a similar approach with one of her boys, David Walters.

DAVID WALTERS

"This child wishes to kill himself." So commented David's minister as he referred the boy to the program. "He frequently wishes he might be run over. Three times he has been hit by an automobile. We do not know whether he stepped in front of them deliberately, but we do know that he has attempted to jump out of a window at school."

In 1938 David, a chubby, oversized boy of twelve, came into the project. His teacher described him as "standing outside of the group. He often gets into trouble when he is saucy or aggressive; at other times, he daydreams and lives in a world of make-believe." The psychologist who first interviewed him found that David had a low-borderline intelligence and was a "very unhappy, frustrated child." He added: "Unless he can secure understanding and affection, I am certain he is headed for difficulty."

A social worker went to the Walters' home and later described the father as a vain show-off. He had readily agreed to let David become a subject: "Someone needs to do something about him!" During the home visit, David's family fought continuously. David's mother was a large, lethargic woman. She described David (one of three sons) as "not having enough pep. He is very hard to manage. I have trouble with him being saucy. He is cowardly and ungenerous, sensitive for himself but not for others." The social worker recorded her reaction to this visit: "I felt the queerest sensation in this home, something strange and unhealthy."

Interviews with school officials filled out a picture of David as listless, withdrawn, and perhaps pre-psychotic. His principal commented, "I find him a very attractive child but quite pathetic and at times annoying in the way he paws and picks at himself and scratches here and there." A former teacher described the boy as "destructive, dull, lacking in attention. He cries easily, daydreams, and is moody. He is a very restless boy."

"Miss Casey," a nurse turned social worker, decided to accept the case. In January, 1939, she made her first visit to the family. The father talked with her about his constant beatings of the child, which failed to give him any "gumption." Mrs. Walters broke in, "You know how you would feel if people made fun of you and didn't like you." The father looked up and sadly replied: "You know, I often have that feeling myself."

Miss Casey's visits continued and she began to form a close bond with the child. Progressively, he revealed his interests and feelings to her. His ambition was to become a "gentleman farmer."

The family minister and school officials concurred in describing David's mother as a strange and mentally disordered woman. The Episcopal priest observed: "The last time I went to their home, the mother was drunk. The little boys clung to me. They were mortally afraid of their mother." In her talks with the mother, Miss Casey noted a pervading feeling of tension: "She made a great effort to keep herself under control . . . she tried to appear at ease, but one could not help feeling that there was real tension and emotional disturbance under all the acting." Mrs. Walters' pronounced rejection of David became more and more apparent; she talked constantly of beating, refused to get glasses for him after they had been suggested, and informed the boy's teacher that she could whip him whenever she wanted because "David is such a brat."

In late 1939, David became seriously ill with pneumonia. He was taken to the hospital, where complications kept him confined for more than five months. During that time, the parents seldom visited the child. Sometimes weeks passed between their visits. The nurses noticed that the mother was markedly cold with the child. Mrs. Walters confessed to Miss Casey: "I am just not able to be affectionate with the children. When they were babies, I could kiss them, but I can't do it now. I can't do it in the hospital. I see all the other mothers doing it, but I can't."

Miss Casey, on the other hand, lavished affection on David while he stayed in the hospital and David yelped with joy whenever he heard she was coming.

As the time approached for his departure, the Walters showed reluctance to take him. Miss Casey finally convinced them to accept David's return and, under her nursing supervision, the boy was brought back to good health. The family came increasingly to depend upon the counselor. The mother found it an effective punishment, for example, to threaten David: "Miss Casey won't come to see you any more if you don't behave."

By 1940, Miss Casey had established a liaison with the school and the community church. Despite the father's attitude about David's school performance ("You are a disgrace to the family!"), an understanding teacher and Miss Casey began to make discernible progress. In school, David formed friendships with the other children and his grades improved markedly. The mother, too, became more understanding, under the guidance of Miss Casey.

As the year drew to a close, Mrs. Walters reported that David was becoming increasingly concerned about sex. At thirteen, he was approaching puberty. "David is getting very modest," the mother said proudly. "He now will not let anyone in the bathroom when he is taking a bath. He is just like me—I like to be alone."

One day David suddenly blurted, "Mother, I have a question to ask you. I hate to because it is a dirty question: Where do babies come from?"

The startled mother said quickly, "Why do you want to know?"

"Jimmy said that you should not take that baloney that they come from heaven. He said your mother and father do dirty things to each other and then they have a baby."

"Well, that is not a nice thing for boys to discuss. Just forget it."

Mrs. Walters informed Miss Casey about the incident and pleaded for her help. The counselor convinced her that David should be given some information about sex and volunteered to do it herself, to the relief of Mrs. Walters.

In weekly interviews, Miss Casey broached the subject with the boy. He responded eagerly. She showed him a book on sex education and answered his questions calmly and simply. David brought up examples of monkeys he had seen in the zoo and Miss Casey used that example for a transition to discussion of human sexual relations. The boy, however, revealed strong anxiety about sex: "Well, I don't think I ever want to get married!"

"But why not?"

"Because I don't want to do those dirty things that Jimmy told me about."

The interviews continued. Despite some progress, David showed continued anxiety. "I don't want the doctor to look at my penis," he said before a hospital examination.

In 1941, David seemed well on the way to the solution of many of his problems. Miss Casey wrote in her annual report, "I am not discouraged with him. He has improved more than any boy in my group." During the summer, David stayed at a camp and received an excellent progress report. "I am delighted with him," Miss Casey exclaimed.

In one tape-recorded interview, David indicated many of his fears: "I want to tell you now something about my fears. I am afraid to swim—afraid I might drown—once I nearly did drown in deep water. My father does not understand me. He gets cross but he doesn't mean to be cross. Tears come into my eyes and I start to cry. I just cannot help it. I don't like people to call me Baby or Stupid. I don't know what's wrong with me. I guess I am queer. Oftentimes I do not know what to say. I won't turn out very well. No one will want to have me. No one will want to marry me. I just cannot do anything."

David's moods shifted from depression and withdrawal to elation. In school, David's work continued at a high level and his relations with other children had improved. His love for Miss Casey, his dependence upon her, was revealed again and again in his conversations. Once, when asked what he had gained from their relation, he said, "You have given me a better disposition . . . I don't hate my father as much . . . I know more about the world . . . I do better in school."

The day after Miss Casey had written, "I am proud of David and think he is worth the effort of the whole study," she received a telephone call from the police. They informed her that David Walters had been arrested on suspicion of murder. His cousin, Richey Jones, had disappeared and David was the last person known to have been in Richey's company.

As the police grilled him, David admitted that he had frequent sexual relations with other boys. David confessed to having had sexual relations with Richey Jones on the day of his disappearance, but he stubbornly denied having committed murder. Four months later, when the ice broke on the Charles River, the police recovered Richey's body. Circumstantial evidence pointed to David, yet there was no proof that David had pushed Richey into the river.

The police booked David on a charge of sodomy and psychiatrists recommended his commitment for observation to the Boston Psychopathic Hospital. There, examiners found David to be essentially sane. A Rorschach analysis, however, showed pronounced obsessional qualities and a sadistic trend in his personality: "He is obsessed with sucking and blood letting, the touching of fluffy textures and the killing of chickens."

Miss Casey visited David in the mental hospital, and David insisted on his innocence: "The cops tried to make me say that I pushed Richey into the river. I did not. I liked Richey. Why should I kill him? I finally said to the police, 'What are you trying to do, frame me?' I did not kill Richey."

In 1942 he was released from the hospital and diagnosed as "without psychosis." In the next year, David was shifted from mental hospital to reform school and back to the hospital. Finally, Miss Casey arranged for his placement at a center for disturbed children. At the home, he was caught wringing the neck of a chicken. Several times he threatened children with a knife. The center, complaining strongly about his seduction of other children and his sadism, soon returned him to the city.

Miss Casey questioned David about his behavior. He answered candidly:

"I like to use knives and I guess I feel like sometimes cutting chickens down the middle and watching their guts spew out. Sometimes I feel that way about people."

"Do you try to control these feelings?" Miss Casey asked.

"Yes, I guess I do, but when people make me mad I want to do something."

With David's permission, Miss Casey arranged for incarceration of the seventeen-year-old boy in a state hospital. He corresponded with her often and seemed relatively content. An older inmate, a former drunkard, became David's protector.

During Miss Casey's last visit in 1947, she thanked the older man for the attention he had been giving David. The old man responded: "Well, I like David. He is good to me too. He waits on me. You know I am lame and it is hard for me to move quickly. I would like to talk to you about him." He added pathetically, "I would like to talk to you about myself, too, if you have a minute."

At twenty-two, David Walters was a seriously maladjusted man, a marked sex deviant, pursued by fears and a sense of inferiority. Diagnosis of him ranged from "an obsessed, sadistic neurotic" to "schizophrenic." His criminal record marked him as a sexual offender.

In terms of the goals set by the Cambridge-Somerville project, Miss Casey had failed. Perhaps David's problems—blatant rejection by the mother, numerous traumas concerning sex, a prepsychotic condition—were too serious for even the most skilled social worker to manage. Perhaps, though no one can know, another form of therapy would have accomplished more. Or perhaps David's deviant tendencies had been too deeply inlaid before the treatment began.

Mrs. Walters had ample opportunity to transmit her intense sex anxiety to the boy. Prior to his entry into the project, David had felt great concern over relations with his mother and with women in general. David's sex anxiety, feeling of impotency, distaste for "dirty" heterosexual relations, fear of women, feeling of sexual unacceptability, and perhaps castration anxiety may actually have been intensified through his affection for a "pure" mother substitute, Miss Casey.

Thus, the fact that his counselor was a woman may have been a hindrance to treatment (although, in general, Miss Casey was one of the most successful counselors). In any case, Miss Casey's discussions with David failed to give him insight into the nature of his problems.

So far we have examined two boys who received the most intensive therapy offered by the staff. Treatment which centered upon close relations between counselor and boy seems to have worked in preventing Robert's delinquency and to have failed in deflecting David from his deviant behavior. The general results of this approach with other cases, however, give encouragement to those who seek this means to prevent delinquency. Less intensive counseling failed to prevent crime. The case record of a third boy illustrates rather clearly why casual treatment did not accomplish its goal.

ALBERT STANSLOWSKI

In 1939, eight-year-old Albert Stanslowski was referred to the project. School records described him as deceitful and aggressive. He could neither read nor write. His teacher overtly rejected him: "I just can't like that child. He is dull as a hoe. He is immature, crafty, sly, a stealer and a fighter. He loves to be boss."

Albert's father, a Polish immigrant, contributed to his family a paltry WPA salary; his mother, a blond Canadian, supplemented this with a little money from work as a scrubwoman at Harvard University. Albert had two sisters, Lillian and Sandra, and one brother, Robert. The family minister summarized the home situation: "Robert is the fair-haired boy, Albert is the black sheep. The mother dislikes Albert intensively and continually impresses his 'badness' on him."

Albert received the battery of examinations given to all entering cases. Each examiner noted delinquent trends. The social worker who first interviewed him remarked: "He seems to be the kind of child who would get out of hand easily, a child whom you cannot like." The project's nurse questioned him and found deep fantasies of hostility towards his father: "He dreams constantly of handcuffing the father and then beating him." School officials reported Albert to be "disobedient, sneaky, willful, bossy, and a dreamer." The psychologist analyzed him as a "dull, immature, unstable personality, subject to great impulsiveness."

On the other hand, there were points of leverage for constructive work within the family. Although Mrs. Stanslowski barely controlled her hostility toward Albert, she seemed to have an extraordinary desire to prevent him from becoming delinquent. The father, although a gruff man, appeared fond of all his children. His playfulness with them, his refusal to use a whip as discipline, his hearty welcome of aid from the project presaged a responsive attitude.

EFFECTS OF TREATMENT

Albert's first counselor, "Mr. Ryan," explained the purposes of the program and found that the parents offered enthusiastic support. The counselor himself reported that they seemed eager for help.

After his first visit early in 1939, however, Mr. Ryan waited two months before approaching the family once again. Quite naturally the parents had forgotten him, and Albert was out on the streets. Meanwhile, the counselor volunteered his services to the school. Four months later, the counselor again returned to the home and found Albert there. The two took a ride to the airport.

During the years that Mr. Ryan remained Albert's counselor, he concentrated on improving Albert's school work. He explained the boy's background to his teachers and tried to influence their attitudes toward him.

The director of the Cambridge-Somerville project questioned Mr. Ryan's concentration on the school and the infrequency of his visits with Albert. The counselor later described this interview: "He wondered if I felt this [Albert's school behavior] was isolated from other patterns and if there were not possibly other causes for the behavior in school. I agreed this was true. But dealing with causes per se was, in my opinion, an impossible task. How can we know the causes? If we knew them, how could we remove them?"

Mr. Ryan was drafted shortly after Pearl Harbor and another counselor replaced him. Pleading the pressure of a heavy case load, "Mr. White" allowed a year to pass without giving any attention to Albert—a year in which Albert's father left the family for the Navy, in which truant officers and police came to know the boy, in which Albert's misbehavior in school increased to the point where he was suspended.

After his debacle in public school, Albert was transferred to a parochial school. There, late in 1942, the boy first met his new counselor. One of the teaching nuns introduced Albert to the counselor with the order: "Now tell the man what a bad boy you are!"

Albert's face colored and he refused to answer. The nun, in quick succession and biting tones, repeated a list of Albert's "crimes" in school: his "hook-jacking" (truancy), stupidity, laziness, disobedience, and aggression. When Albert began to cry, the counselor intervened with reassuring remarks.

Three months later the police arrested Albert on a charge of trespassing. Alarmed by this, the counselor went to see Albert once again. On meeting the counselor at his home, the boy asked: "When are we going to the airport?" In his mind, the Cambridge-Somerville counselors had become the "plane-men."

The counselor tried to explain his function in talks with the boy and his family. Mrs. Stanslowski had developed severe psychosomatic headaches and her disgust with Albert and the girls had increased. A month later, when the older daughter was apprehended for shoplifting, the mother committed the girl to a school for delinquent girls. The younger daughter soon followed her sister into exile.

Mr. White made an effort to touch on some of Albert's problems. He offered, for example, to discuss the boy's reasons for disliking school. Albert responded: "I don't know. I guess there is something wrong with me." To this Mr. White replied: "Too bad if a boy doesn't like school. It makes it hard on him." During the brief period when they saw each other regularly, Albert's conduct in school improved. He reported proudly to his counselor: "I ain't hook-jacking no more."

By the end of 1943, Albert's taste of a close relationship ended with his second counselor's departure for the Army. As he left, the counselor wrote: "Albert is a happy-go-lucky, gregarious boy, whose chief interest is pleasure and how to attain it. He strongly resents authority and is easily led into mischief. He will probably participate in delinquent activities."

Seven months later the third counselor found Albert working in a grocery store to supplement the family's meager funds. Like the former counselors, the third man concentrated his efforts on the school. In the course of a year, he saw Albert only twice. During this time, Albert's school problems had increased and he appeared in court on a larceny charge. Albert and some other boys had snatched a woman's purse as she walked home from work late one night. Albert was placed on probation. The counselor wrote: "I made many attempts to see the family and [my failure] was most unfortunate because on the few occasions when I have seen the boy, I have found him very easy to develop a relationship with. He was always happy to see me."

Albert's fourth and final therapist took over the case early in 1945. He conducted several interviews with the family and made a genuine attempt to work with Albert. He found that the boy could not remember the names of his last two counselors, and his mother reported that Albert had run from the house whenever he saw Mr. Ryan coming down the street.

Albert's mother evidenced a profound discouragement with the situation. "I cannot never bring that boy up," introduced a recital of his misdeeds, as Albert listened uncomfortably. She berated him in front of other boys as well as his fourth counselor. Albert later exclaimed: "My mother is always talking about something like that. I hate it!"

The fourth counselor encouraged Albert to talk of his problems and worked toward winning his confidence. Evidence of progress came when Albert confessed: "I can tell you some things I cannot tell my mother. Yesterday, I hopped a cement truck and the police chased me. She would be very mad if she knew about that."

The counselor, however, failed to solidify the relationship and Albert skipped several appointments. After sending Albert a few letters, the counselor gave up his efforts to see the boy. Four months passed before he again visited the family. The mother's hostility toward Albert had not decreased. With little time remaining, the counselor attempted to mediate between them. In late 1945, as the project ended, he too concluded: "I have not been able to do much with Albert."

The family tried to keep in touch with the counselor. In 1946, although he had an I.Q. of only 80, Albert graduated from high school. His mother sent a graduation invitation which the counselor refused. In the same year, Mrs. Stanslowski called the counselor requesting his help. Albert, accused of setting fire to a neighborhood store, was being held on the serious charge of arson. The counselor saw "little to do in the situation" and declined his services. Lacking substantial proof, the police released the boy.

In 1948, the court committed Albert Stanslowski to five years in Concord prison for attempted rape and larceny. After his release from prison, Albert was charged with several more crimes (primarily larceny) but the prosecutors could not furnish sufficient evidence to convict him.

With Albert, as with David, the Cambridge-Somerville program failed. It failed this time, however, for different reasons. Albert could relate well to adults and was anxious for help. He responded eagerly to signs of affection from his counselors. Albert's case offered no greater problems than that of the first child we discussed, Robert. None of Albert's counselors, however, established a close relation with the boy; indeed, the counselors seldom saw him. In no sense, then, can Albert's case be considered a test of the hypothesis that close, continuous support from an understanding adult can prevent delinquency.

The Stanslowski case, unfortunately, typifies much of the Cambridge-Somerville treatment. Negligible attention followed thorough examination of each child and his background. Counselors concentrated their efforts after emergencies had occurred. Preventive efforts consisted primarily in establishing smooth relations with the school, tutoring, talks with the family, trips for the children, securing medical aid, and arranging for participation in various community groups. Few counselors interviewed their boys with regularity. Few attempted to touch upon the psychological problems of either the boys or their families.

Again and again, Albert had given indications of his impending criminality. The harangues of his mother, his teachers, and the nuns could have been seen as danger signs. His constant failures in school, his early truancy and delinquencies, as well as the fact that his was a socially disorganized neighborhood, were further signals of danger. The counselors, however, consistently failed to heed them. They accepted defeat rather than the challenge of prevention.

In sum, the Cambridge-Somerville project applied methods utilized by many social work agencies. Only 12 boys were given intensive individual therapy. For a variety of reasons, the less intensive methods of the majority of the staff failed to prevent criminality. Evidence—i.e., the fact that twice as many control as treatment boys were incarcerated in jail and prison—but evidence which is perhaps debatable, hints that the program might have deflected a few individuals from experience in a penal institution. Under certain conditions, however, the experiment appears to have had more beneficial results. Younger boys and those few children who received intensive, supportive counseling had a lower crime rate.

This research, then, suggests that intensive counseling may prevent delinquency; yet few boys in the treated group of the Cambridge-Somerville Youth Study received that kind of therapy. Thus the program failed to achieve its fundamental goal of preventing crime.

CHAPTER IV

THE ORIGINS OF CRIME

IF IT IS NOT TO BE UTOPIAN, SOCIAL POLICY MUST BE GROUNDED ON a fundamental knowledge of the causes of human action. It is the task of psychologists, sociologists, and anthropologists to furnish this knowledge. Fortunately criminology, as one branch of contemporary social science, has made unusual progress in recent years. Such researchers as Sheldon and Eleanor Glueck, Edwin Sutherland, Robert Lindner, and Walter Bromberg have, during the last three decades, developed a substantial fund of knowledge, particularly concerning the effects of disorganized urban areas and familial conditions upon the rate of crime. Sociologists in general have emphasized a delinquent subculture (a group characterized by a unique set of values and customs), "differential association," and a deviant code of values as causative forces. Psychologists, especially psychoanalysts, have concentrated upon individual drives and their origin in traumatic familial situations.

Yet both psychological and sociological researchers have, too frequently, focused upon single causal explanations. Even more important, research into the etiology of crime has almost universally been performed in a "retrospective" fashion; the subjects of the studies have almost always been convicted delinquents or criminals. Since the memories of the subjects may have been faulty and their current position in society (such as membership in a gang) may have been influenced by prior events, these studies are open to criticism—particularly since the natural tendency of the social scientist is to find convincing reasons for psychological or social "abnormality." Consequently, the legacy left to social science by the Cambridge-Somerville Youth Study is invaluable because, in the very nature of the experiment, retrospective biases were eliminated.

ORIGINS OF CRIME

Moreover, the extensive observations by psychologists, social workers, and psychiatrists form a massive source of evidence. Although these observations were obviously not free of bias, no single theoretical viewpoint governed the recording of data. In addition to these recordings on the early lives of the boys, we also possessed one measure—criminal records—of their later experience. An average of seventeen years separated the two sources of information. If significant connections could be discovered, important evidence would be added to support those who affirm the importance of early environmental experience in the formation of adult behavior.

The absence of a single viewpoint in the gathering of information had the disadvantages, of course, that certain hypotheses could not be tested because there was insufficient data. Nevertheless, since the interviews and recorded information were in "raw" form, the present researchers were furnished with an unrivaled fund of behavioral observations.

We carefully read each of the cases and extracted relevant information regarding intelligence, physical constitution, social environment, discipline, home atmosphere, and the character of each child's parents. We recorded this information for each boy and then compared the groups in terms of crime rate. We used the Chi-square test, two-tailed, to determine the level of statistical significance.

Information about the boys who received treatment was more detailed than that about control boys. The treated group had been observed for two to eight years, while the control boys had been studied only for one short period in their lives. For our analysis of causative factors, therefore, we concentrated on the 253 boys who had received treatment. We used the control group primarily for confirmation of those relationships which appeared significant. This chapter is a discussion of our findings with the treated boys. In Appendix B figures are presented for the control group.

One possible objection to this approach is that treatment may have disrupted or obscured causal patterns. For two reasons, we do not agree with this argument: first, treatment seemed to affect only a small minority of the children; second, trends within the control group, as Appendix B shows, confirm our findings with the treated group (although the patterns did not reach the same high level of statistical significance).

The following sections report our discoveries concerning why some of the 253 treated boys became criminal.

Intelligence, Physical Constitution, and Crime

At the turn of the century, many social scientists thought they had discovered a basic cause of criminal behavior in mental defectiveness. Spurred by Ceasare Lombroso's opinions concerning the "born criminal," they contended that no man of intelligence could look on crime as a legitimate way of life; thus, *ipso facto*, criminality derived from stupidity.

Research by certain scientists lent weight to the prevalent belief. In 1896, for example, C. E. Dawson examined 52 inmates of American industrial schools and concluded that 76 percent of the boys and 74 percent of the girls had subnormal intelligence.[1] In the early 1900s, Dr. H. H. Goddard's investigation of feeblemindedness led him to assert that at least 50 percent of all criminals could justifiably be classified as mentally defective.[2]

Carl Murchison, in 1926, was one of the first to doubt a direct relationship between crime and intelligence. After hearing the guards in a prison deride the intelligence of convicts, Murchison decided to compare their mental test scores with those of the inmates. He found that the convicts had a significantly higher average score than the guards.[3]

Simon Tulchin, making one of the most comprehensive studies of the hypothesis, compared test scores of 4,748 reformatory and 5,512 prison inmates with an equal number of Army recruits. In 1939, he reported that equal numbers of inmates and soldiers had been judged "inferior."[4] Some critics claimed that the Army sample reflected biased selection (in the general direction of lower intelligence); Tulchin countered that the prison sample, too, was

---

[1] C. E. Dawson, "A Study in Youthful Degeneracy," *Pedagogical Seminary* (December, 1896).
[2] Henry H. Goddard, *Feeblemindedness*.
[3] Carl Murchison, *Criminal Intelligence*.
[4] Simon H. Tulchin, *Intelligence and Crime*.

biased since it contained only those criminals not clever enough to escape detection.

Recently, H. R. Weiss and Richard Sampliner studied 189 adolescent first offenders. They found a distribution of intelligence scores closely approximating that of the general population.[5]

As recently as 1953, however, an Egyptian investigator reaffirmed the relationship between low intelligence and crime. Mukhtar Hamza found that most of the delinquents in a group of 160 boys were subnormal, and that at least 25 percent were mentally defective.[6]

Contradictory reports still left the relationship between intelligence and delinquency open to question. The Cambridge-Somerville project offered an opportunity to introduce fresh data into the controversy and also, perhaps, to explain the divergent conclusions of preceding studies. Stanford-Binet intelligence tests had been administered to most of the children early in the study. From examination of the scores for only those boys who later became criminal, an apparent relationship between crime and intelligence emerged.

Forty-two percent of the criminals had below-average intelligence. Similar figures in other studies had led to the theory that low intelligence and criminality bore a close relationship. Yet 44 percent of the total sample of 239 boys with recorded I.Q. scores had below-average intelligence. Thus, almost equal proportions of criminal and non-criminal boys could be tabbed as having low intelligence.

Table 21 shows the proportion of boys in each level of intelligence who became criminal. The table indicates that no significant relationship exists between criminal behavior and low intelligence. It appears that the child of average intelligence is slightly more "prone" to criminality.[7] Interestingly, children with superior intelligence never served terms in reform school, jail,

[5] H. R. Weiss and Richard Sampliner, "A Study of Adolescent Felony Violators," *Journal of Criminal Law, Criminology, and Police Science*, 34 (1944), 377–91.

[6] Mukhtar Hamza, "The Dynamic Forces in the Personality of Juvenile Delinquents in the Egyptian Environment," *British Journal of Psychology*, 44 (1953), 330–38.

[7] Chi-square comparison of superior, average, and subnormal boys shows that the difference is not statistically significant (X^2 4.1; d.f. 2).

or prison. Approximately the same proportion was, however, convicted of crimes. Perhaps judges, influenced by a belief that high intelligence somehow mediates against a criminal career, were less inclined to confine them in an institution. Perhaps, the boys' superior brains gave them better tools for escaping the revenge of the law; or it may be that they actually committed fewer serious crimes.

TABLE 21. RELATION OF INTELLIGENCE LEVELS TO CRIME RATE AND INCARCERATION RATE

Intelligence Quotient		Percent of Boys Convicted of Crimes	Percent of Boys Sentenced to Penal Institutions
Superior (I.Q. over 110)	(N: 23)	26	0
Average (I.Q. 91–110)	(N: 111)	46	16
Dull Average (I.Q. 81–90)	(N: 59)	44	15
Sub-normal (I.Q. below 81)	(N: 46)	35	19

The conclusion is that low intelligence does not lead a boy into crime, although high intelligence may prevent him from going to a penal institution.

Intelligence is, presumably, an inherited trait. At times in the history of social science, certain other "constitutional" factors have been described as contributing to crime. Since all our subjects underwent complete (and usually repeated) physical examinations, a brief mention of our findings in respect to these other variables seems warranted.

1. Difficulties at birth (prematurity, Caesarian section, and so forth) were not significantly related to later criminality.

2. The child's general health bore no relation to later criminal tendencies; equal proportions of healthy and unhealthy boys became criminal.

3. Boys who had definite neurological handicaps (brain damage, epilepsy, and so forth) had a statistically significantly greater tendency to turn to crime. Fifty-seven percent of boys with neurological difficulties, as opposed to 36 percent of "normal" children, became criminal ($P < .05$).[8] Whether this result is due to the lessened inhibition of the boys or to the resulting psychological handicaps is open to question.

[8] X^2 4.6; d.f. 1.

4. Glandular abnormalities—long touted as the basic cause of crime by certain over-enthusiastic endocrinologists—were not significantly related to crime. Approximately equal proportions of children with and without glandular difficulty became criminal (45% and 35%, respectively).

5. Although other body deformities were not significantly connected with crime, we found that 75 percent of those boys who suffered from severe acne later developed criminal records ($P < .02$).[9] While it is conceivable that some underlying physiological deficiency led to both crime and acne, it is more probable that acne was another sign of the same emotional stress which gave rise to criminality.

6. Prolonged enuresis was not significantly related to crime.

Thus, while boys with neural damage and severe acne are more likely to become criminal, there seems little basis for attributing criminality to physical causes.

Societal Influences and Crime

Most sociologists today look upon crime as primarily, if not entirely, a group phenomenon. They use as evidence such facts as: (1) crimes are seldom committed by single individuals; (2) crime concentrates in certain deteriorated urban sections; (3) delinquent gangs have their own unique deviant code of values; and (4) the techniques of crime must be learned. Delinquents adopt the values and learn the methods of crime, sociologists maintain, through association with a particular sub-culture; sociological and economic factors, rather than psychological conditions, are the essential causative elements in crime.

This explanation of criminal behavior came into prominence during the 1920s, when numerous studies proved that crime centered in certain urban slum areas. Research at the University of Chicago pioneered in this. Professors William Park and Ernst Burgess, authors of the *Urban Community,* were among the first to turn to the social milieu as a unit for investigation. Under their tutelage a series of works emerged, perhaps the most important being those of Frederick Thrasher and Clifford Shaw. Thrasher

[9] X^2 5.0; d.f. 1.

examined 1,313 delinquent gangs in Chicago and showed that they centered in certain "interstitial," culturally changing areas, which were encroached upon by new industrial developments and were characterized by deteriorated housing and inhabitants stricken with mental disease and poverty.[10] Such areas appeared to be on the edge of civilization culturally, economically, and socially.

In the 1930s, Clifford Shaw and Henry McKay meticulously examined the case histories of individual criminals and also the areas in which the criminals had matured.[11] They too found that delinquency prevailed in districts characterized by physical decline, decreasing population, and high rates of dependence upon charity. Large proportions of foreign-born and Negro elements inhabited these "ghettos." A clash of conflicting cultures, added to physical ugliness and economic poverty, destroyed the foundations for instilling conformity. Neither parents nor neighborhood organizations functioned as agents for social control. The prestige and values of youth gangs replaced those of more traditional institutions.

The work of the "Chicago school," of Mailer, Faris, and Reckless, emphasized social disorganization, lack of community control, and the absence of a "moral consensus" as the source of criminality.

Other writers have added new interpretations. Edwin Sutherland, for example, held that disorganization alone would not lead to the inculcation of criminal values. He pointed to the new forms of social organization which arose in the slums. Pressures from these unique slum groups, he believed, pushed children into delinquency. Sutherland viewed delinquency as the sharing with others of certain attitudes toward the law, society, and oneself. These attitudes are first injected into the person through "differential association" (the learning of deviant values through association with criminals).[12]

In 1955, a most provocative and sophisticated presentation of

[10] Frederick M. Thrasher, *The Gang*.

[11] Clifford Shaw and Henry McKay, "Social Factors in Juvenile Delinquency," in National Commission on Law Observance in Enforcement, *Report on the Causes of Crime*, Vol. 11.

[12] Edwin H. Sutherland, *Principles of Criminology*, pp. 3–99.

this theoretical orientation appeared. Albert Cohen, in his *Delinquent Boys*, defended the view that the "transcending" factor in the causation of crime is the influence of the delinquent sub-culture.[13] Noting that delinquency centered in certain areas and in the lower class, Cohen asked why such a deviant sub-culture existed. He maintained that emphasis on certain values by the dominant group in America (the middle class) creates an anxiety about their status among those who are debarred from successful participation in the system (the lower class).

Cohen delineated an American society dominated by values which reward ambition, financial achievement, academic success, self-control, respect for property, and "worldly asceticism." The terms for success, set by the middle class, cannot be met by particular groups, which therefore establish other systems with different definitions of prestige and status. Delinquent gangs, according to Cohen, are the result of a search for status among those to whom society has given little. Crime is a compensation for "status anxiety."

Despite the fact that delinquent gangs are centralized in specific areas, many children living in such areas do not join these activities. Although Cohen tackled the task of explaining the existence of delinquent sub-cultures, he specifically disavowed any attempt to explain why certain children in the slums do not subscribe to the delinquent sub-culture. Why one child from a poor environment becomes a Bernard Baruch and another an Al Capone has not been explained by sociological investigations. This weakness in the sociological position has been criticized by psychologists, psychiatrists, and criminological researchers such as Sheldon and Eleanor Glueck.

Consequently, in contemporary social science there are two opposing positions regarding the importance of neighborhood influence upon delinquency. On the one hand, there are those who argue that deviant sub-cultures are the primary source of criminality. On the other hand, there are those who, pointing to individual variations within a deviant culture, insist that the primary explanation must come from an examination of psychological or hereditary roots nourished by the family. This is an

[13] Albert K. Cohen, *Delinquent Boys*.

important controversy, for community defense against delinquency depends on its solution.

Although the Cambridge-Somerville experiment did not specifically record the effects of delinquent sub-cultures upon the boys, certain measures of neighborhood influence were developed. As each child entered the program in 1938 or 1939, social workers ranked his home neighborhood on an eleven-point scale. The ratings were based upon the area delinquency rates, degree of physical deterioration, influence of gangs, and the presence or absence of "positive" community organizations. For statistical reasons, we consolidated the ratings into four categories: the "good neighborhood" (plus 5, 4, 3, 2), the "fair neighborhood" (plus 1, 0, and minus 1), the "poor neighborhood" (minus 2, 3) and the "worst neighborhood" (minus 4, 5).

The "good" areas had low delinquency rates, well-functioning community organizations, and a relatively high economic standard. The "fair" neighborhood contained more socially disruptive elements (saloons, pool houses, bars) and generally had a lower economic level. "Poor" areas were actual slums, characterized by material poverty, the existence of gangs, and a distinct lack of community organizations. The "worst" areas lacked neighborhood pride or organization, were socially heterogeneous, dominated by gangs, and plagued by unemployment and bitterness. It should be remembered that none of these areas, not even the "good," approached the upper-middle-class standards of some of Boston's suburbs or the "gold coast" level of certain sections in Chicago.

To test the relationship between neighborhood influences and crime, we divided the total group into their respective social classifications and then computed the proportions of boys in each category who had been convicted for crimes (other than traffic offenses) as well as the proportions of boys who had been committed to penal institutions (Table 22). The pattern revealed, although not statistically significant, hints that neighborhood consistently influences crime causation. Seventy-seven percent of all the boys who served time in a penal institution had neighborhood classifications of "poor" or "worst." (Sixty-seven percent of the total sample were from the poorer neighborhoods.) [14]

[14] Chi-square comparison of boys sentenced to penal institutions from worst and from all other neighborhoods: 3.5; d.f. 1.

It is difficult to discern whether boys from the poorer areas—those with the highest rates of delinquency, the least degree of social cohesion, and the greatest poverty—actually committed more serious offenses. Children from the worst areas probably ended in an institution more often for two reasons: police in slum areas tend to press charges with greater severity and, in addition, judges hesitate to return children to debilitating slum influences.

TABLE 22. RELATION OF TYPE OF NEIGHBORHOOD TO CRIME RATE AND INCARCERATION RATE

Type of Neighborhood	Percent of Boys Convicted of Crimes	Percent of Boys Sentenced to Penal Institutions
Good (N: 37)	38	8
Fair (N: 41)	37	10
Poor (N: 96)	40	13
Worst (N: 59)	46	20

We recognized that the Cambridge-Somerville area represented a fairly restricted socio-economic region. Although the bitter wave of the depression had passed, it had left in its wake large numbers of unemployed. Ten years after its onset, Cambridge and Somerville still showed the effects of the depression. Even the best neighborhoods in this study were lower middle class. Consequently, our results represent only a section of the class structure.

In our sample, however, there is not a *highly* significant relation between "delinquent areas," or sub-cultures, and crime. If we had predicted that every child who lived in the poorer Cambridge-Somerville areas would have committed a crime, we would have been more often wrong than right. Thus, current sociological theory, by itself, cannot explain why the majority of children, even those from the "worst" areas, never became delinquent.

Despite our failure to substantiate those theories which place primary emphasis on disorganized neighborhood conditions, we did find evidence in support of those which emphasize the importance of a deviant sub-culture in the promotion of crime. Seventy-five percent of the boys who were regular members of delinquent gangs in childhood developed criminal records; 56 percent of those who irregularly accepted delinquent gangs as their reference groups became criminals; and only 30 percent of those who, during childhood, looked to their homes or to nondelinquent peers as their reference group became criminal ($P < .001$).[15] Certainly, membership in a delinquent gang reinforces deviant values. Yet the question remains: Why did certain youngsters join these gangs while others did not?

In an attempt to answer this question, we examined other "cultural" variables. It is often assumed that the birthplace of the father bears on delinquency: Sons of immigrants, one reads, have difficulty in adjusting to American standards. In our group of boys, we found, on the contrary, that sons of immigrants are less likely to become criminal. Whereas 46 percent of American-born fathers produced criminal sons, 33 percent of immigrants' sons had been convicted for a crime ($P < .05$).[16] Perhaps, one might argue, it is the parents' "ethnic maladjustment" that produces crime. If a father cannot speak English and rejects "American" values, does this behavior produce more crime in the boys? Ethnic maladjustment does not produce more crime: we found that equal proportions of sons of "adjusted" and "maladjusted" fathers became criminal.[17]

We did, however, find a marked difference between those boys who accepted their father's culture and those who rejected the language, customs, and values of their parents' original culture: only 16 percent of those who accepted their parents' culture, as opposed to 40 percent of those who rejected the culture, became criminal ($P < .01$).[18]

To trace the relationship between parental religion and crime, we recorded both the religious faith of the parents (Protestant, Catholic, Jewish, or none) and the strength of their religion (in terms of attendance at services).

Few families in our sample were either Jewish or agnostic, and these few produced no serious criminals. The mother's religion was significantly related to her son's criminal tendencies in only one way: those boys reared by strongly religious Catholic mothers had a significantly lower rate of crime than those reared by Catholic mothers who attended church irregularly or not at all

[15] X^2 25.9; d.f. 1. Reliability of classification: 83.3%.   [16] X^2 4.0; d.f. 1.
[17] There was no significant relation between the mother's ethnic maladjustment and the son's crime.
[18] X^2 6.6; d.f. 1; Reliability of classification: 86.7%.

ORIGINS OF CRIME

TABLE 23. RELATION OF MOTHER'S RELIGION TO CRIME RATE

	PERCENT OF BOYS CONVICTED OF CRIMES	
Mother's Affiliation	Strongly Religious Mother	Weakly Religious Mother
Protestant	(N: 26) 42	(N: 66) 44
Catholic	(N: 61) 28	(N: 96) 45

($P < .05$) [19] (Table 23). The father's religion, however, had no significant relation to crime (Table 24).

TABLE 24. RELATION OF FATHER'S RELIGION TO CRIME RATE

	PERCENT OF BOYS CONVICTED OF CRIMES	
Father's Affiliation	Strongly Religious Father	Weakly Religious Father
Protestant	(N: 14) 29	(N: 63) 43
Catholic	(N: 40) 33	(N: 116) 39

Neither the education of the father nor the education of the mother significantly influenced their sons' rates of crime.

In this brief analysis of social factors, the background of criminals has been partly delineated. Our studies show that the criminals tend to have grown up in neighborhoods with a high crime rate; that they are more often reared by native-born fathers; that they revolt more often against their fathers' values; and that, religiously, they are raised either by Protestant parents or Catholic mothers who adhere only weakly to their religion. Yet these "causative" relationships are illusory, we believe, for they are largely the result of conditions within the family. In our opinion, it is the basic socialization process in the early years of life which determines whether a boy will be prone to criminal acts. It is these factors which we analyze in the following sections.

Parental Discipline and Crime

Discipline has long been viewed as a key to the problem of crime. Every parent consciously or unconsciously exerts control over his child, but disciplinary methods differ radically both in form and in consistency. For many years, disciplinary techniques have been a focus of attention for speculation and scholarly studies. Most issues of women's magazines include advice for mothers about how to discipline their children. Many newspapers

[19] X^2 4.5; d.f. 1.

carry columns attributing delinquency to incorrect parental discipline. Benjamin Spock's *Baby and Child Care*, with its many admonitions about discipline, has an acknowledged place beside the Bible on many family bookshelves. But these sources of advice often disagree: whereas Spock advocates parental permissiveness, Bishop Fulton Sheen demands greater parental authority. It is no wonder that the American parent is confused.

Empirical research has indeed shown a relationship between discipline and crime. Cyril Burt conducted one of the first attempts to support theory with evidence. In 1925 he studied the familial disciplinary techniques which had been used with a group of British delinquents. Burt concluded that certain types of "defective" discipline led directly to crime. Almost seven times as many parents of delinquents as of non-delinquents were indifferent to discipline or lax in its administration, disagreed with each other over methods, or used overly strict forms. Discipline, Burt contended, was the most important differentiating factor between the homes of delinquents and non-delinquents.[20]

In another pertinent investigation in 1950, Maud Merril, at Stanford University, directed a study of two hundred delinquents. Her findings supported those from England. Three fourths of the delinquents came from homes where discipline had been very lax, or very severe, or highly erratic. Only one fourth of the delinquents were found to have been treated with consistency or normal firmness.[21]

One of the most comprehensive studies of the relationship between delinquency and discipline was that conducted by Sheldon and Eleanor Glueck. Examining, over a ten-year period, 500 boys incarcerated in Massachusetts reform schools and 500 non-delinquent boys living in Boston's slums, the Gluecks searched for factors which might differentiate the two groups.[22] One of the many variables which concerned them was disciplinary practices. Securing information from psychiatric interviews, home visitor reports, and interviews with social workers, the Gluecks compared the disciplinary approaches used within the homes. The contrast was striking: only 5.7 percent of the fathers of the de-

---

[20] Cyril Burt, *The Young Delinquent*.
[21] Maud A. Merril, *Problems of Child Delinquency*.
[22] Sheldon and Eleanor T. Glueck, *Unraveling Juvenile Delinquency*.

linquents were "firm but kindly," though 55.5 percent of the fathers of the non-delinquents could be described in that way. More than twice as many fathers of delinquents as fathers of non-delinquents were erratic in their discipline, and more than three times as many were overly strict. About the same proportions were lax.

Relatively few mothers from either group were overly strict. Among the mothers of the incarcerated boys, the majority were lax in discipline and about one third were erratic. Sixty-six percent of the mothers of the non-delinquents, on the other hand, were "firm but kindly."

The delinquents' parents depended largely on physical punishment as their method of controlling the children: 56 percent of the delinquents' mothers and 68 percent of their fathers utilized physical punishment as a primary technique, compared to 35 percent of the non-delinquents' mothers and 35 percent of their fathers. The mothers and fathers of the non-delinquents depended more often on reasoning with the child. Noting these sharp contrasts, the Gluecks concluded: "The analysis is a revealing commentary on the relative effectiveness of physical punishment as opposed to an appeal to reason in the control of child behavior." [23]

Such evidence indicates a strong relationship between criminality and discipline. Burt's research suggested that laxity, disagreement or inconsistency, and excessive strictness promoted delinquency; Merril's findings concurred. The Gluecks, who had a control group to which they could compare the delinquents, found that neither paternal laxity nor maternal over-severity differentiated their two groups of five hundred boys. They showed, however, a connection between delinquency and erratic or overly strict discipline by the father and one between laxity or erratic discipline by the mother. In addition, use of physical punishment had a positive relationship to crime. Other studies, more general in nature, of the link between discipline and personality have shown a connection between discipline based upon the "withdrawal of love" and acceptance of parental standards.[24]

In past research it has been difficult to obtain accurate information. Studies have often depended upon the retrospective (and

[23] *Ibid.*, p. 133.
[24] Robert Sears, Eleanor Maccoby, and Harry Levin, *Patterns of Child Rearing*.

necessarily biased) views of the individuals themselves or upon reports by investigators who already knew that the children had become criminal. The Cambridge-Somerville families were observed by social workers and counselors in many situations over a period of at least two years. As a result, we could glean from the records an extensive and objective account of disciplinary practices. For analysis, we decided upon three major divisions of the methods: discipline based on the withdrawal of love, discipline dependent upon physical punishment, and marked laxity.

We considered verbal signs of disapproval for specific acts, withholding privileges, threats of isolating the child, or "reasoning" with the child as all representing one fundamental technique: the withdrawal of love. These "love-oriented" methods depended upon a bond of affection for their effectiveness. Direct attacks upon the child, whether verbal or physical, fell into our "punitive" category. These attacks included beatings, displays of violent anger, and aggressive threats. A lax parent was one who was indifferent to controlling the child. Typical of this type was the mother who said: "His father is always drunk and I am too busy to bother with him. It is too much trouble to keep up with him." The lax parents made very little attempt to discipline their children.

We did not assume that these three categories were exhaustive. In some families, for example, one parent was consistently punitive and the other lax or indifferent. Sometimes the same parent would be erratic in his disciplinary methods. About one such mother, a counselor wrote:

One minute the mother was ignoring their tantrums. Then she suddenly got up . . . smashed both children with a strap, yelled and screamed . . . . then she left them, came back to the room . . . and ignored their further acts. The boy is often threatened with the strap. To avoid this he runs out of the house or hides under the beds. The family laughs at this, considers it a "riot" and then often leaves him alone.

We classified these inconsistent methods into a series of "erratic" groupings. Thus, we had six final types of discipline.[25]

[25] We were able to categorize 250 of the cases according to methods of discipline. Three judges agreed on the ratings of 88 percent of the cases selected at random from the sample.

1. *Love-oriented discipline.* Both parents consistently used methods based on withholding love, rewards, or privileges in combination with "reasoning."
2. *Punitive discipline.* Both parents consistently used beatings, physical isolation, violent anger, or aggressive threats.
3. *Lax discipline.* Neither parent exerted control.
4. *Erratic discipline A* (love-oriented and lax). One parent used love-oriented methods and the other was lax, or they varied inconsistently between the two types.
5. *Erratic discipline B* (love-oriented, lax, and punitive). One or both parents wavered inconsistently in using these methods, so that all three were combined.
6. *Erratic discipline C* (punitive and lax). One parent used punitive methods and the other was lax, or they varied inconsistently between the two methods.

Examining the criminal rates of the men who had been disciplined in the various ways (Table 25), we found that lax disci-

TABLE 25. RELATION OF PARENTAL DISCIPLINE TO CRIME RATE AND INCARCERATION RATE

Type of Discipline		Percent of Boys Convicted of Crimes	Percent of Boys Sentenced to Penal Institutions
Punitive	(N: 14)	21	7
Love-oriented	(N: 60)	27	5
Erratic A (love-lax)	(N: 40)	35	5
Erratic B (love-lax-punitive)	(N: 41)	49	19
Lax	(N: 52)	50	19
Erratic C (punitive-lax)	(N: 43)	56	30

pline or erratic discipline involving punitiveness had a strong relationship to high criminality. Children who had been disciplined consistently (whether by punitive or by love-oriented techniques) or with a mixture of laxity and love-oriented methods had a significantly lower rate of crime ($P < .005$).[26] In addition, significantly more children who had been disciplined punitively or with laxity went to a penal institution than those children who had been controlled by love-oriented methods ($P < .001$).[27]

Contrary to our expectations (and to the findings of previous

[26] X^2 17.5; d.f. 5.
[27] Love-oriented and love-lax categories compared to all others: X^2 12.19; d.f. 1.

studies), we found no evidence that consistently punitive discipline leads to delinquency. In fact, we were surprised to discover that the 14 children who had been severely but consistently treated had the lowest rate of crime. Consistent use of love-oriented techniques also seems to produce non-criminality. These figures indicate that the *consistency* of parental behavior is more important than the methods parents use for enforcing their demands.

Why should this be so? Contemporary psychology contends that a child's conscience stems primarily from his identification with his parents. When a child is disciplined by the withdrawal of love he feels an anxiety about his act; this anxiety soon accompanies other behavior similar to that which was disciplined. A child who is physically beaten, it appears, also develops a conforming attitude—an attitude presumably based on his experience that swift and sure pain attends acts of which his parents disapprove.

Consistent discipline, of whatever type, appears to decrease the chances of criminality; the effects of inconsistent discipline, on the other hand, depend upon the particular form in which it is administered. Discipline which varied between laxity and being love-oriented resulted in a relatively low crime rate: approximately equal proportions of the criminals and non-criminals fell into this grouping (14 and 18 percent, respectively). Discipline which was totally erratic, involving both love-oriented and punitive techniques, seemed to promote delinquency: more criminals than non-criminals had been disciplined in this manner (26 and 17 percent respectively).

Erratic discipline which varied between laxity and punitiveness proved to have the most harmful effect upon children. Such discipline contained no love-oriented element. Nearly twice the proportion of criminals as of non-criminals had been so treated (23 and 13 percent, respectively). In all probability, this erratic discipline produced such bad results because the punitiveness caused a feeling of rebellion in the children and the laxity failed to control the rebellion.

Two variables seem to play primary roles in the relationship between discipline and crime. On the one hand, the "withdrawal of love" backed by consistent demands strongly tends to decrease criminality. On the other hand, punitiveness combined with inconsistent demands tends to increase crime. If love-oriented discipline is used, the child will accept the parental values; if the parents are consistent, the child will have a stable awareness of these values. The absence of either consistency or love-oriented discipline, it would appear, leads strongly to criminality, while the presence of consistency leads strongly, on the contrary, to conformity. A child who has undergone extremely lax discipline seems to have a fundamental unsureness of "correct" values; this child is, consequently, more open to other influences in his subculture.

As the next sections will demonstrate, disciplinary techniques are closely related to other factors in the environment of the child. The effect of discipline frequently depends upon these other important factors.

Home Atmosphere and Crime

Psychoanalytic thought has, for many years, concentrated upon the early familial environment as the determinant of adult personality. Psychoanalysts have maintained that the individual repeats, throughout his life, the basic patterns of social action established in his youth. Yet few psychoanalysts—Walter Bromberg, Robert Lindner, Benjamin Karpman, Richard Jenkins, and David Abrahamsen are prominent exceptions—have directly tested the relation between family atmosphere and criminality.[28]

Sociologists have done extensive research in this area of causation. They have been particularly struck with the importance of a break in the family as a criminogenic influence. The "broken home" has often been tabbed by sociologists as a prime villain in the causation of criminal behavior. In 1918, Ernst Shideler was one of the first to investigate the problem. Shideler examined the backgrounds of 7,598 boys in state industrial schools of 32 states. He found that over half had come from broken homes. Six out of

[28] See Walter Bromberg, *Crime and the Mind;* David Abrahamsen, "Study of 102 Sex Offenders at Sing Sing," *Federal Probation,* 14, No. 3 (September, 1950), 26–32; Robert Lindner, *Rebel Without a Cause;* Benjamin Karpman, *The Sexual Offender and His Offenses;* Richard Jenkins, "Motivation and Frustration in Delinquency," *American Journal of Orthopsychiatry,* Vol. 27, No. 3 (July, 1957).

ten boys confined to such institutions had lost one or both of their parents.[29]

In a contemporaneous study, S. P. Breckinridge and Edith Abbott noted that 43.3 percent of 584 delinquent cases came from homes split by death, desertion, divorce, separation, or commitment of one parent to an institution.[30] During the next decade, John Slawson confirmed the previous findings: 45.2 percent of 1,649 boys committed to New York penal institutions came from broken homes. The proportion among non-delinquent boys was much smaller: only 19.3 percent of 3,198 New York City public school children had lived in such homes.[31] At about the same time, William Healy and Augusta Bronner of the Judge Baker Clinic announced that 49 percent of delinquents whom they had studied lived in broken homes.[32] And in 1940, Ashley Weer recorded a history of family disintegration in the backgrounds of 39.6 percent of the criminals in his research.[33]

Nevertheless, Clifford Shaw and Henry McKay challenged the conclusions of the other investigators. In 1931 they published the results of an examination of 7,278 cases. They failed to find a highly significant statistical relationship between broken homes and delinquency.[34]

Unfortunately, except for the Shaw and McKay research, all of these early studies linking familial conditions and delinquency failed to establish the incidence of broken homes in the background of non-delinquents from the same social class. (Slawson's control of socio-economic classes is open to question.)

Social scientists have increasingly looked upon the broken home not as a direct cause of delinquency but as a sign of deep tension and unsatisfying emotional relationships. This familial conflict

[29] Ernst Shideler, "Family Disintegration and the Delinquent Boy in the United States," *Journal of the American Institute of Criminal Law and Criminology*, 8 (1918), 709–32.
[30] Sophonisba P. Breckinridge and Edith Abbott, *The Delinquent Child and the Home*, pp. 91–92.
[31] John Slawson, *The Delinquent Boy*.
[32] William Healy and Augusta Bronner, *Delinquents and Criminals*, p. 263.
[33] H. Ashley Weer, "Male and Female Broken Home Rates and Types of Delinquency," *American Sociological Review*, 5 (1940), 601–9.
[34] Clifford Shaw and Henry McKay, "Social Factors in Juvenile Delinquency," in National Commission on Law Observance and Enforcement, *Report on the Causes of Crime*, Vol. 11.

ORIGINS OF CRIME

and disruption, they believe, lies at the heart of delinquency. Studies by John Bowlby, Dorothy Baruch and Annie Wilcox, Claude Mullins, David Abrahamsen, and Lauretta Bender, and our own work on the psychopathic personality have focused upon the early familial relationships as the progenitors of criminality. These studies have consistently found that many criminals come from frustrating, tense, conflictful homes.[35]

Perhaps the best-known work in this area has been done by Sheldon and Eleanor Glueck. *Unraveling Juvenile Delinquency* (1950) reports several important differences between the homes of delinquents and non-delinquents. About half of the parents of the delinquents lived apart, while only about a quarter of the non-delinquent families were separated. Furthermore, the quality of family life differed substantially. Many more of the delinquents' parents were incompatible; few of their families were cohesive. The parents of the delinquents less often demonstrated affection to their children and the emotional ties between parents and child were loose.[36]

In the Cambridge-Somerville research, we expected that the same patterns would emerge, as they had in other studies. Basing our judgments on the intangible factors of general family life (the bonds of affection between the members of the family, their pride in the family, the degree of conflict among them), we categorized the Cambridge-Somerville families into four broad groups.[37]

Many of the children came from *cohesive* homes. We considered a home cohesive if the parents had affection for each other and for their children, if each member took some pride in the family unit, and if the family participated together in many of their recreations. These families were not necessarily free from conflict or argument. Nor were they free of "role conflicts" among the members of the family. Nevertheless, arguments did not dominate the family gatherings or involve lasting bitterness. The comments

---

[35] For a summary of this material, see William and Joan McCord, *Psychopathy and Delinquency*, Chapter IV.

[36] Sheldon and Eleanor T. Glueck, *Unraveling Juvenile Delinquency*, Chapters IV–VI.

[37] Three judges, independently rating a random sample of the homes, agreed in 80 percent of their categorizations.

of a counselor concerning one of these families illustrates their traits:

> Although parental discipline may be a little severe, his home is a wholesome one, and he is given good treatment and a certain amount of freedom. They are careful to keep him away from delinquent companions and manage this by doing many things together.
> I am very impressed by the genuine devotion and solidarity of this family group. Although the mother was out of the home working because of the father's inability to find work, there was no evidence of deprivation or frustration. The mother secured a job . . . and the family unit was kept intact with the father not losing face or his position as head of the family.

We considered a home as *quarrelsome but affectionate* if conflict was the keynote of the atmosphere but if, nevertheless, family pride and unity and a degree of affection were still evident. On her first visit to such a home, one social worker noted:

> The household was chaotic, the children chasing around uproariously. The mother was arguing loudly and snapped at the children.
> The mother and her mother-in-law were constantly at each other. The mother-in-law says her son never lived in such squalor . . . . the mother herself remains indifferent, but apologized for the looks of the house. She said that neither she nor the children could ever find anything.

After subsequent visits, the social worker added:

> The house has been dirty, untidy, cold, and tumultuous with irregular and inadequate meals and care. Discipline was very inconsistent. Money was not carefully spent. But the mother in her loud, vulgar, noisy way worked hard and valiantly to keep her family intact, and there was a warmth of sympathy and loyalty uniting the noisy group and the mother as they worked their stormy passage together.

The third type of home would be characterized as *quarrelsome and neglecting*. Affection, cohesiveness, and a sense of mutual pride seemed absent. Parents neglected their children and disliked each other. In many of these homes, even the physical needs of the children were untended.

Finally, there were *broken* homes. In this category we placed only those families which had been permanently (or for a very long period of time) ruptured by death, desertion, divorce, or separation. If a family had once been broken but then reunited, we categorized it under one of the other three types.

Figuring the proportions of boys from each type of home who later became delinquent and who were incarcerated in penal institutions, a wide divergence appeared (Table 26). As expected,

TABLE 26. RELATION OF HOME ATMOSPHERE TO CRIME RATE AND INCARCERATION RATE

Home Atmosphere		Percent of Boys Convicted of Crimes	Percent of Boys Sentenced to Penal Institutions
Cohesive	(N: 114)	30	9
Quarrelsome-affectionate	(N: 56)	38	16
Broken	(N: 43)	51	11
Quarrelsome-neglecting	(N: 37)	70	30

a significantly lower proportion of men from cohesive homes than from the other types of homes became criminal ($P < .005$).[38] Quarrelsome-neglecting families actually had a higher crime rate than homes in which a permanent separation had disrupted the family. A significant difference, following the same pattern, also appeared in the proportions of boys from quarrelsome-neglecting homes, and those from broken homes, who were incarcerated in penal institutions ($P < .01$).[39] Table 26 clearly indicates that conflict and neglect within the home predispose a child to crime (even more so than do broken homes), while cohesiveness and affection lead toward conformity. It should also be noted, in passing, that those homes which were broken when the child was young (in infancy or before five years old) did not produce a greater proportion of criminals than those homes which were broken later in the child's life. This fact contradicts, of course, some psychoanalytic generalizations concerning the dire effect of an early separation of the child from his parents.

Earlier, we mentioned that the form and consistency of discipline depend, to a large extent, on other aspects of the familial environment. Home atmosphere and discipline are distinctly related, cohesive homes emphasizing love-oriented techniques and quarrelsome homes utilizing erratically punitive methods ($P < .001$).[40] Holding either discipline or home atmosphere constant, we were

[38] X^2 14.75; d.f. 3. [39] X^2 11.55; d.f. 3. [40] X^2 37.3; d.f. 6.

able to determine the effects of each upon criminality (Table 27) with several interesting results. Boys who had been disciplined by love-oriented techniques had generally lower crime rates than their counterparts who had been disciplined by lax or punitive measure. Only for quarrelsome-neglecting homes, however, is this difference statistically significant ($P < .001$).[41]

TABLE 27. RELATION OF HOME ATMOSPHERE AND PARENTAL DISCIPLINE TO CRIME RATE

	PERCENT OF BOYS CONVICTED OF CRIMES		
Home Atmosphere	Love-oriented Discipline	Punitive Discipline	Lax Discipline
Cohesive	(N: 66) 26	(N: 26) 42	(N: 19) 32
Quarrelsome-affectionate	(N: 12) 33	(N: 33) 39	(N: 11) 36
Broken	(N: 14) 50	(N: 16) 56	(N: 12) 50
Quarrelsome-neglecting	(N: 7) 14	(N: 20) 75	(N: 10) 100

Viewing Table 27 in another way, one may see that home atmosphere exerts an influence, except when discipline is love-oriented, in the causation of crime. Every boy with a background of both lax discipline and a quarrelsome-neglecting home had a criminal record. The crime rate for this combination was decidedly greater than for lax discipline in combination with any other type of home atmosphere ($P < .001$).[42] Not only did boys with lax discipline and quarrelsome-neglecting homes have the highest crime rate, but among boys who had lax discipline, the crime rate significantly and progressively increased from a low for cohesive homes to a high for quarrelsome-neglecting homes ($P < .005$).[43]

The effect of home atmosphere on boys disciplined punitively was less pronounced. A significantly higher proportion of such boys with quarrelsome-neglecting homes became criminal ($P < .02$).[44] Except for this comparison, however, punitive discipline resulted in similar crime rates for boys from other types of homes.[45]

Home atmosphere seemed to have relatively little effect on criminality when discipline was love-oriented. Surprisingly, for this group, boys from quarrelsome-neglecting homes had the lowest rates. None of the differences, however, were significant.[46]

[41] X^2 12.7; d.f. 1. [42] X^2 12.4; d.f. 1. [43] X^2 13.4; d.f. 3. [44] X^2 6.0; d.f. 1.
[45] X^2 7.2; d.f. 3. [46] X^2 4.49; d.f. 3.

ORIGINS OF CRIME

We therefore conclude that although quarrelsome-neglecting homes usually generate delinquency, love-oriented discipline can counteract this influence. On the other hand, cohesive homes reduce the possibility of crime among boys with lax discipline.

Many opponents of the sociological explanation of crime have contended that the higher rate of delinquency found in certain slum areas is due to the concentration of disorganized families in the worst areas. It seems reasonable to suppose that the frustrations inherent in the worst neighborhoods would tend to create tension and disruption in the family structure. This disruption in the family, not the deviant values of the neighborhood, is the basic cause, some investigators claim. One would expect, consequently, that the quarrelsome or non-cohesive homes would be heavily concentrated in those urban areas with the highest rates of crime and the greatest degree of economic and physical deterioration.

We recognized that our sample contained a limited socio-economic range and that we could not fully test this hypothesis. In terms of the lower-middle and lower class, however, we found each type of home approximately equally distributed in the various neighborhood areas (Table 28).

TABLE 28. PERCENT OF EACH TYPE OF HOME WITHIN EACH TYPE OF NEIGHBORHOOD

Home Atmosphere	NEIGHBORHOOD			
	Good (N: 36)	Fair (N: 40)	Poor (N: 96)	Worst (N: 58)
Cohesive	47	45	46	43
Quarrelsome-affectionate	11	18	20	14
Broken	22	20	22	28
Quarrelsome-neglecting	20	17	12	15

Earlier, in discussing the relationship between neighborhood and crime, we mentioned the necessity for distinguishing those characteristics which led some children within a delinquent area to become criminal while others did not. Recognizing that influences of the sub-culture may be the decisive factor under certain conditions, we hoped to estimate their effect by holding constant either neighborhood or home atmosphere. In our findings, as shown in Table 29, we believe, lies a key to the understanding of criminality. The highest crime rates appear in poor neighborhoods among families which are not cohesive. In deteriorated urban areas, the cohesiveness of a family militates against criminality: significantly fewer boys from cohesive families than from non-cohesive families became criminal—even though their immediate neighborhood contained a delinquent sub-culture ($P < .005$).[47] A cohesive home seems to be decisive in crime prevention; a broken or quarrelsome home leads to criminality especially if coupled with adverse neighborhood influences.

TABLE 29. RELATION OF HOME ATMOSPHERE AND TYPE OF NEIGHBORHOOD TO CRIME RATE

Home Atmosphere	PERCENT OF BOYS CONVICTED OF CRIMES	
	Good-Fair Neighborhood	Poor-Worst Neighborhood
Cohesive	(N: 35) 34	(N: 69) 29
Non-cohesive	(N: 41) 39	(N: 85) 53

Although the difference is not significant, boys with non-cohesive homes in better neighborhoods have less chance of becoming criminals than boys from these types of homes in poor neighborhoods. Apparently, many children from non-cohesive homes in good neighborhoods relieve tensions aroused by their family atmospheres in other ways.

Although delinquency tends to be concentrated in specific areas, it is the person's home which seems to be the critical factor. The child who lives in an emotionally frustrating home seeks gratification elsewhere. Our research indicates that children living in a cohesive home have no need for the attractions of delinquent life. Backed by the security given them by their parents, they can resist the temptations of gang membership.

The general family ethos appears to be one important reason that particular children in disorganized neighborhoods do or do not turn to crime; but to understand the dynamics of the family's influence, we must look more closely at the central figures, the father and the mother.

The Father and Crime

Since Freud's discovery of Oedipus hostility, the attitudes, personality, and actions of the father have become a center of interest

[47] X^2 8.9; d.f. 1.

in the analysis of deviant behavior of boys. Psychoanalysts such as Walter Bromberg, Benjamin Karpman, and Robert Lindner have described in fascinating detail how male criminal patients transfer resentment felt for their fathers to rebellion against society. Clinical cases, however, are a select sample from which generalizations are necessarily inconclusive, and few non-clinical analyses of the importance of the father's role in causation have been made.

One excellent study stands out as an exception. In their important research on the backgrounds of delinquents, Sheldon and Eleanor Glueck isolated several influences of the father upon criminality.[48] They found that many of the delinquents' fathers had serious physical handicaps, mental disease, or records of alcoholism and criminality. A higher proportion of the delinquents' fathers had poor work records, and a considerably greater proportion were "unacceptable models" for their sons' emulation. The Gluecks found, furthermore, that affectional relations between fathers and sons were significantly poorer in the delinquent group. Only 40 percent of the fathers of delinquents, compared to 80 percent of the fathers of non-delinquents, gave evidence of "warm affection" for their children. Fewer of the delinquent boys had close emotional ties to their fathers, and significantly more expressed open hostility. The delinquent boys more often demonstrated a feeling that their fathers were not concerned about their welfare. The Gluecks concluded that delinquents had been emotionally deprived and stunted in personality through poor father-son relations.

Other investigators, not specifically concerned with delinquents, have studied the effects of paternal behavior upon children. In research conducted at the Harvard Laboratory of Human Development, Judson Shaplin found that the father was more influential as a support for the mother and as a contributor to her prestige than as an independent source of warmth. Shaplin concluded that the son's identification with parental attitudes was less closely linked to the father's interaction with his son than with either the father's regard for his wife or the mother's interaction with the son.[49]

---

[48] Sheldon and Eleanor T. Glueck, *Unraveling Juvenile Delinquency.*

[49] Judson T. Shaplin, "Child Training and the Identification of Pre-Adolescent Boys with Their Parents."

The Glueck and the Shaplin results yielded apparently contradictory hypotheses. From the first, we would expect to find a strong relationship between the father's personality and crime; from the second, we would expect to discover that the relationship between father and son was not particularly significant in the causation of crime.

Evidence from the Cambridge-Somerville experiment, we assumed, could provide further information regarding the specific influence of paternal attitudes and character upon criminality. We tried to isolate the fathers, as individuals, in an attempt to discern the effects of their personalities [50] upon the children. Inevitably, in categorizing the fathers, we focused on their relations with the boys.[51]

The largest group, consisting of 95 fathers, was broadly classified as *warm*. Such men ranged widely in the manner in which they showed their affection for the boys. A small number were overly-protective, anxious about their children, restrictive, and highly demonstrative. Others were more taciturn. As a group, they were cordial, friendly, relaxed, and open in their dealings with the children. One counselor described a warm, but reserved, father in this way:

> The father is a strong, hard-working man, given to little emotionalism, and very interested in his boys.
> The boys were obviously fond of their father and showed him the greatest respect. On the whole, it was a happy family. The father was friendly, hardworking, concerned about his children's welfare and willing to help wherever possible.

The warm fathers had certain traits: they enjoyed their children, they were kind in their treatment, and they showed an affectionate concern for the boys.

We labeled a second group of fathers, which numbered 37, as *passive*. These men played a subsidiary role in family life, and were generally withdrawn and introverted. Nonetheless, many of these mild men, in their quiet way, loved their boys. Here is a de-

---

[50] We use the word "personality" throughout this chapter in a non-technical manner to designate both "traits" (such as anxiety) and "attitudes" (such as cruelty).

[51] Eighty percent agreement in the ratings of three independent judges indicates that the typology was applied in a reliable fashion.

scription of such a man who failed to play a dominant role within the family:

> The father is a gentle, retiring man—good-natured, keeping to himself. He does not play a very active part in the family but he apparently is fond of S. and while he has little to say either about the raising of S. or affairs in general, he plays ball with him whenever possible.

Another father of this type left discipline and the control of the family entirely under the direction of his wife; yet she described him in glowing terms: "He gets tired easily but he is quiet with an even disposition, thoughtful, kind, and good. He listens to the children's prayers."

A third type of father stood in stark contrast to the passive males. Thirty-four *cruel* fathers overtly and vehemently rejected and terrorized their children. They ruled the family with a firm grip and were verbally and physically violent with their children and their wives. The cruel fathers were aggressive men who dominated the lives of those around them.

Another 34 male parents could reasonably be called *neglecting*. These fathers did not cruelly berate their children; rather, they seemed completely indifferent to their welfare. The neglecting fathers ignored their sons or overtly rejected them. One such father stole the shoes which his son had been given by the school. Another periodically deserted the family, returning at intervals for sexual relations with his wife. Absence of either attention or concern for their families typified these men.

Of the fathers who were away from home we formed two groups, because we felt that the role played by them *in absentia* might be very different. The 21 fathers who had died fell into an obvious category. The 24 who had been more or less permanently separated from their families by divorce, desertion, or incarceration we called the *absent* fathers.

We theorized that one of these paternal types, the "warm" fathers, would account for a very small number of criminals. Such fathers offered their children the emotional security which seems necessary for socialization. This hypothesis was partially substantiated (Table 30), although unexpectedly the passive fathers turned out the smallest proportion of criminals. As we anticipated, the warm fathers, too, had few criminals among their sons. Neglecting fathers, rather than overtly cruel fathers, produced the highest number of delinquents. Divided by type of father, a significant difference appeared in the proportions of children who later became criminal ($P < .05$).[52] In addition, the cruel, dead, absent, and neglecting fathers contributed a significantly greater proportion of their sons to penal institutions than did the warm or passive fathers ($P < .001$).[53]

TABLE 30. RELATION OF FATHER'S PERSONALITY TO CRIME RATE AND INCARCERATION RATE

Father		Percent of Boys Convicted of Crimes	Percent of Boys Sentenced to Penal Institutions
Passive	(N: 37)	32	8
Warm	(N: 95)	34	5
Absent	(N: 24)	42	0
Cruel	(N: 34)	47	32
Dead	(N: 21)	52	19
Neglecting	(N: 34)	62	24

It seems, therefore, that the influence of the father depends very much upon the role he plays within the family. The fathers can be broadly grouped on the basis of Table 30 into two general types: those whose presence usually produced conformity and those who usually produced rebellion. The actions of two types of fathers —the warm and the passive—tended to produce non-criminal sons. The warm fathers furnished the prerequisites for their sons' introduction to social life. Presumably, these fathers did not cause emotional frustrations among their children and did not engender a feeling of revolt against authority.

At first glance, it seems more difficult to account for the success of passive fathers. These men were weak, ineffectual, and uninfluential in family affairs. Nevertheless, the figures indicate that paternal passivity is strongly related to low criminality. We believe that the passive fathers, in most relevant respects, closely resembled the warm fathers. Even though they were markedly withdrawn men, many of them gave evidence of an affectionate attitude toward their children. Their over-all passivity did not destroy their sons' affection or respect, perhaps because the normal role of the

[52] X^2 12.12; d.f. 5.
[53] X^2 11.25; d.f. 1 (loving and passive fathers as opposed to all others).

father in American family life is a rather passive one. The father is away from home most of the day, and the mother usually takes over the more important aspects of discipline and guidance. The greater passivity of these fathers did not strongly violate their children's conception of the paternal role.

There seems to be an additional reason why the passive fathers produced conformist children. If the boys identified with their fathers and adopted the paternal attitudes of withdrawal and passivity, they would be well insulated from the attractions of delinquent life. Gang membership involves adventuresomeness, assertion, and extroversion—traits which are antithetic to passivity.

Two types of fathers, at the other end of the scale, had a decidedly adverse effect upon the criminal proclivities of their boys. The neglecting fathers had the worst influence. These men were present in the home and actively rejected their sons. They constantly frustrated the basic emotional and material needs of their boys. It is little wonder that these children grew up in revolt against their fathers and their society.

Evidently, the constant frustrations caused by the neglecting fathers had a more serious effect than the brutal actions of the cruel fathers (although the difference between the two is not statistically significant). Both types rejected their children, but apparently the cruel fathers instilled just enough fear of retribution to keep many of their sons from becoming criminal.

Separation of the father from the home, regardless of the reason, also resulted in a high proportion of criminals. We assume that these boys lacked an acceptable male ideal for emulation. In addition, of course, they lacked a certain degree of affection which might have countermanded other adverse factors in their environment.

Since we knew that disciplinary practices bore on the causes of crime, we wished to learn whether the influence of the father's personality was only a reflection of disciplinary methods. Does the father's personality have an effect independent of the disciplinary methods which he uses? Does discipline have an effect independent of the father's character? As one would expect, a significant connection links the father's personality and the way his son is disciplined. A significantly higher proportion of families led by "warm" fathers used consistently love-oriented techniques (P < .005).[54] Families with passive and those with absent fathers seemed to select no particular form of discipline. Boys with cruel fathers, not surprisingly, were subjected to punitive discipline (P < .001).[55] And those reared by neglecting fathers were, usually, completely undisciplined (P < .01).[56] By holding constant either the father's personality or the type of discipline, we could correct any possible contamination between the ratings.

In order to test the relation of each variable to crime, we divided the fathers into the two categories which most directly reflected their influence upon criminality. In the "loving" group we placed warm and passive fathers. In the "non-loving" category we put cruel, absent, and neglecting fathers. The pattern which emerged is shown in Table 31. Loving fathers who used erratic discipline produced fewer criminal sons than non-loving fathers who used erratic discipline (P < .02).[57]

TABLE 31. RELATION OF PARENTAL DISCIPLINE AND FATHER'S PERSONALITY TO CRIME RATE

Type of Discipline	PERCENT OF BOYS CONVICTED OF CRIMES	
	Loving Fathers	Non-loving Fathers
Consistently punitive	(N: 7) 29	(N: 7) 14
Consistently love-oriented	(N: 38) 32	(N: 19) 11
Erratically love-oriented	(N: 26) 19	(N: 13) 61
Erratically punitive	(N: 35) 40	(N: 47) 66
Lax	(N: 25) 44	(N: 26) 62

It appears that unless discipline is consistent boys raised by non-loving fathers are prone to crime. If the father was not loving, significantly fewer boys who had been disciplined consistently became criminal (P < .001).[58] If the father was warm or passive, however, the crime-rate variation was not statistically significant.

The importance of discipline can best be seen in relation to other conditions within the home. Consistent and kindly methods of control are most important when other factors are conducive to rebellion.

We have assumed that acceptance of family values plays a large

[54] X^2 9.7; d.f. 1.   [55] X^2 26.4; d.f. 1.   [56] X^2 7.2; d.f. 1.
[57] X^2 12.4; d.f. 1. For erratic love-oriented discipline alone (X^2 7.2) and for erratic punitive discipline alone (X^2 5.4) the differences were significant.
[58] X^2 22.2; d.f. 1.

part in the prevention of crime. Those forces which are related to low criminality—consistent discipline, a cohesive home, a warm or passive father—all seem to lead the child to close identification with family values. These values need not, however, be identical with those of society at large. One often hears the aphorism: "Like father, like son." If a father acts as a deviant model, does his son, too, become deviant? We attempted to answer this question by grouping the fathers in accordance with what was known of their behavior.

Forty-five fathers had criminal records. An additional 69 fathers were either alcoholic or blatantly unfaithful to their wives. The remaining 139 fathers, for purposes of this study, were classified as non-deviant in behavior. An examination of the father's "role model" (together with his personality) revealed an expected pattern of causation (Table 32). The numbers in each category were

TABLE 32. RELATION OF FATHER'S PERSONALITY AND ROLE MODEL TO CRIME RATE

	PERCENT OF BOYS CONVICTED OF CRIMES		
Father's Personality	Criminal Father	Alcoholic or Sexually Unfaithful Father	Non-deviant Father
Warm	(N: 13) 46	(N: 15) 27	(N: 67) 33
Passive	(N: 6) 50	(N: 15) 40	(N: 16) 13
Cruel or neglecting	(N: 13) 85	(N: 25) 60	(N: 30) 40
Absent	(N: 11) 55	(N: 13) 38	(N: 21) 48

unequally represented; yet one could see the influence of the paternal role model on crime: There is a general tendency for boys with criminal fathers to have criminal sons ($P < .005$).[59] Sons of criminals become criminals themselves, especially if their fathers have been cruel or neglecting ($P < .01$).[60] In addition, crime rates are highest for boys raised by alcoholic or sexually unfaithful fathers if these fathers have also been cruel or neglecting ($P < .05$).[61]

A review of Table 32 indicates that the father's role model exerts the greatest influence when the father is either cruel or neglecting. This finding tends to contravene one psychological interpretation of the phenomenon of identification: that theory which places major emphasis upon the need for love as the basis

[59] X^2 9.7; d.f. 1. [60] X^2 4.6; d.f. 1 for criminal fathers.
[61] X^2 3.9; d.f. 1 for alcoholic and sexually unfaithful fathers.

for internalization of values. The finding tends to lend support, on the other hand, to those investigators who maintain that a child "identifies"—patterns his behavior after—that individual who exerts aggressive power over him. Interestingly, however, the son appears to identify with a cruel or neglecting father only if the father's behavior is deviant. Thus, perhaps, the child's "identification with the aggressor" occurs only when the model provides a "permissible" outlet for the aggressive feelings created by aggression—that is, when the father himself encourages by his behavior the child's aggressive urges.

By holding constant discipline, we hoped to discover more about the effects of the paternal role model on crime. Table 33

TABLE 33. RELATION OF PARENTAL DISCIPLINE AND FATHER'S ROLE MODEL TO CRIME RATE

	PERCENT OF BOYS CONVICTED OF CRIMES					
Type of Discipline	Criminal Father		Alcoholic or Sexually Unfaithful Father		Non-deviant Father	
Consistently punitive	(N: 2)	0	(N: 1)	100	(N: 11)	18
Consistently love-oriented	(N: 11)	18	(N: 8)	25	(N: 41)	29
Erratically love-oriented	(N: 3)	67	(N: 14)	43	(N: 23)	26
Erratically punitive	(N: 17)	76	(N: 26)	54	(N: 41)	44
Lax	(N: 12)	75	(N: 20)	35	(N: 20)	50

indicates that consistent discipline militates against criminal tendencies, even though the father himself may be criminal. Of the boys reared by criminal fathers, those who were disciplined consistently had a lower crime rate than those disciplined erratically ($P < .001$).[62]

These several analyses indicate that fathers arouse a tendency toward criminal behavior in their children if the child is deprived of paternal affection through absence, cruelty, or neglect. The likelihood of crime is increased if the child is disciplined in an erratic fashion or is left undisciplined. The son's drive toward crime is increased even more if the father himself is criminal. On the other hand, warmth or passivity on the part of the father, combined with consistent discipline and a non-deviant role model, helps to insulate the son against criminality.

From analyses of paternal influence, disciplinary methods, and

[62] X^2 17.0; d.f. 1.

family atmosphere, we have found that emotional support from within the family can do much to prevent crime. As we turn to the mother, often the pivot of family life, the causes of delinquency can be understood more fully.

The Mother and Crime

To assert that the mother's relation to her child plays a critical part in the development of personality expresses a platitude accepted wholeheartedly by psychologists as well as by the general population. Maternal influence has recently received considerable scrutiny from social scientists. The psychologist David Levy has investigated one aspect, maternal overprotection,[63] while many researchers have examined its counterpart, deprivation of maternal affection. Some investigators, particularly psychiatrists, would generalize their clinical findings to the conclusion that the mother's attitudes (particularly her unconscious encouragement of "acting-out" behavior) play the primary, if not the sole, role in causation.

Only a handful of studies, however, have directly linked maternal attitudes to criminality. Research has too frequently been based on a limited number of boys, selected by criteria which may have biased the results. (Cases found in child guidance clinics, for example, are usually delinquents whose parents have sought psychological aid.)

In this area, too, Sheldon and Eleanor Glueck have performed notable service through their extensive comparisons of delinquent and non-delinquent boys.[64] Their research in *Unraveling Juvenile Delinquency* is undoubtedly the best known of the studies relating emotional deprivation to delinquency. In their study, although 28 percent of the 500 delinquents' mothers were either indifferent or rejecting toward their children, only 4 percent of the non-delinquents' mothers had these attitudes. The delinquent children less often demonstrated a strong emotional attachment to their mothers. Only 23 percent of the delinquents compared to 71 percent of the non-delinquents believed that their mothers were genuinely concerned for their welfare.

[63] David Levy, *Maternal Overprotection*.
[64] Sheldon and Eleanor T. Glueck, *Unraveling Juvenile Delinquency*.

The Cambridge-Somerville experiment provided material for a somewhat different form of analysis. First, the Gluecks' sample of delinquents was composed of boys already sentenced to reform school; our criterion of criminality consisted in conviction by the courts, regardless of sentence, for crimes other than traffic violations. Second, in our project the social investigators who gathered material about the boys did not know the outcome of their lives. Third, the fact that their records covered a number of years and contained many interviews with the boys' mothers allowed rather fine distinctions concerning maternal attitudes and personality.

In a first broad classification, we found 174 mothers who seemed to love their children and to be actively concerned about their welfare. The records, however, indicated basic differences among these women. Some were overprotective, others markedly anxious, others neurotic, and still others could be typed as "loving-normal." We divided the remaining 77 mothers into four categories: the passive, the neglecting, the cruel, and the absent.[65]

We found a high proportion of *overprotective* mothers among the Cambridge-Somerville families. Fifty-nine mothers had strong anxiety about their children, strenuously attempted to "protect" them, and rigorously restricted their sons' activities. The children of these mothers were treated as if they were still in an infantile stage. One of the overprotective mothers resisted "intervention" by the study. The caseworker reported her words:

"P is the kind of boy who likes to stay around the house and I want him to stay there. I don't want him going off any place with you." . . . She then added that she did not want her boy to go to camp or go away from her at any time though it was permissible for us to provide him with some of the necessities he is lacking.

The record of another overprotective mother illustrates the extremes of restriction which these women set upon their boys:

"I don't allow A. to go outdoors anymore after school." She went on to say that she keeps him in the house under her supervision so that "he won't associate with those bad boys." She said that he could, however, bring his friends to the house but A. immediately countered, "But you don't like any of my friends."

[65] Three judges reached 88 percent agreement regarding categorization of the mothers.

Thirty-three mothers, similar in personality to the overprotective mothers, differed from the first group in the extent to which they restricted their children's activities. Not only in relation to their sons but in other areas of their lives, they exhibited an inordinate degree of anxiety. One such *loving-anxious* mother was described by a psychologist in this way:

> The mother is very talkative and excitable. She is extremely concerned about C. She considers her responsibility toward her son very seriously and is often worried about him to ridiculous extremes. Though she will not restrict him, she will not hesitate to call me at any hour to discuss her fears.
> She is fairly bright and rather warm and affectionate in her relationships. "You know, I have not been sleeping well; he asks so many questions. What shall I do? I let him go where he wants but I get worried and nervous." In such continuous instances, she expresses her devotion to the boy but also shows undue concern over the petty details of his behavior.

Permeating anxiety in 23 of the mothers had reached the level of an apparent neurosis or latent psychosis. Although these women were affectionate toward their boys, they were preoccupied with their own emotional problems and the symptoms caused by these conflicts. A social worker described one of these *loving-neurotic* mothers:

> The mother is very concerned about the boy but seems to exhibit an unusual degree of possessiveness. "I might as well be dead" is a typical comment among her continual threats of suicide. In addition, she is usually morose and pessimistic and extreme in self-pity. Though constantly talking of E., she seems to be really jealous of any attention paid to him.
> She has a cleaning compulsion and an obsessive fear of dirt and germs. Everything in the house must be scrubbed constantly and hands washed frequently. If a cat enters the apartment, she takes a rag and cleans every place the cat has touched. Walls and floors have to be continually scrubbed even though she is physically exhausted. Every speck of dust must be cleaned up and apologized for.

The group of mothers whom we classified as *loving-normal* were, in general, kindly and affectionate. They were not overly restrictive, nor did they exhibit any signs of marked anxiety or neurosis. They enjoyed the company of their children and had a zest for life. The description below typifies the 59 loving-normal mothers:

> A strong bond of affection exists between mother and son. She is young, excitable, friendly, and enthusiastic, warm-hearted and extremely cordial. She is continually trying to provide the best life has to offer her son, even though it entails a good deal of sacrifice on her part. She commented, "E. is really a very good boy. It makes me feel good to see him grow up. I can't thank you enough for helping him and I do all I can too."

Besides establishing four types of "loving" mothers, we grouped together 22 women in the *passive* category. Like the passive fathers, as parents these women were weak and ineffectual. Phlegmatic in manner, they played only a minor role within the family, leaving direction and discipline of the children to other people in the home. An "I cannot be bothered" attitude governed their relationship with their sons. The personality of the passive mothers is illustrated in this description of one of them:

> Mrs. A. is acquiescent and tends to be easy going, taking the path of least resistance. Her chief wish seems to be to have a little peace. It is difficult to make her talk about the boy in any way though she expresses fondness for him. She does not seem to want to be bothered by anything that looks like another problem and prefers to assume that everything is all right.
>
> She seems to protect and indulge the child without any outward sign of affection. She does not see the child as presenting any difficulty and seems to expect very little of him. She gives the impression of having already used up her energy in bringing up her other children.

Not just emotional passivity, but total indifference to their children, characterized the 25 parents whom we described as *neglecting* mothers. These women neglected the physical and psychological needs of their offspring. Seldom did they exhibit any sign of affection. One boy who had a neglecting mother exclaimed to his counselor: "What a cheap bunch! They even forgot my birthday. No present, not even a card, nothing!" A teacher described another of the neglected children in school:

> B. was very humiliated because he had to clomp around the classroom in rubber-boots that came up to his knees. When asked if his mother had not been able to get his shoes repaired he first said that she was too busy and then muttered that she didn't really care about him anyway.

Another group of mothers, through verbal and physical abuse, made clear to their sons that the boys were heartily disliked. These 22 *cruel* mothers dominated their boys and showed no affection toward them. When asked about his mother, one of these cruelly treated children replied: "She can go to hell . . . . she even hits me with a stick. . . . I will do anything to get away, even go to a training school." A social worker described another of the cruel mothers in action:

She got unduly excited whenever A. was around and when he hesitated to leave she smashed him, yelled, and screamed till the boy was in fact, too petrified to move.

Finally, a small number of mothers were permanently absent from the home. There were only 8 individuals in this category. Separation and divorce were frequent, but there was a high degree of replacement. If the natural mother had left the home but had been replaced by a stepmother or a mother-substitute, we classified the substitute mother in the appropriate category.

An examination of the maternal backgrounds of the criminals and the non-criminals in the Cambridge-Somerville study showed some interesting differences (Table 34). In general, if the mother

TABLE 34. RELATION OF MOTHER'S PERSONALITY TO CRIME RATE AND INCARCERATION RATE

Mother		Percent of Boys Convicted of Crimes	Percent of Boys Sentenced to Penal Institutions
Loving-normal	(N: 59)	27	9
Loving-anxious	(N: 33)	34	12
Overprotective	(N: 59)	37	7
Loving-neurotic	(N: 23)	43	0
Cruel	(N: 22)	45	20
Absent	(N: 8)	50	13
Passive	(N: 21)	57	29
Neglecting	(N: 25)	72	40

gave affection to her children, crime rates remained low: variation between the four "loving" categories was not statistically significant. On the other hand, neglect on the mother's part led to a high rate of criminality. Boys who had loving mothers were not only less often convicted of crimes ($P < .01$),[66] but they also

[66] X^2 18.53; d.f. 7.

were significantly less frequently sentenced to penal institutions than were boys with non-loving mothers ($P < .001$).[67]

Loving mothers, regardless of their other personality characteristics, apparently gave their children enough emotional security for the internalization of moral controls. Several of the factors which we analyzed testify to the importance of emotional security. Cohesive homes, warm or passive fathers, consistent discipline, as well as loving mothers, tended to give the boys enough inner security so that they did not turn to delinquency for recognition.

Forty-five percent of the boys who had cruel mothers became criminals. The fact that this percentage was not higher indicates that despite physical abuse and overt rejection, this cruel attention instilled at least a fear of retaliation by the law.

Paralleling the father's influence on criminality, the highest proportion of criminals came from homes in which the mother was neglecting. The basic foundations of conformity were absent. But in contrast to our previous findings about the father, the passive mothers produced a very high proportion of criminal sons. Passivity in the father tended to decrease crime; passivity in the mother seemed to increase it. Moreover, almost a third of the sons of passive mothers served time in a penal institution, compared to only 8 percent of the sons of passive fathers.

The contrast in influence of maternal and paternal passivity may be due to the different expectations which the child has concerning each parent. Given the fact that the father is often absent from the home (that passivity is, in a sense, his normal role), the child does not view paternal passivity as rejection. When the mother is passive, however, the child's expectations are distinctly violated. The mother's role within the family is normally a very active one in American society. To the child, a passive, indifferent, withdrawn mother must appear to be rejecting him, when he compares her to his friends' mothers.

We found previously that the effects of disciplinary methods varied according to general home atmosphere, the personality of the father, and his role model. We then wished to discover the relationship between the mother's personality and disciplinary

[67] X^2 19.49; d.f. 1.

control. Of course, we recognized that the categorization of disciplinary techniques and of mother's personality overlapped to some extent. Yet some loving mothers disciplined their children punitively, and some non-loving mothers disciplined their children in a "love-oriented" manner (e.g., by withholding privileges).

Not surprisingly, we found love-oriented discipline in general use by loving mothers ($P < .001$).[68] Boys raised by cruel mothers were most frequently subjected to punitive discipline ($P < .005$).[69] And a significantly higher proportion of boys whose mothers were either absent or neglecting were left almost entirely undisciplined ($P < .001$).[70]

As in analyzing the influence of the father, by holding constant either the mother's personality or her method of discipline, we could correct any possible contamination between the ratings. More important, we could examine the effects of discipline and maternal personality as they interact in the causation of crime. We divided the mothers into two large groups: loving mothers and non-loving mothers (including cruel, absent, passive, and neglecting). Table 35 reveals the influence of discipline and maternal personality on crime. Despite the disproportionate distribution

TABLE 35. RELATION OF PARENTAL DISCIPLINE AND MOTHER'S PERSONALITY TO CRIME RATE

	PERCENT OF BOYS CONVICTED OF CRIMES	
Type of Discipline	Loving Mother	Non-loving Mother
Consistently punitive	(N: 10) 10	(N: 4) 50
Consistently love-oriented	(N: 56) 25	(N: 4) 25
Erratically love-oriented	(N: 34) 38	(N: 6) 17
Erratically punitive	(N: 45) 44	(N: 37) 65
Lax	(N: 29) 38	(N: 23) 70

among the various categories, two findings emerge from the table: crime rates among boys who had been raised by loving mothers were significantly lower if discipline was consistent ($P < .01$);[71] and crime rates among boys who had been reared by non-loving mothers were significantly lower if their discipline was love-oriented ($P < .01$).[72]

The table also shows that unless discipline was love-oriented,

[68] X^2 20.3; d.f. 1. [69] X^2 9.0; d.f. 1. [70] X^2 16.3; d.f. 1. [71] X^2 6.6; d.f. 1.
[72] X^2 7.3; d.f. 1.

absence of maternal love resulted in higher criminal rates. Significantly more boys among those who received punitive discipline became criminal if their mothers were non-loving ($P < .025$).[73] Similarly, for boys with lax discipline, a significantly larger proportion became criminal if their mothers had been non-loving ($P < .025$).[74]

We therefore conclude that a combination of lax or erratically punitive discipline with a lack of maternal affection greatly increases a tendency to criminality. On the other hand, consistent discipline coupled with maternal love greatly reduces the chances of criminality.

From our examination of the father's influence, we noted the effects of the father's role model on the behavior of his son. To examine the influence of the mother's role model, we categorized the mothers into three groups: those with criminal records, those known to be either alcoholic or sexually promiscuous, and those who were (to our knowledge) not deviant. Table 36 demonstrates

TABLE 36. RELATION OF MOTHER'S ROLE MODEL TO CRIME RATE

Mother's Role Model		Percent of Boys Convicted of Crimes
Criminal	(N: 15)	60
Alcoholic or sexually unfaithful	(N: 30)	67
Non-deviant	(N: 206)	36

that if the mother is deviant, there is a pronounced tendency for her son to become criminal ($P < .001$).[75]

To discover whether the role model represented by the mother was more crucial in the causation of crime than her affectional relationship to the son, we divided those mothers who were present in the home into four groups (omitting the eight absent mothers) as shown in Table 37. From the table it is clear that the mother's personality and her role model influence her son's criminal tend-

TABLE 37. RELATION OF MOTHER'S PERSONALITY AND ROLE MODEL TO CRIME RATE

	PERCENT OF BOYS CONVICTED OF CRIMES	
Mother's Personality	Deviant Role Model	Non-deviant Role Model
Loving	(N: 24) 50	(N: 150) 31
Non-loving	(N: 21) 81	(N: 48) 48

---

[73] X^2 5.0; d.f. 1. [74] X^2 5.0; d.f. 1. [75] X^2 12.4; d.f. 1.

encies in the following ways: if a mother is non-loving, her son's chances of becoming criminal are significantly increased if she is also a deviant role model ($P < .005$); [76] if a mother is loving, her son's chances of becoming criminal appear to be slightly increased if she is also a deviant model (non-significant); whether the mother is deviant or not, her son's chances of becoming criminal are significantly increased if she is non-loving ($P < .05$).[77]

The effect of a deviant mother on her son varied according to the form of discipline. Clearly, from Table 38, erratically punitive

TABLE 38. RELATION OF PARENTAL DISCIPLINE AND MOTHER'S ROLE MODEL TO CRIME RATE

	PERCENT OF BOYS CONVICTED OF CRIMES	
Type of Discipline	Deviant Role Model	Non-deviant Role Model
Consistently punitive	(N: 1) 0	(N: 13) 23
Consistently love-oriented	(N: 7) 29	(N: 53) 26
Erratically love-oriented	(N: 10) 40	(N: 30) 33
Erratically punitive	(N: 18) 94	(N: 66) 42
Lax	(N: 9) 67	(N: 43) 44

discipline combined with a deviant mother led to criminality. Holding constant erratically punitive discipline, criminal rates varied significantly according to the mother's role model ($P < .001$).[78] In addition, the table shows that the general tendency toward higher criminality for sons of deviant women was diminished through consistent discipline ($P < .01$).[79]

As a result of these statistical tabulations, it seems fair to assume that maternal affection and role model are two primary determinants of criminality. In summary, a child is very likely to become criminal (1) if his mother is rejecting, (2) if the mother herself is deviant, and (3) if the son undergoes erratically punitive discipline. On the other hand, a boy is unlikely to turn to crime (1) if his mother is loving, (2) if he undergoes consistent discipline, and (3) if his mother is not deviant.

The results of our examination of both the mother and the father have underlined the importance of parental influence in the causation of crime. The following chapter presents our findings concerning the combined, interacting influence of both parents on the child.

[76] X^2 8.2; d.f. 1.
[77] X^2 4.7; d.f. 1 for deviant mothers. X^2 4.4; d.f. 1 for non-deviant mothers.
[78] X^2 15.5; d.f. 1. [79] X^2 7.0; d.f. 1.

CHAPTER V

FAMILY STRUCTURE AND CRIME

MANY STUDIES HAVE, LIKE OURS, STRESSED THE IMPORTANCE OF THE family in the etiology of crime. It is seldom, however, that these studies have progressed beyond the level of broad generalization. In this chapter, we plan to examine in more specific detail the relative effects of father and mother on the causation of crime. We will present at least tentative answers to such questions as: (1) If the personalities of a child's parents differ, whose influence predominates with respect to criminality? (2) In terms of crime, is there a more pronounced influence upon the child if the father or if the mother is rejecting? and (3) If one parent's behavior is non-deviant but the other's is deviant, is the child more likely to follow one rather than the other? In general, therefore, we are examining the problem of how the influence of one parent depends upon the affectional attitude and role model of the other parent.

We have found that the affection of the parents for their child generally determines the son's chances of becoming criminal. We found low crime rates in families reared by either passive or warm fathers, and particularly high criminality in families with neglecting fathers. In families with loving or overprotective mothers we found low crime rates, but in families with passive or neglecting mothers we found a strong tendency toward criminality. Which of the parents, we wondered, had the greater influence in causation?

Before estimating the relative importance of the parents, we ascertained the correlations in parental personality. After dividing the mothers into the three personality types of loving, overprotective, and non-loving (which included passive, absent, cruel, and

FAMILY STRUCTURE AND CRIME

neglecting mothers), we divided each group according to the personalities of their husbands (Table 39).

TYPE 39. PERCENT OF MOTHERS OF EACH PERSONALITY TYPE MARRIED TO FATHERS OF EACH PERSONALITY TYPE

Father	MOTHER		
	Loving (N: 112)	Overprotective (N: 60)	Non-Loving (N: 72)
Warm	52	37	19
Passive	11	18	18
Absent	18	20	18
Cruel	7	15	24
Neglecting	12	10	21

Performing the same analysis in terms of the husbands of each type of woman (Table 40), we found that, not surprisingly, the

TABLE 40. PERCENT OF FATHERS OF EACH PERSONALITY TYPE MARRIED TO MOTHERS OF EACH PERSONALITY TYPE

Mother	FATHER				
	Warm (N: 94)	Passive (N: 37)	Absent (N: 45)	Cruel (N: 34)	Neglecting (N: 34)
Loving	62	35	44	24	38
Overprotective	23	30	27	26	18
Non-loving	15	35	29	50	44

relationship between the personality of the mother and that of the father is highly significant ($P < .005$).[1] Pre-marital selection may well have given rise to the correlations; yet post-marital behavior could easily have influenced the attitudes of both parents.

Whether because warmth of personality led to mutual attraction or because the affection of one parent brought forth affection from the other, more than half of the families with loving mothers had warm fathers. An even higher proportion of the warm fathers were married to loving mothers ($P < .001$).[2]

One could hypothesize that passive males lean toward women who have strong maternal instincts, reflected in overly restrictive care of their children. Yet only a slightly higher proportion of passive fathers than of other types were married to overprotective wives and less than one third of the passive fathers had overprotective wives. Overprotectiveness might be thought of as a response

[1] X^2 25.1; d.f. 8.   [2] X^2 15.5; d.f. 1.

to the husband's absence, yet only a fourth of the wives of absent fathers were overprotective. In addition, it should be noted that only 10 percent of the overprotective mothers had neglecting spouses; and of neglecting fathers, the smallest proportion were married to overprotective women. Thus, overprotectiveness did *not* seem to be a compensation for neglect by the father. Nor was it a compensation for paternal absence or passivity.

A significant relationship appeared between non-loving mothers and husbands who were cruel ($P < .005$).[3] The reason for this may be that neither parent wanted children and their rejection was reflected in cruelty. Perhaps, too, non-loving mothers were cold wives, both sexually and in other ways, and their husbands gave vent to their frustration through cruelty to their children. Similar reasoning might account for the connection between non-loving mothers and neglecting fathers ($P < .05$).[4]

Without attempting to explain why there was a link between mothers' and fathers' personality, it can be seen that the two variables were certainly not independent. Loving mothers tended to be paired with warm fathers, and rejecting mothers tended to be married to cruel or neglecting fathers.

As a first step in isolating various influences of the parents upon the child, we analyzed the relative effects of maternal as opposed to paternal passivity. Earlier, we reported the discovery that paternal passivity militated against crime while maternal passivity promoted it. Conceivably, these results might be explained by the influence of the mates of the passive parents. Yet when one examines this problem, an orderly phenomenon appears: passivity in one parent, without love from the other parent, correlates differently with crime according to whether the mother or the father has a passive personality (Table 41). Criminality occurred sig-

TABLE 41. RELATION OF PARENTAL PASSIVITY TO CRIME RATE WHEN NEITHER PARENT WAS LOVING

Parents		Percent of Boys Convicted of Crimes
Mother passive	(N: 8)	88
Father passive	(N: 9)	22
Both parents passive	(N: 4)	75

[3] X^2 8.0; d.f. 1.   [4] X^2 4.1; d.f. 1.

FAMILY STRUCTURE AND CRIME

nificantly more frequently among boys cared for by passive mothers than among boys raised by passive fathers, despite the fact that the spouse was non-loving in all cases. ($P < .01$).[5]

We found a second contrast between maternal and paternal passivity: if the mother is passive, her effect on the son depends upon the father's personality. Table 42 demonstrates this phe-

TABLE 42. RELATION OF FATHER'S PERSONALITY AND MATERNAL PASSIVITY TO CRIME RATE

Father		Percent of Boys Convicted of Crimes
Warm	(N: 8)	38
Neglecting, absent, or cruel	(N: 8)	88

nomenon. The numbers in each category in the table are small; yet it would appear that among these few children raised by passive mothers, boys cared for by "warm" fathers had a strikingly lower crime rate than boys subjected to non-loving fathers ($P < .05$).[6] Paternal warmth, therefore, seems to deter the bad effects of maternal passivity (or, conversely, maternal passivity is particularly harmful if the father is not loving toward his son).

When, on the other hand, the father was passive, there was no statistically significant pattern; the crime rate remained low regardless of the mother's personality (Table 43). We can hypoth-

TABLE 43. RELATION OF MOTHER'S PERSONALITY AND PATERNAL PASSIVITY TO CRIME RATE

Mother		Percent of Boys Convicted of Crimes
Loving	(N: 24)	29
Non-loving	(N: 13)	38

esize that the relatively low crime rate among boys raised by passive fathers is directly due to the father's behavior. It may have been imitation of the father's timidity, introversion, and withdrawal which resulted in non-delinquent sons.

Next, we wished to investigate the influence of each parent's affectional relationship with the son and its effect on crime. We divided the families into four groups: both parents loving (including passive fathers), both parents rejecting (omitting absent

[5] X^2 7.5; d.f. 1.   [6] X^2 4.2; d.f. 1.

parents), a loving father and a rejecting mother, and a rejecting father and a loving mother. We computed the rate of crime of the sons in each combination (Table 44). As one would expect,

TABLE 44. RELATION OF PARENTAL AFFECTION TO CRIME RATE

Mother	PERCENT OF BOYS CONVICTED OF CRIMES	
	Loving Father	Rejecting Father
Loving	(N: 104) 32	(N: 36) 36
Rejecting	(N: 24) 46	(N: 40) 70

families in which both parents were loving produced the lowest proportion of criminals; families in which both were rejecting produced the highest proportion of criminals ($P < .001$).[7] But one result was unexpected: rejection by one parent did not produce a significantly higher crime rate than that for those boys whose parents were both loving. So long as the mother was loving, crime rates rose only slightly if the father was rejecting. Children who were raised by a loving mother and a rejecting father did not become criminal significantly more often than those children who were raised by two loving parents.[8] If, on the other hand, the father was loving, the attitude of the mother did not make a significant difference in the rate of crime. The combination of a loving father and a rejecting mother did not produce significantly more criminals than did the combination of two loving parents.

Maternal rejection appeared to be more criminogenic than paternal rejection. In a comparison of rates among children with rejecting mothers, fewer who had loving fathers than those who had rejecting fathers became criminal; yet this difference was not statistically significant. If the father was rejecting, however, the attitude of the mother significantly affected the rate of crime. A comparison of the rates among men who were subjected to rejecting fathers shows that significantly fewer who were reared by loving mothers became criminal ($P < .005$).[9]

From this analysis, one can see that maternal attitudes were of primary importance in the genesis of crime. If the mother was loving, her sons had only a small chance of becoming criminal

[7] X^2 17.5; d.f. 1.
[8] The relatively higher rates of crime for sons of overprotective or loving-neurotic mothers were not lowered when the father was loving or rejecting.
[9] X^2 9.3; d.f. 1.

FAMILY STRUCTURE AND CRIME

—regardless of the father's attitude. If the mother was rejecting, her sons were likely to become criminal, especially if the father was rejecting.

Because of the obvious importance of maternal love in determination of criminality, we wished to hold this factor constant in a reassessment of the relationship between father's personality and crime. Table 45 again demonstrates how paternal passivity

TABLE 45. RELATION OF FATHER'S AND MOTHER'S PERSONALITY TO CRIME RATE

Father	PERCENT OF BOYS CONVICTED OF CRIMES	
	Loving Mother	Non-loving Mother
Warm	(N: 80) 33	(N: 14) 43
Passive	(N: 24) 29	(N: 13) 38
Absent	(N: 32) 41	(N: 13) 62
Cruel	(N: 17) 24	(N: 17) 71
Neglecting	(N: 19) 47	(N: 15) 80

tends to reduce criminality: holding constant an absence of maternal love, we found that if the father was either passive or warm, crime rates were lower than if he was absent, cruel, or neglecting ($P < .02$).[10] And if the father was either passive or warm, the mother's love made very little difference in terms of criminality.

As would be expected, crime rates varied in accordance with maternal love if the father was either absent or neglecting ($P < .025$).[11] But maternal love appeared even more important as the critical condition for families dominated by cruel fathers: holding constant paternal cruelty, criminality appeared significantly less frequently if the mother was loving ($P < .01$).[12] Paternal cruelty apparently leads to crime only if not counteracted by maternal love.

The crime-rate variation corresponding to the father's personality was not statistically significant if the mother was loving. Thus, it appears that the father's personality strongly affects criminality only as a secondary condition—that is, providing that the mother is non-loving.

Since paternal warmth or passivity seems to have a tendency to reduce criminality among boys with non-loving mothers, we

[10] X^2 6.5; d.f. 1. Absent parents were not included in the previous analysis.
[11] X^2 5.1; d.f. 1.   [12] X^2 7.6; d.f. 1.

wondered if, perhaps, paternal love (as found in warm or passive fathers) reduced the criminogenic force of certain types of mothers more than of others. This question is answered in Table 46. Pre-

TABLE 46. RELATION OF MOTHER'S AND FATHER'S PERSONALITY TO CRIME RATE

Mother	PERCENT OF BOYS CONVICTED OF CRIMES	
	Warm or Passive Father	Non-loving Father
Loving	(N: 104) 32	(N: 68) 38
Passive	(N: 12) 50	(N: 8) 88
Absent	(N: 3) 0	(N: 5) 80
Cruel	(N: 8) 13	(N: 12) 67
Neglecting	(N: 4) 100	(N: 20) 65

viously, we found that if the father was loving, absence of maternal love did not result in significantly higher crime rates. Yet when we considered variations in the mothers' personality types, we found that despite paternal love, if the mother was passive or neglecting, significantly greater criminality resulted than if the mother was loving ($P < .02$).[13] Furthermore, still holding constant paternal love, maternal passivity or neglect led to significantly higher crime rates than did maternal cruelty ($P < .02$).[14]

The effects of maternal cruelty, as of paternal cruelty, seem to depend upon the other parent's personality. Given maternal cruelty, if the father was non-loving, criminality occurred significantly more frequently ($P < .02$).[15] It therefore seems reasonable to conclude that the effects of parental cruelty may be counteracted by love. Perhaps this is because the child learns to avoid the cruel parent, whereas he cannot "avoid" neglect.

This analysis of the interaction of the mother's and the father's personality points to three conclusions: (1) maternal love is a strong antidote to crime; (2) paternal love, unless coupled with maternal neglect, also tends to prevent crime; and (3) absence of love from either parent, coupled with other factors, is strongly conducive to criminality.

The influence of parental role models on crime was discussed in Chapter IV. There we found that if the father was criminal or

---

[13] X^2 5.8; d.f. 1.   [14] X^2 5.5; d.f. 1.
[15] X^2 5.7; d.f. 1. Unfortunately, the evidence regarding maternal absence is too slight to be more than suggestive.

if the mother's behavior was deviant, high crime rates resulted. Table 47 shows how paternal and maternal role models interact

TABLE 47. RELATION OF PARENTAL ROLE MODELS TO CRIME RATE

	PERCENT OF BOYS CONVICTED OF CRIMES		
Mother's Role Model	Criminal Father	Alcoholic or Sexually Unfaithful Father	Non-deviant Father
Deviant	(N: 16) 88	(N: 17) 59	(N: 12) 42
Non-deviant	(N: 29) 31	(N: 52) 42	(N: 127) 34

in the causation of crime: If the father was criminal, high crime rates resulted only if the mother's behavior was deviant. If the mother's role model was non-deviant, criminal rates were significantly lower than if the mother was deviant ($P < .001$).[16] On the other hand, if the mother's role model was deviant, crime rates varied according to the father's behavior. Holding constant the deviant behavior of the mother, crime rates were highest if the father was criminal; and if the father was alcoholic or sexually unfaithful, criminality was more frequent than if the father was not deviant ($P < .05$).[17]

We supposed that disciplinary methods would be influential in determining whether or not the child would imitate a deviant model. One would expect that punishment for imitation of deviance would be a preventive measure against criminality (Table 48). We found that although consistent discipline seemed to deter

TABLE 48. RELATION OF PARENTAL DISCIPLINE AND ROLE MODELS TO CRIME RATE

	PERCENT OF BOYS CONVICTED OF CRIMES		
Type of Discipline	Both Parents Deviant	One Parent Deviant	Neither Parent Deviant
Consistent	(N: 4) 25	(N: 22) 23	(N: 48) 27
Erratically love-oriented	(N: 6) 50	(N: 15) 40	(N: 19) 26
Erratically punitive	(N: 16) 94	(N: 29) 48	(N: 39) 41
Lax	(N: 7) 71	(N: 26) 46	(N: 19) 47

crime if one parent was deviant (and either consistent or love-oriented discipline seemed to deter crime if neither was deviant), the differences are not statistically significant. Again, discipline

---

[16] X^2 13.2; d.f. 1.   [17] X^2 6.6; d.f. 2.

appeared to be most relevant to criminality in conjunction with adverse conditions. If discipline was erratic (whether punitive or love-oriented), the role model strongly affected criminality ($P < .005$).[18] If discipline was consistent, however, the parental role model did not seem to influence criminal behavior. If both parents were deviant, either lax or erratically punitive discipline increased the criminogenic effect ($P < .001$).[19] Thus, consistent discipline does seem to deter criminality.

In discussing the relationship between criminality and the influence of each parent, we noted that a child was apt to become criminal either if the mother's role model was deviant or if she was rejecting. We saw also that criminal fathers had a high proportion of criminal sons. One would expect that maternal rejection coupled with a criminal paternal model would lead to crime. We wondered if boys would be less apt to pattern their behavior after a criminal father if their mothers were loving (Table 49).

TABLE 49. RELATION OF MOTHER'S PERSONALITY AND FATHER'S ROLE MODEL TO CRIME RATE

PERCENT OF BOYS CONVICTED OF CRIMES

Mother	Criminal Father	Alcoholic or Sexually Unfaithful Father	Non-deviant Father
Loving	(N: 27) 41	(N: 45) 42	(N: 102) 28
Rejecting	(N: 15) 87	(N: 23) 48	(N: 31) 52

We found, as we had hypothesized, that the father's role model is most crucial when the mother is rejecting: if the mother was rejecting, criminal fathers had a higher proportion of criminal sons than did non-deviant fathers ($P < .025$).[20] If the mother was loving, however, the role model of the father was not significantly related to criminality. Secondly, maternal love tends to negate the influence of a criminal father. Among boys with criminal fathers, those with loving mothers had a significantly lower crime rate ($P < .005$).[21] Third, we found that maternal rejection leads to criminality even if the father's role model is non-deviant. In

---

[18] X^2 13.3; d.f. 2.   [19] X^2 12.2; d.f. 1.
[20] X^2 5.2; d.f. 1. Boys with absent mothers were omitted from this analysis. One out of two who had criminal fathers and three out of five who had non-deviant fathers became criminal.
[21] X^2 8.3; d.f. 1.

Chapter IV, we saw that the father's personality was not related to his son's criminality if he was non-deviant; yet boys with non-deviant fathers had a higher crime rate if their mothers were rejecting than if their mothers were loving ($P < .02$).[22]

We previously found that absence of maternal love was a primary condition for criminal behavior on the part of a son. Under certain circumstances, however, paternal love appears to compensate for the lack of maternal love and act as a deterrent to crime. To ascertain the interaction between paternal affection and the maternal role model, we divided deviant and non-deviant mothers according to the father's personality (Table 50). The

TABLE 50. RELATION OF FATHER'S PERSONALITY AND MOTHER'S ROLE MODEL TO CRIME RATE

	PERCENT OF BOYS CONVICTED OF CRIMES	
Father	Deviant Mother	Non-deviant Mother
Warm	(N: 13) 38	(N: 82) 33
Passive	(N: 4) 75	(N: 33) 24
Rejecting	(N: 18) 94	(N: 50) 40

mother's role model, not surprisingly, was most critical if the father was rejecting: if she was deviant, a significantly higher crime rate resulted ($P < .001$).[23] Conversely, when the mother was a deviant model, paternal warmth did seem to deter criminality. Although the father's personality was not significantly related to criminality when the mother was non-deviant, there were significantly lower crime rates among boys with warm fathers when she was deviant ($P < .001$).[24] It therefore seems that a deviant role model encourages criminality, especially if it is combined with rejection. Both maternal and paternal love tended to negate the criminogenic effects of deviant role models.

In the analysis of role models and of parental personality, we found that boys with neither parent loving and boys with two deviant parents had high crime rates. At the other extreme, boys with two loving parents and boys with neither parent deviant had low crime rates. These two variables were found in different com-

[22] X^2 5.7; d.f. 1.
[23] X^2 14.5; d.f. 1. Boys with absent fathers were omitted from this analysis. Four out of nine who had deviant mothers and seventeen out of thirty-six who had non-deviant mothers became criminal.
[24] X^2 11.7; d.f. 1.

binations among the families we had studied. To test their interaction, we divided the group into nine divisions and computed criminal rates (Table 51).

TABLE 51. RELATION OF PARENTS' PERSONALITIES AND ROLE MODELS TO CRIME RATE

PERCENT OF BOYS CONVICTED OF CRIMES

Parents' Personalities	Both Parents Deviant	One Parent Deviant	Neither Parent Deviant
Neither parent loving	(N: 16) 81	(N: 13) 69	(N: 16) 69
One parent loving	(N: 11) 64	(N: 39) 41	(N: 45) 29
Both parents loving	(N: 6) 67	(N: 38) 29	(N: 60) 28

We had, of course, expected to find vast differences in criminal rates between families in which both factors were positive and those in which both factors were negative. And indeed, crime rates for boys with two deviant, non-loving parents were considerably higher than crime rates for boys with two non-deviant, loving parents ($P < .001$).[25]

Unfortunately, only six boys had two deviant parents, both of whom were loving. We were therefore unable to determine whether the positive effects of love or the negative effects of deviant models would have the greater influence under these circumstances. The tendency, nevertheless, suggests that criminality is likely to result. That is, despite the presence of love from both parents, two deviant models might be expected to have criminal sons.

We did find that if neither parent was loving, although neither was deviant, criminality occurred significantly more frequently than if one or both were loving and neither was deviant ($P < .001$).[26]

The intermediate groups (one deviant or one loving parent) further illustrate the way in which parental role models and personalities interact in relation to criminality. If only one parent was loving, the parental role model was related to crime: boys with two deviant models had a higher crime rate than did boys with no deviant models ($P < .05$).[27] If only one parent was deviant, crime rates varied according to parental personality: boys with two loving parents had lower crime rates than those with only

[25] X^2 14.8; d.f. 1. [26] X^2 11.0; d.f. 1. [27] X^2 4.8; d.f. 1.

one loving parent; these, in turn, had lower crime rates than did boys with no loving parent (P < .01).[28]

Because of the disproportionate distribution of boys among these nine categories, our conclusions must be regarded as tentative. Yet the pattern is consistent: if both parents were deviant *or* neither was loving, high criminality resulted. If both parents were loving *and* neither was deviant, low crime rates resulted. If only one parent was loving or one was deviant, criminality varied sharply according to the other variable. If one parent was non-loving, but neither was deviant; or if one parent was deviant, but both were loving, crime rates were low. We hypothesize that when any two of these negative factors (deviant model or absence of love) are present, they result in greatly increased criminogenic tendencies.

To illustrate this hypothesis through our sample, we combined the groups in Table 51. We considered a deviant model or a nonloving parent as one negative factor in each case. When we added various combinations of negative factors, we found that two negative factors resulted in a significantly greater crime rate than did one negative factor (P < .01)[29] (Table 52). The pattern, showing

TABLE 52. RELATION OF PARENTAL DEVIANCE AND ABSENCE OF LOVE TO CRIME RATE

Number of Negative Factors Present		Percent of Boys Convicted of Crimes
None	(N: 60)	28
One	(N: 83)	29
Two	(N: 61)	51
Three	(N: 24)	67
Four	(N: 16)	81

Note: The negative factors considered were maternal deviance, paternal deviance, maternal rejection, and paternal rejection.

a sharp rise in criminality between one and two negative factors, suggests that perhaps there is a "tolerance level" for adverse influences.

This study of parental influence points to the fact that maternal love is a primary socializing force. However, paternal warmth is

[28] X^2 9.9; d.f. 2.   [29] X^2 7.1; d.f. 1.

generally effective as a substitute for maternal love. If, on the other hand, either parent's behavior is deviant, rejection is likely to cause criminality.

More specifically, we have shown that:

1. Maternal and paternal passivity differ in their relationships to criminality. Maternal passivity is similar in effect to maternal neglect. Paternal passivity resembles paternal warmth in its relation to crime.

2. Love from either parent tends to compensate for rejection by the other. Yet maternal love appears to be more important as a socializing force.

3. The effects of paternal absence, neglect, and especially cruelty depend largely upon the mother's attitude. If she is loving, crime rates remain relatively low.

4. The effects of maternal absence or cruelty depend largely upon the father's personality. If the father is warm or passive, sons are not likely to become criminal.

5. Boys with neglecting mothers seem to become criminal despite the presence of love from their fathers; boys with passive mothers tend to become criminal unless they have warm (not passive) fathers.

6. Only when both parents' role model is deviant does criminality appear to be primarily a reflection of role model.

7. Consistent discipline generally negates the influence of deviant models; erratic-punitive discipline coupled with deviant models greatly increases criminality.

8. Maternal love tends to negate the influence of a criminal father. Sons of criminals with loving mothers are less likely than sons of criminals with non-loving mothers to become criminal.

9. Even though the father's behavior is not deviant, absence of maternal love leads to criminality.

10. Paternal warmth tends to negate the influence of a deviant mother.

11. If the mother's behavior is not deviant (or if she is loving), the father's personality is not significantly related to crime.

12. Both parental role model and parental personality influence criminal rates. These variables seem to interact so that any com-

bination of two negative factors (non-loving parent or deviant parental model) results in sharply increased criminal rates.

The Son's Position in the Family and Crime

The reader may well ask why, if the parental personalities and role models are so vitally important, one child in a family turns to crime when another does not. The answer seems to depend on the fact, so well documented by psychoanalysts, that parents have different relationships with each of the children in their family. In rating parental personality, we tried to account for differences by judging the parent in relation to each child. Parents who had several children in the project might be considered to have very different attitudes toward each of their sons. Furthermore, children may be given different roles within their families. And, of course, they are born at different times.

We classified the boys according to the roles assigned to them within their families. Only 115 boys were clearly pictured as either "pets" or "troublemakers." When we compared the criminal rates of these two groups, a predictable phenomenon resulted ($P < .01$).[30] Table 53 indicates that more boys regarded as "troublemakers"

TABLE 53. RELATION OF SON'S ROLE IN THE FAMILY TO CRIME RATE

Son's Role		Percent of Boys Convicted of Crimes
"Pet"	(N: 64)	30
"Troublemaker"	(N: 51)	57

than as "pets" became criminal. These assigned roles were apparent before the onset of criminality. The conclusion seems to be that when the parents view their children as "troublemakers," they make a self-fulfilling prophecy.

Alfred Adler first argued that such a seemingly commonplace fact as the child's place in birth order may well make a deep imprint upon his personality. Table 54 (omitting twins) shows how the son's ordinal position in the family is related to criminal

[30] X^2 8.6; d.f. 1.

tendencies ($P < .05$).[31] The greater propensity of middle children to commit crimes, as revealed there, may be explained in several ways. Only children and youngest children, in general, receive more parental attention. Oldest children have once been "only children," and they are frequently given status (which the middle child misses) through the responsibility of caring for younger children. Furthermore, the middle child may arrive at a time in his parents' lives when the burdens of a family are most pressing. In several ways, therefore, birth order itself seems to stack the cards against a middle child.

TABLE 54. RELATION OF BIRTH ORDER TO CRIME RATE

Birth Order		Percent of Boys Convicted of Crimes
Only child	(N: 11)	27
Youngest child	(N: 72)	27
Middle child	(N: 121)	47
Oldest child	(N: 44)	34

We believe that the etiology of crime must be discovered through large-scale studies which incorporate control groups for comparison. Yet once these statistical links have been detected, there may be a tendency to view criminal causation as a static relationship between a cause and the consequent behavior. Through a closer examination of two families, for whose names we will substitute pseudonyms, perhaps some of the forces behind criminality may be illuminated.

THE JONES FAMILY

This family had a record well known to community officials. The family consisted of four boys. Two of the older children had criminal records when Dick and Russ, the younger boys, were small children. One of the older brothers was already in prison. Mrs. Jones was an anxious, vacillating person, torn by inner conflict. Mr. Jones was a harsh but irresponsible parent.

The father consistently neglected Dick; he was indifferent to Dick's welfare and ignorant of his needs. Occasionally both parents expressed overt rejection of the young boy. Yet the mother was not consistent in her treatment of Dick. At times, she smothered

[31] X^2 8.2; d.f. 3.

him with affection and behaved in an overprotective manner. She restricted his activities, encouraged feminine tendencies, and defended him against the attacks of his brothers and father.

Although confused by his mother's sudden changes in behavior, Dick clung to her. "Dick is very fond of his mother. He is the youngest of a large family and she treats him like a baby," the social worker commented. As Dick grew older, his counselors noted a general tendency for him to withdraw from life and to act the role of a coddled baby. He gave up the usual activities of boys his age and turned increasingly to identification with the female role. During the study, when Dick's counselor was changed, his original therapist expressed concern about his future:

> It would appear that Richard is a strange child, the pet of the mother. In his more personal friendships, he tended to play with little girls. He preferred cutting out pictures or playing with dolls. His mother was inclined to approve. Dick was comparatively weak and was definitely effeminate. Ahead lies the danger of homosexuality, or a release into other forms of delinquent behavior.

The counselor's worries with respect to delinquency were unjustified. According to official criminal records, Dick has not committed a crime (although we have no knowledge of his personal adjustment in other ways).

While Mrs. Jones varied between overprotection and neglect of Dick, her attitude toward the other younger brother, Russ, was consistent. A psychologist noted: "There seems to be complete rejection of Russ by his mother. She looks upon him as a bad one." Mr. Jones neglected Dick, but he maintained an attitude of blatant hostility toward Russ. In his frequent alcoholic rages, the father vented his anger on Russ.

Russ found himself isolated in the family, neglected by his mother, hated by his father. His counselor reported: "Russ constantly fights with Dick, showing a strong rivalry, with the mother taking the younger child's part against Russ. In addition, there is no masculine ideal in the home. The father is a drunkard, with little concern for his children. Russ finds that he has no one to whom he can turn when confronted by a particular problem."

As he grew older, Russ consciously imitated his older brothers. He pictured himself as a hardened criminal, a lone wolf standing against the world, embittered but strong. Another counselor commented: "Russ would like to be a tough guy like his brother who formerly spent time in a reformatory."

Russ achieved this goal: he committed his first crime, breaking and entering, at the age of thirteen. At twenty-seven, he was serving time in prison on a charge of assault.

Encouraged by his mother, Dick had developed a concept of himself revolving around babyhood and femininity. Such a role excluded toughness and aggression as valued modes of behavior. Russ, on the other hand, could not gain attention through acting the "baby." Whatever role he played, his parents rejected him. Through identification with his older brothers (despite their absence from the home), Russ found a place for himself in the world. By denying a need for parental affection, by rejecting all that his brother Dick represented, by placing himself outside the "respectable" orbits of life, Russ achieved a significance which he could not obtain from his family. Thus, even though their general environment was similar, the two boys were subjected to very different parental attitudes and actions.

THE MARTIN FAMILY

In a more complicated way, another family demonstrates the varying effects of parental treatment. At first, the Martins appeared to be a remarkably compact family. The mother, father, and six sons talked alike and looked alike. When the family was criticized by outsiders, a general call to arms occurred, and each came to the aid of the others. When one of the sons was scolded in school for having dirty hands, Mr. Martin took it as a direct insult and shouted: "I'll go down to the school tomorrow and knock the teacher's head off."

Constant arguing and bickering within the family, however, marred the superficial cohesiveness. The sons fought among themselves with a bitterness born of jealousy. The parents often did not speak to each other for weeks. The mother, particularly, showed great swings in mood and a highly inflammable temper. At times she was elated and buoyantly happy; but often her elation turned to morbid depression. Three of the Martin sons were participants in the Cambridge-Somerville project.

William, the youngest of the sons, was his mother's favorite. Since infancy his health had been delicate. Consequently, Mrs. Martin seldom exerted any control over him and gave way to all his whims. She had desired a girl, and treated William in a coddling, indulgent way. He received many privileges which were denied to the other boys. Mrs. Martin herself commented: "William is more spoilt than any of them. He gets mad if I pay any attention to the others." Mr. Martin, too, regarded William as the favorite son. Although strict and puritanical, he softened his demands when dealing with the boy. William, according to our records, has never committed a serious crime during his thirty years of life.

Arthur, the second son, had also been a sickly infant. Plagued by a series of diseases, he had become a weak, pale, passive child. Both parents disliked him because of the trouble he had caused them. Although inhibition prevented concrete displays of their hostility toward him, the parents covertly expressed rejection of Arthur. Compared to William, Arthur was neglected by the parents. He received no new clothes, gifts, or special cuts of food. Whenever Arthur demonstrated his physical weakness (as he did both in school and in the neighborhood), his father berated him and condemned him as a "coward." Arthur was often truant from school. When his father was informed of this, he threatened Arthur with terrible beatings, and the child meekly promised never to be absent again.

Counselors noticed that Arthur was well aware that he was not the favored son. He constantly strove to win the attention of his mother. Arthur temporarily responded well to the solicitous care of his counselors. Certain neurotic symptoms (such as enuresis which had continued into adolescence) stopped after he had established a relationship with his counselor. But unlike William, as an adult Arthur committed several serious crimes. In 1956, he was serving a prison sentence.

The third son, John, was subjected to outright hostility by both his parents. His father regarded him as "a moron," "a crybaby," and a "squealer." Both parents "washed their hands" of the boy and treated him with sullen indifference. Only when John caused trouble at school or in the community, did the parents shed their apathy toward him. Every misdemeanor on his part provoked rage and brutality from his father. Because of their early sickness, the cowardice of William and Arthur was relatively tolerated; but every sign of weakness on John's part brought forth condemnations. The father encouraged his favorite boy, William, giving him playful boxing lessons. John, however, was excluded from these sessions because he "could not take it."

In school, John developed a reputation as a figher and a bully. His argumentativeness kept him from making friends. He sought affection through displays of toughness. The Cambridge-Somerville counselors made little progress with him.

In adolescence, after a severe automobile accident, John's feelings about his rejection became apparent. His counselor visited him in the hospital and later described their conversations:

He said that he hated his mother. He refused to do anything the doctor ordered. He said that he would like to stick a knife in his brother, William. He showed an ambivalent attitude toward his father, though he expressed no outright hostility, possibly through fear. He did not care what happened to him. He didn't care if he ever got well and even said that he was thinking of jumping out the window: "After all, who cares anyway."

By the end of adolescence, John developed a criminal record. When he was eighteen, he received his first court conviction for drunkenness. In 1958, his record showed another conviction for drunkenness, a serious traffic violation, and a conviction for burglary.

In the Martin family, the dissatisfactions of the parents converged particularly on this one boy. John became convinced, early in life, of his worthlessness and insignificance. He may have believed that his aggression in school and depredations in the community proved that he was not the coward his father detested. The role of bully in the community made up for his insignificance at home. Arthur had an excuse, in his early illness, for a lack of strength. But his father's constant pressure on him to prove his masculinity eventually had its effect and Arthur became a prison "tough guy." Unlike his two brothers, William found affection and recognition in the family. For this reason, perhaps, he had no need for additional demonstrations of his strength.

The drunkenness and burglaries of John and Arthur Martin and the crimes of Russ Jones can be traced, we believe, to tensions within the families of these men. Their brothers, however, found security through vastly different emotional experiences. These differences were reflected in their behavior as adolescents and adults.

The behavior and personality of parents in relation to their children are certainly primary factors in the causation of crime. As we turn from discussion of criminality in general to the causation of particular types of crime, we will see how these factors and others are related to the choice of a criminal act.

CHAPTER VI

THE CHOICE OF THE CRIMINAL ACT

ALBERT COHEN RECENTLY WROTE: "THE ASSUMPTION SEEMS TO BE common that delinquency, like measles, is a homogeneous something that people either have or have not." [1] In practice, of course, criminality can be of many varieties—violent or non-violent, sexual or sexless, dangerous or relatively harmless. Yet research has taken little cognizance of these obvious differences.

Few social scientists today believe that the criminal act is a rational one; rather, they believe that a subtle complex of causes and motives, largely of an irrational or unconscious nature, leads to crime. But our knowledge takes us little further than acceptance of this general position. Although reliable information has been reported regarding the causation of crime in general, little has been done to uncover specific determinants for particular types of crime. Cohen has summarized this deficiency:

The analogy of delinquency to a "symptom" meriting little investigation in its own right has been much overworked. If we wish to retain it, however, we would do well to remember that physicians, from whose vocabulary the term is borrowed, do not lump together fevers, rashes, boils, aches and pains, jaundice, vertigo and spots before the eyes as symptoms, differences among which may be safely ignored. The syphilis spirochete is not considered a satisfactory explanation for violent sneezing in the month of August. For the understanding of delinquency as well, we must discover the significant respects in which this behavior may vary, describe our delinquents in terms of these dimensions of variation, and construct our theories to fit the richness and particularity of the data.[2]

Some psychiatric investigators, such as William Healy and Augusta Bronner, have insisted that this task is impossible. They

[1] Albert K. Cohen, *Delinquent Boys*, p. 172.
[2] *Ibid.*

CHOICE OF THE CRIMINAL ACT

maintain that the specific crime is a random choice. Prompted by an anti-social tendency, a man can commit any crime from rape to speeding, they argue.[3]

Other researchers, particularly psychoanalysts, agree that the detection of any determinant in the choice of crime is extremely difficult. But, they would add, it can be done through extensive psychological analysis. The work of Benjamin Karpman, Walter Bromberg, and Robert Lindner is based on the assumption that sufficient investigation can unearth the causal sequence which leads to a particular criminal action. Lindner's "hypno-analysis" of "Harold," a federal convict, represents such an attempt. In *Rebel Without a Cause*, Lindner traces Harold's burglaries, assault, and hysteric blindness back to a strong hostility toward his father, a castration complex, and the trauma of viewing the "primal scene."[4]

With our unique and rich source of information, we approached this problem in a different manner. Using the psychological and sociological categories with which previous sections of our books have dealt, we sought relationships to particular types of crime.

Unfortunately, court records furnished only the legal titles of crimes for which the boys had been convicted. They reported none of the circumstances surrounding the acts; neither fine distinctions nor very subtle analyses could be made from our information. Despite these defects, we felt that important facts could be gleaned from studying the types of crimes reported in the official records.

Using the legal designations as a base, we grouped crimes into five categories. The largest and most amorphous of the categories comprised those acts we regarded as primarily *crimes against property*. Crimes so classified could be broadly described as those whose target was (ostensibly) either material property itself or a violation of general rules safeguarding property. Cambridge-Somerville men committed a variety of crimes of this type: breaking and entering, larceny, malicious destruction, forgery, trespassing, fraud or embezzlement, car robbery or use of an automobile without authority, illegal possession of firearms, arson, vagrancy, non-support, injury to property, violation of game laws, conspiracy to steal or access before the fact. In addition, we categorized another group of seven

---
[3] William Healy and Augusta Bronner, *Delinquents and Criminals*, p. 263.
[4] Robert Lindner, *Rebel Without a Cause*.

criminals under this same heading. These had committed acts, few in number, which could be fitted under no other heading and involved, in some way, the violation of general social rules. These few crimes were disturbing the peace, truancy, violation of probation or parole, false alarm, running away from home or the scene of an accident, "stubbornness," violation of the school committee rules, "use of profane language" and "threats."

Crimes against the person involved those acts which, so far as we could discern, were directed against individuals and involved a violent attack. The legal titles of these crimes were homicide, assault, robbery with a weapon, kidnaping, and injury to the person.

Sex crimes included the homosexual or heterosexual acts described as carnal abuse, sodomy, rape, impairing the morals of a minor, lewd and lascivious behavior, illegitimacy, abusing a female child, accosting a person of the opposite sex, exposure, and "peeping Tom."

Because of the large number of such offenses and their rather unique nature, we kept *drunkenness* a separate category.

Although we did not consider *traffic violations* as crimes in the tabulations of the preceding sections, such offenses formed our fifth category of legal violations. Since these violations had appeared on the docket of a higher court, we assumed that they were relatively serious acts.

Obviously, these are very broad categories which include a variety of acts differing widely in the particular subjective meaning they hold for the individual. Yet each of these types had a different "target" and, even though the classifications were far from subtle, they did offer a rare opportunity for studying the long-term causes of different crimes.

Are there specific causal syndromes behind each of these five general types of crime? To answer this question, we used two forms of analysis. First, we examined the backgrounds of all 253 boys in relation to each type of crime. Because such influences as maternal neglect or familial conflict produced high proportions of criminal sons, these factors naturally appeared in the genesis of almost all kinds of crime.

In order to eliminate the pervasive criminogenic influence of these factors, we called upon a second form of analysis. Here, we

CHOICE OF THE CRIMINAL ACT 127

wished to answer the question: If a man, whatever the cause, becomes criminal, is it possible to discover early influences which predisposed him to particular criminal acts? Therefore in this second form of analysis, we concentrated upon the men who had been convicted for any type of crime.

As the first step in the investigation, we computed the proportion of boys convicted for each variety of crime who came from a particular early environment—e.g., to test whether maternal attitudes were significantly related to drunkenness, we compared the proportions of boys convicted for that offense who had been raised by loving, passive, cruel, and neglecting mothers. It immediately became apparent that early environmental influences bear a strong relationship to the selection of the criminal act; boys who committed different crimes came from very different backgrounds. This is what we found.

Crimes Against Property

Eighty-six boys had been convicted at least once for crimes against property. A high proportion of these criminals had been raised by neglecting mothers and fathers; they had either not been disciplined at all or had been controlled by erratically punitive measures; their homes were characterized by neglect and conflict; and their intelligence usually fell in the normal range. Furthermore, the majority had criminal fathers. How each of these influences tended to produce these criminals can be seen more graphically in the following figures: 64 percent of the maternally neglected men committed property crimes; only 31 percent of the sons of all other types of mothers did so ($P < .001$).[5]

The relationship between mother's personality and property crimes is shown in Table 55.[6] Significantly more criminals raised by loving-anxious or loving-neurotic mothers than criminals raised by loving-normal or overprotective mothers were convicted for

---

[5] X^2 11.1; d.f. 1. The mother of one man convicted for a property crime could not be classified.

[6] The reader should keep in mind that the tables given in this chapter describe only criminals. Since neglecting mothers, for example, had sons who committed all types of crimes, it is valuable to "hold constant" criminality as such in order to see if differences appear in type of crime.

property crimes (P < .05).[7] Among the unloved children who became criminal, neglect led more often to property crimes than did other forms of maternal "lovelessness."

TABLE 55. RELATION OF MOTHER'S PERSONALITY TO PROPERTY CRIMES

Mother		Percent of Criminals Convicted of Property Crimes
Overprotective	(N: 33)	54
Loving-normal	(N: 25)	56
Passive	(N: 16)	63
Cruel	(N: 11)	64
Loving-neurotic	(N: 11)	73
Absent	(N: 4)	75
Loving-anxious	(N: 12)	83
Neglecting	(N: 18)	89

Paternal neglect, like maternal neglect, instilled a tendency to commit property crimes. Fifty-six percent of sons neglected by their fathers committed crimes against property; 31 percent of all other men committed such crimes (P < .005).[8] As Table 56 shows, crim-

TABLE 56. RELATION OF FATHER'S PERSONALITY TO PROPERTY CRIMES

Father		Percent of Criminals Convicted of Property Crimes
Warm	(N: 43)	56
Cruel	(N: 20)	60
Absent	(N: 27)	67
Passive	(N: 15)	73
Neglecting	(N: 22)	86

inals who had been subjected to neglecting fathers were more apt to commit crimes against property than were other criminals (P < .05).[9]

The role model presented by the father also influenced the boy's criminality. Fifty-one percent of the criminal fathers had sons who committed property crimes, whereas 35 percent of the alcoholic or sexually unfaithful fathers and 28 percent of the non-deviant men had sons who committed property crimes (P < .01).[10] Yet

[7] X^2 4.2; d.f. 1.
[8] X^2 8.1; d.f. 1. The fathers of two men convicted for property crimes could not be categorized.
[9] X^2 4.7; d.f. 1.   [10] X^2 7.1; d.f. 1.

among criminals, those who had criminal fathers were not more prone than those who had alcoholic or promiscuous, or those who had non-deviant fathers, to commit property crimes.

Certain types of discipline and of general home atmosphere were also significantly related to crimes against property. Forty-three percent of the men who had experienced lax discipline or who had been subjected to erratic punitiveness committed property crimes, compared to only 24 percent of those disciplined in any other manner ($P < .005$).[11] Analysis of the 130 men who became criminal shows that consistency of discipline also played a role (Table 57). Consistent discipline, whether of a love-oriented or a

TABLE 57. RELATION OF PARENTAL DISCIPLINE TO PROPERTY CRIMES

Type of Discipline		Percent of Criminals Convicted of Property Crimes
Punitive	(N: 7)	43
Love-oriented	(N: 26)	50
Love-lax	(N: 19)	63
Lax	(N: 30)	73
Love-punitive-lax	(N: 23)	74
Punitive-lax	(N: 25)	80

punitive nature, militated against property crimes. A significantly lower proportion of criminals who had been consistently disciplined than of criminals disciplined in a lax or erratic manner were convicted for crimes against property ($P < .005$).[12]

As one might expect, a family atmosphere characterized by conflict and neglect was particularly related to property crimes. Sixty-five percent of the men reared in quarrelsome and neglecting homes committed property crimes, whereas only 31 percent of those who lived in other types of homes committed such acts ($P < .001$).[13] Criminals who came from cohesive homes, we found, were least likely to commit property crimes [14] (Table 58).

Unexpectedly, we also found a relationship between intelligence and crimes against property. Considering the range of I.Q. scores between 81 and 110 as average, we found that 39 percent of the

[11] X^2 10.7; d.f. 1.   [12] X^2 8.7; d.f. 1.   [13] X^2 17.88; d.f. 1.
[14] Comparison of rates for criminals from all types of homes: $P < .025$; X^2 9.5; d.f. 3. Comparison of rates for criminals from quarrelsome-neglecting homes and from all other types: $P < .01$; X^2 7.86; d.f. 1.

men with average intelligence committed property crimes, although only 25 percent of those with either high or low intelligence did so (P < .05).[15]

TABLE 58. RELATION OF HOME ATMOSPHERE TO PROPERTY CRIMES

Home Atmosphere		Percent of Criminals Convicted of Property Crimes
Cohesive	(N: 50)	54
Broken	(N: 27)	63
Quarrelsome-affectionate	(N: 26)	69
Quarrelsome-neglecting	(N: 27)	89

We may conclude that this most common form of crime stems from neglect and insecurity in the home, and, apparently from following the example of a criminal father. These crimes are also slightly influenced by intelligence. It is important to note that we found *no* significant relationship between property crimes and neighborhood—in other words, property crimes are not simply a result of economic poverty.

In the life of a boy whom we will call Oswald James, one can see more specifically how these varied influences combined to produce a "property criminal."

The Cambridge-Somerville staff first contacted Oswald James in 1939, when he was twelve years old. Although a healthy boy, Oswald was lethargic, shy, and mentally retarded. The Cambridge police had suggested that the boy be included in the program, for he came from a family which had already produced several delinquents. Oswald had four brothers, one of whom had been arrested for burglary, and four sisters, two of whom became prostitutes by 1945.

The James family lived in a three-room apartment on an income of $93 a month. The social worker who first visited the family described the home as the filthiest she had ever seen. The children were crawling with lice and their faces were covered with acne, cold sores, and boils.

Mrs. James was a huge person, equipped with several fatty chins. Her clothes were ragged and dirty. Most of the time she lay, face down, on a small bed in the living room. The children were given

[15] X^2 4.3; d.f. 1.

free rein to roam the neighborhood; no control was exerted over them. Slow, sloppy, indifferent to her children, the mother spent most of her energy in drinking.

For years Oswald's father had been known to various social agencies in Boston. Several times he had been convicted for drunkenness. Once, his alcoholism became so serious that he was committed to the Boston Psychopathic Hospital. There he was diagnosed as suffering from an alcoholic psychosis and was transferred to another hospital where he spent a year. Because he was afflicted with cirrhosis of the liver and heart disease, the father had given up all pretense to earning a living. He was supported by public welfare and by the earnings of a brother in the CCC. Like many drunkards, the father had a razor-sharp temper. He bitterly condemned his children and, when he could summon the energy, whipped them unmercifully.

Because of his low intelligence, Oswald failed several grades in school. (During one year, only one of the eight James children was promoted.) His teachers regarded him as a stupid, incredibly dirty, and "hopeless" child. Nevertheless, Oswald caused little trouble in school. Occasionally the school furnished the boy with shoes or other clothing to supplement the meager supply from the WPA.

Because of his home and the fact that he lived in the worst slum neighborhood, Oswald associated with boys in several delinquent gangs. Early in life he began to adopt their ways. He started by stealing milk from the doorsteps of houses, eagerly drinking his loot; then came a series of incidents involving "malicious mischief" (such as throwing a crowbar through a window). As the years passed, Oswald's truancy and misbehavior at school increased.

Oswald's counselor and his Episcopal priest intermittently attempted to meliorate the situation. The counselor saw the boy about once a month and tutored him in reading. The priest arranged for scholarships to send the boy to camp and also entered him in several settlement houses. Oswald accepted these ministrations quietly but unenthusiastically.

By 1941, the family had begun to split up. Two older boys went off to the CCC; both were eventually "dishonorably discharged." Together with another brother, they joined the Army when the war came. One sister was arrested for larceny and imprisoned at a girls' reform school. Two other sisters became involved in serious sexual delinquencies. Meanwhile, the mother was brought to court on a charge of neglect and warned by the court to "change her ways" (to no avail). The father's addiction to alcohol affected him deeply: his thinking became slow and confused, his speech blurred, and his fits of anger more brutal.

Oswald's first counselor left the program and others successively replaced him; none was able to establish a close relationship with the boy. As the years passed, Oswald's crimes became more serious. In 1943 he was arrested for two larcenies and a traffic offense; in 1944 he was placed on probation for stealing a truck; in 1945 he stole an automobile. Because of the car theft, Oswald was committed to reform school, where the staff described him as "slow, willing, timid, pleasant, obedient." Yet he spent his entire term at the school in the "discipline cottage." In late 1945, Oswald ran away from school three times. He was caught and returned each time.

In 1946, after a series of burglaries which occurred following his release from reform school, Mrs. James surrendered Oswald to the police. When the police arrived at the house Oswald was firing a .38 caliber pistol into a bed, but he did not attempt to put up a fight. The police took him away to reform school once more.

By 1947, Oswald had served another sentence (this time for illicit sexual relations with a married woman) and, after parole, joined the Army. In 1956, Oswald James was twenty-seven; in recent years he had been convicted for two serious traffic violations, but his property crimes had apparently ceased.

Crimes Against the Person

Only 14 boys committed acts which we classified as crimes against the person. We found a causal syndrome in the background of these men which differed in certain fundamental ways from the influences which produced "property criminals." A high proportion of men who committed these acts of violence had been raised by overprotective or neglecting mothers and by cruel or neglecting fathers. Their discipline had been lax or erratically punitive. They had come most often from either broken homes or homes rent by conflict and neglect.

None of the men who had been cared for by loving-normal, loving-neurotic, or passive mothers committed crimes against the person. Sons of overprotective or of neglecting mothers, on the other hand, were six times as likely to commit such crimes as the sons of all other types of mothers: 12 percent of those raised by overprotective or neglecting mothers committed violent offenses, compared to 2 percent of the sons raised by other kinds of mothers ($P < .005$).[16]

Of those mothers who produced criminal sons, certain types contributed relatively high proportions of violent criminals (Table 59). Among those criminals who had been raised by loving

TABLE 59. RELATION OF MOTHER'S PERSONALITY TO CRIMES AGAINST THE PERSON

Mother		Percent of Criminals Convicted of Crimes Against the Person
Loving-normal	(N: 25)	0
Loving-neurotic	(N: 11)	0
Passive	(N: 16)	0
Cruel	(N: 11)	9
Loving-anxious	(N: 12)	17
Overprotective	(N: 33)	18
Neglecting	(N: 18)	22
Absent	(N: 4)	25

mothers, a significantly higher proportion of those brought up by loving-anxious and overprotective mothers committed crimes of violence ($P < .01$).[17] Of those criminals who had not received maternal love, significantly more whose mothers had been neglecting or absent rather than passive or cruel committed these crimes ($P < .05$).[18]

The father's role model, too, was related to crimes against the person. Thirteen percent of the boys with criminal fathers, compared to only 4 percent of all other boys, had been convicted for

[16] X^2 9.6; d.f. 1. All the neglecting mothers whose sons became violent criminals were married to cruel or neglecting fathers. This was not true of the overprotective mothers.
[17] X^2 7.2; d.f. 1.   [18] X^2 4.1; d.f. 1.

these direct and violent attacks (P < .02).[19] Analysis of the criminals (Table 60) confirms this relationship (P < .05).[20]

TABLE 60. RELATION OF FATHER'S ROLE MODEL TO CRIMES AGAINST THE PERSON

Father's Role Model		Percent of Criminals Convicted of Crimes Against the Person
Criminal	(N: 28)	21
Alcoholic or sexually unfaithful	(N: 38)	11
Non-deviant	(N: 65)	6

Twelve of the 15 criminals convicted for this type of crime had undergone lax or punitively erratic discipline. Nine percent of boys disciplined in this manner became "violent criminals," compared to only 2 percent of boys disciplined in any other way (P < .02).[21]

An even more interesting relationship emerges in the examination of these criminals (Table 61). Love-oriented methods militated

TABLE 61. RELATION OF PARENTAL DISCIPLINE TO CRIMES AGAINST THE PERSON

Type of Discipline		Percent of Criminals Convicted of Crimes Against the Person
Love-oriented	(N: 26)	0
Love-lax	(N: 19)	5
Lax	(N: 30)	13
Punitive	(N: 7)	14
Punitive-lax	(N: 25)	16
Punitive-love-lax	(N: 23)	17

against crimes of violence: a significantly lower proportion of criminals whose parents had utilized love-oriented techniques without punitiveness, as compared with criminals whose parents had been lax or punitive, were convicted for crimes against the person (P < .025).[22] This finding contrasts with the background of those convicted for crimes against property, where consistency, regardless of technique, made a critical difference.

As with the "property criminals," quarrelsome and neglecting homes accounted for a large share of the violent criminals. But, surprisingly, the broken home provided an equally high propor-

[19] X^2 6.4; d.f. 1.   [20] X^2 4.3; d.f. 1.   [21] X^2 5.9; d.f. 1.   [22] X^2 5.20; d.f. 1.

CHOICE OF THE CRIMINAL ACT

tion. Thirteen percent of the men raised in such homes became "violent criminals." This is six times more than the tiny proportion (2%) of those raised in other kinds of homes who committed violent criminal acts (P < .005).[23]

The presence of at least some affection in the home militates against crimes of violence (Table 62). A significantly lower pro-

TABLE 62. RELATION OF HOME ATMOSPHERE TO
CRIMES AGAINST THE PERSON

Home Atmosphere		Percent of Criminals Convicted of Crimes Against the Person
Quarrelsome-affectionate	(N: 26)	4
Cohesive	(N: 50)	6
Broken	(N: 27)	19
Quarrelsome-neglecting	(N: 27)	19

portion of criminals from quarrelsome but affectionate or cohesive homes committed crimes against persons (P < .02).[24]

We found that neighborhood was an unimportant factor in the genesis of violent crimes. Our study indicates that this type of criminal comes primarily from a love-starved home; yet the personality of both mother and father, and the father's behavior, must be taken into account. Ninety-three percent of these "violent criminals" had overprotective mothers or cruel or neglecting fathers.[25]

The case of one boy convicted for crimes against the person, whom we will call Ralph Burley, illustrates the typical causal syndrome:

In 1953, when he was twenty-four years old, Ralph Burley was convicted by a Massachusetts court for assault with a deadly weapon. This was not Burley's first offense. He had previously been convicted of several robberies, drunkenness, and a traffic violation.

Burley came to the attention of the Cambridge-Somerville staff because of a history of physical and mental illness. In 1939, when he was ten, Burley was just recovering from a long bout with pneumonia. The disease was complicated by an asthmatic condition and by the possibility of tuberculosis. Upon his release from

[23] X^2 10.5; d.f. 1. [24] X^2 5.75; d.f. 1.
[25] The father of the remaining violent criminal was absent from the home. Less than half of all the men in our sample, and approximately half the criminals, had parents of these types.

the hospital, his bad luck continued: he was struck by an automobile and his skull was fractured.

Ralph's mother was solicitous. Under her constant supervision, his health slowly improved. His mother devoted herself to him, ignoring her second child, a little girl. The mother was a plump, industrious, and restless woman. Her energy bordered on hysteria. She was subject to violent changes in temper, intense anxiety, and an overpowering desire to "keep busy." "I die when I have to sit around with nothing to do," she said to the social worker visiting her home.

Counselors assigned to the case immediately noted the mother's complete dependence on her boy. She restricted his friendships and activities, refused to allow him to leave her for camp, and constantly questioned him about his feelings and thoughts. She hesitated to punish the boy for fear that discipline would turn him against her. Yet at times her volatile temper exploded and she did physically punish him.

Excusing her attitude on the grounds that it was due to her son's frequent illnesses, the mother constantly showed her partiality for Ralph as opposed to her daughter. The little girl responded with bitter jealousy toward her brother and with exhibitionistic demands for affection. When Ralph "showed off"—as he did constantly—his mother laughed at his restless antics. If the daughter copied the son, however, the mother burst into a fit of anger.

Ralph's father had deserted the home when the boy was seven. When he was living with the family, Mr. Burley was alcoholic; he had been arrested fifteen times for drunkenness. Even when sober, the father was sadistic toward the children and his wife. When he fell into a rage, Mr. Burley broke furniture, smashed windows, and severely beat his wife and the children. He particularly hated Ralph because the child bore a close physical resemblance to his mother.

Thus, after the desertion of the father, the family was composed of the overprotective, extremely excitable mother, the rejected daughter, and Ralph. As the boy grew up, he became increasingly unstable. His teachers described him as "rattle-brained," boastful, egoistic, totally erratic. His minister found him to be a "good churchgoer," but highly impulsive, restless, and an uninhibited seeker for recognition. When Ralph was twelve these traits, together with an uncontrollable head twitching, brought him to a public mental health clinic. Neither mother nor child kept their appointments and the case was dropped.

Ralph's counselors strove to help improve the child's physical and mental condition. They succeeded in securing treatment for his asthma and, eventually, cured this. Work with the mother proved unavailing, however, for her anxiety about her son was too extreme. She tried to make the boy forget his father; finally, the child told other people that his father was "dead." As Ralph reached adolescence, the mother increased her supervision of him. She constantly impressed upon him that if he left her, if he roamed the streets against her orders, he would be killed in a traffic accident.

When Ralph was fifteen, Mrs. Burley suddenly changed in behavior, becoming sexually promiscuous. Often she brought men home to spend the night. The Cambridge-Somerville staff, aware of her activities, removed the daughter from the home and arranged placement in a foster home. Ralph, however, remained with his mother.

Burley became involved in a series of petty crimes: setting off fire alarms, stealing from other children at school, and trespassing on factory property. As he reached manhood, he committed a violent assault which resulted in imprisonment. At twenty-seven, he was out of prison. Yet he had been convicted recently for a serious traffic offense and for drunkenness. His background of overprotection, cruelty, a broken home, and highly erratic discipline is typical of other criminals who committed crimes against the person.

Sex Crimes

The etiology of sexual offenses rather closely resembles that of property crimes. (One could even speculate about the sexual motivation for property crimes.) Yet there is a salient and important difference: whereas maternal neglect leads to both property crimes and to sexual crimes, maternal passivity bears a relationship to sexual offenses but not to property offenses. In addition, sexual crime is promoted by paternal neglect, erratic or lax discipline, and a quarrelsome-neglecting home atmosphere. In these latter causal characteristics, sexual crimes are similar to property crimes, but differ in certain important respects from crimes of violence.

Twelve men committed sexual crimes. The majority of them had been raised by neglecting or passive mothers. These two types of mothers instilled deviant sexual tendencies in a much higher proportion: 15 percent of the sons of passive or neglecting mothers committed sexual crimes as opposed to only 2 percent of the sons of other kinds of mothers ($P < .001$).[26] None of the sons of loving-neurotic, absent, or cruel mothers committed sexual crimes. Among criminals, this relationship can be seen clearly, as in Table 63.

TABLE 63. RELATION OF MOTHER'S PERSONALITY TO SEX CRIMES

Mother		Percent of Criminals Convicted of Sex Crimes
Loving-neurotic	(N: 11)	0
Absent	(N: 4)	0
Cruel	(N: 11)	0
Loving-normal	(N: 25)	4
Overprotective	(N: 33)	9
Loving-anxious	(N: 12)	8
Passive	(N: 16)	19
Neglecting	(N: 18)	22

Neglect by the father also tended to produce sexual crimes. Eleven percent of the paternally neglected men, compared to 4 percent of all others, had been convicted for sex crimes ($P < .05$).[27] Although a higher proportion of the criminal sons of neglecting fathers committed sex offenses, the difference here is not statistically significant (Table 64).

TABLE 64. RELATION OF FATHER'S PERSONALITY TO SEX CRIMES

Father		Percent of Criminals Convicted of Sex Crimes
Absent	(N: 27)	4
Cruel	(N: 20)	5
Warm	(N: 43)	9
Passive	(N: 15)	13
Neglecting	(N: 22)	18

---

[26] X^2 13.5; d.f. 1.   [27] X^2 3.8; d.f. 1.

CHOICE OF THE CRIMINAL ACT

The father's personality (as an independent factor) does not seem to be a particularly important influence in the causation of sexual crimes. All the sex criminals with neglecting fathers had either passive or neglecting mothers. Fifty percent of the sex criminals had passive or neglecting mothers *and* passive, neglecting, or absent fathers; men with these backgrounds composed only 9 percent of our total sample ($P < .001$).[28]

Discipline bore a stronger relationship to sexual offenses. Seven percent of the men who had been disciplined in a lax or an erratically punitive manner committed sex crimes, as opposed to 2 percent of those men disciplined by other methods ($P < .05$).[29] The consistency of discipline, whether punitive or love-oriented, seemed to differentiate these criminals from other types (Table 65).

TABLE 65. RELATION OF PARENTAL DISCIPLINE TO SEX CRIMES

Type of Discipline		Percent of Criminals Convicted of Sex Crimes
Love-oriented	(N: 26)	0
Punitive	(N: 7)	0
Lax	(N: 30)	10
Love-lax	(N: 19)	11
Love-punitive-lax	(N: 23)	13
Punitive-lax	(N: 25)	16

A significantly lower proportion of criminals who had been consistently disciplined (either by love-oriented or by punitive measures) than of criminals who had been disciplined in a lax or erratic manner were convicted of sexual crimes ($P < .05$).[30]

Quarrelsome-neglecting homes were the breeding ground for one half of the sexual criminals. Sixteen percent of men who had lived in quarrelsome and neglecting homes, compared to a total of 3 percent of those from broken, quarrelsome-affectionate, or cohesive homes, committed sexual offenses ($P < .001$).[31] Quarrelsomeness and conflict in a family produced criminals who had a distinct tendency to become sexual deviants ($P < .01$)[32] (Table 66).

Sex crimes, like crimes against the person, involve direct attack upon individuals. Yet violent crimes, unlike sex crimes, seem to

[28] X^2 25.24; d.f. 1. [29] X^2 4.3; d.f. 1. [30] X^2 4.48; d.f. 1. [31] X^2 12.1; d.f. 1.
[32] X^2 6.82; d.f. 1 (quarrelsome-neglecting homes compared to all others).

be a consequence of negative attention. Sex criminals had little guidance or attention of any kind. Furthermore, the father's personality and role model are of relatively little importance in the genesis of sex crimes, but are a major factor in causation of violent crimes.

TABLE 66. RELATION OF HOME ATMOSPHERE TO SEX CRIMES

Home Atmosphere		Percent of Criminals Convicted of Sex Crimes
Broken	(N: 27)	4
Cohesive	(N: 50)	6
Quarrelsome-affectionate	(N: 26)	8
Quarrelsome-neglecting	(N: 27)	22

The case of Paul Liston (a pseudonym) illustrates the emotional coldness, particularly on the mother's part, which seems characteristic of the environment of sex criminals.

A social agency first referred Paul to the Cambridge-Somerville project. He was plagued by persistent eczema which no physical treatment had been able to cure. Moreover, all of his brothers had been in reform schools and the agency feared that Paul would imitate his brothers.

Eight years old when he first entered the project, Paul was seclusive, highly anxious, and withdrawn (a personality syndrome characteristic of all the sex criminals in the study). His teacher described him as "unusually depressed, timid, unresponsive, slovenly." His first counselor found him to be "different, nervous, and inactive." Psychologists noted that Liston maintained a façade of emotional insensitiveness and indifference, primarily because of a pervasive fear of rejection. Paul offered a stoical mein to the world, but clammy hands, nail-biting, nightmares, and petty stealing revealed the emotional turmoil underneath his placid exterior.

Liston's home was a chapter out of Dickens—incredibly poor, barren, and cold. The children were emaciated, ill, and underfed. Although Mr. Liston earned a meager salary as school janitor, the family was given aid by public welfare. One Christmas the counselor surprised the Listons with a turkey and found them eating bread and beans.

Paul's mother spent most of her day sleeping in a chair or on her bed. Mrs. Liston seemed to be suffering from a chronic cold; a convenient excuse for abdicating from the care of her children and the worries of her household. She was a complaining and very unhappy woman whose only release came from occasional sexual relations with other men.

Liston's father was also passive and withdrawing, overburdened with the cares of his job and the problems of his family. His marriage had been necessary because of pregnancy, and he talked continually of divorce. His religion, however, prevented this threat from being carried further than occasional desertions.

The counselors tried to correct the boy's irritating eczema. They had no success until he was placed in a foster home—then the skin disease disappeared completely. The mother welcomed Paul's absence from the home, and the father reluctantly agreed to the placement.

After a year in the foster home, Paul returned—against his will—to his family. Mr. Liston's economic position had improved, and he demanded the return of his son. Paul's skin disease reappeared, more virulent than before. During this period, when he was eleven, he became involved in some minor property crimes. These culminated in threatening an arresting policeman with a knife. Paul, like his brothers, went to reform school. Because of his passivity and lack of aggression, he made a favorable impression and was soon released on parole. Paul refused to return to his family and was placed in an institution for homeless boys. He disliked this almost as much as living with his family.

In 1949 he joined the Navy and seemed to make a good adjustment to military life. Upon release, he held a succession of jobs. Each of them ended when he stole from his employers.

In 1954, Liston committed a sexual assault and was convicted before a Boston court. Since his release he has not been convicted again for a sexual crime, but he has been convicted several times for traffic offenses and drunkenness. His father has left his mother and Paul sees little of either of them.

Drunkenness

Twenty-two men had been arrested more than once, and an additional 24 had been arrested once, for drunkenness. We cannot argue that every one of these 46 individuals was alcoholic; nevertheless, in practice, seldom is a man charged with drunkenness unless he is a rather continual public nuisance. A conviction for drunkenness indicates a socially unacceptable degree of public display.

In several ways, the "drunks" resembled those men convicted for property crimes. Maternal neglect was particularly conducive to drunkenness. On the paternal side, if a father was either absent from the home or neglecting, his son's chances of drunkenness increased. As children, the drunkards had been disciplined in an erratic manner, strongly emphasizing punitiveness. And, typically, they came from homes which were either broken or quarrelsome and neglecting.

A comparison of maternal backgrounds shows that almost half (48%) the sons of neglecting mothers had been convicted for drunkenness, although only 15 percent of the sons of all other types of mothers had been charged with this offense. The difference is, of course, highly significant ($P < .001$).[33] The connection between maternal neglect and drunkenness among criminals is clearly revealed in Table 67 ($P < .005$).[34]

TABLE 67. RELATION OF MOTHER'S PERSONALITY TO DRUNKENNESS

Mother		Percent of Criminals Convicted of Drunkenness
Passive	(N: 16)	19
Loving-anxious	(N: 12)	25
Absent	(N: 4)	25
Cruel	(N: 11)	27
Overprotective	(N: 33)	30
Loving-normal	(N: 25)	36
Loving-neurotic	(N: 11)	45
Neglecting	(N: 18)	67

Almost half (47%) of the drunkards had fathers who were either neglecting or absent from the home. Up to this point, we had not detected any specific relationship between choice of crime and absence of the father. But paternal absence or neglect is significantly related to drunkenness: 27 percent of the sons of absent or neglecting fathers compared to 14 percent of the sons of other fathers were convicted for drunkenness ($P < .025$).[35] Comparison among

[33] X^2 16.1; d.f. 1. [34] X^2 8.8; d.f. 1.
[35] X^2 5.3; d.f. 1. The father of one man convicted for drunkenness could not be classified.

the criminals reveals a similar, but non-significant, pattern (Table 68).

Erratic punitiveness was the type of discipline which produced the highest proportion of drunkards. Twenty-seven percent of the boys disciplined in this manner, as opposed to 14 percent of those disciplined in any other way, were convicted for drunkenness

TABLE 68. RELATION OF FATHER'S PERSONALITY TO DRUNKENNESS

Father		Percent of Criminals Convicted of Drunkenness
Cruel	(N: 20)	25
Warm	(N: 43)	30
Passive	(N: 15)	40
Neglecting	(N: 22)	41
Absent	(N: 27)	44

($P < .01$).[36] Unlike its relation to other types of crimes, laxity did not lead to drunkenness. Punitiveness in itself did not lead to drunkenness, but punitiveness administered in an erratic fashion did. The relationship between erratic punitiveness and drunkenness reappears in the comparison of criminals (Table 69). A sig-

TABLE 69. RELATION OF PARENTAL DISCIPLINE TO DRUNKENNESS

Type of Discipline		Percent of Criminals Convicted of Drunkenness
Punitive	(N: 8)	0
Love-lax	(N: 19)	21
Lax	(N: 30)	33
Love-oriented	(N: 26)	35
Punitive-lax	(N: 25)	44
Love-punitive-lax	(N: 23)	52

nificantly higher proportion of criminals who had been disciplined by erratic measures involving punitiveness as compared to criminals disciplined in other ways were convicted for drunkenness ($P < .02$).[37]

In their general home environment, the drunkards closely resembled men who committed crimes of violence. Broken and quarrelsome-neglecting homes produced disproportionately large numbers of both kinds of criminals. Thirty percent of men raised in quarrelsome-neglecting or broken homes had been convicted for

[36] X^2 6.6; d.f. 1.   [37] X^2 5.2; d.f. 1.

drunkenness, although only 12 percent of the other men had court convictions for drunkenness (P < .001).[38] If one considers the criminals alone, this strong influence of home atmosphere is apparent (P < .05)[39] (Table 70). The men with records of drunkenness

TABLE 70. RELATION OF HOME ATMOSPHERE TO DRUNKENNESS

Home Atmosphere		Percent of Criminals Convicted of Drunkenness
Quarrelsome-affectionate	(N: 26)	27
Cohesive	(N: 50)	28
Broken	(N: 27)	44
Quarrelsome-neglecting	(N: 27)	44

came overwhelmingly from homes which offered little emotional stability.

The life of one man, whom we will call George Genet, a typical and probably confirmed drunkard, illustrates the influences which produce this type of deviance. George Genet lived in one of the most disorganized of the Cambridge-Somerville families. The squalor and disorder of his home can be appreciated from the comments made in 1939 by a social worker who visited the family:

A heavy, nauseating odor hung in the air. The children swarmed about me, begging for pennies. When I didn't give them the money, the children sat on my lap and this was really frightening because their impetigo was virulent. I asked the mother where the boy was and she replied she did not know—probably he was out on the streets. One of the daughters tried to climb in my lap and the other children yelled, "She got bugs! She got bugs! She's been thrown out of school because she's got bugs!"

The mother of this family was careless, casual, dirty, and apparently lacking in any sense of responsibility. She drank heavily. After alcoholic sprees, she sneaked other men into the house to spend the night with her. When police reported to her that her daughter was being paid for sexual perversion by men at a nearby poolroom, the mother responded: "I can't do nothing with her; it is her own business."

[38] X^2 11.5; d.f. 1. The home atmosphere of one man convicted for drunkenness could not be classified.

[39] A significantly higher proportion of men from quarrelsome-neglecting or broken homes committed crimes of drunkenness. X^2 3.94; d.f. 1.

CHOICE OF THE CRIMINAL ACT

Mr. Genet was of French-Canadian origin. By trade a carpenter, he was fired from a variety of jobs because of drunkenness. He took no part in disciplining the children, except for occasional whippings. Often the mother and father drank together, but these bouts usually ended in physical fights. On one occasion they both went to the local police station and turned each other in; each, of course, was totally drunk.

George, one of six children in the family, was relatively intelligent, nervous, suggestible, and plagued by anxiety and nightmares. Although one of his brothers served time in a reform school and then prison (after seventeen burglaries), George did not participate in really serious delinquencies. Much of the credit for this should go to George's counselor, who became a sympathetic father substitute. The counselor worked with George on an intensive basis. He attempted to instill a sense of responsibility in the child by offering him stable and frequent companionship.

Nevertheless, the counselor battled against great odds. The therapy began in 1939, when George was eleven. The boy's personality had already been badly malformed. George was "wise in the way of the streets" (he sold newspapers, ran "numbers" games, and did errands for older gang leaders), but he was tense, withdrawn, and guilt-ridden. He often requested his counselor to slap him in the face as punishment for his minor delinquencies. When he was particularly nervous, George masturbated through his clothing.

George was taken to the Judge Baker Clinic in Boston for psychological diagnosis. There, he described his frightening dreams (usually centering on death), his sexual relations with his sisters, and several incidents of getting drunk on the wine left around the house. He was eleven years old at the time of this interview. The clinic recommended that George be sent to a foster home. This measure was taken when the mother was charged with neglect before a Boston court.

George stayed in a variety of homes. They differed widely in quality. In one he established a close relation with his "parents," but when they tired of him he was switched to another home where he was bedded in a locked dormitory with ten other boys. His counselor continued to work with him through these changes.

In 1941, George was first arrested for drunkenness. He was found unconscious on a city street. Beside him lay his father, equally intoxicated. They were taken to a hospital. Because of his previous delinquencies, the court decided that the best place for George was reform school. He was committed, against the vehement objections of his counselor.

After George's release from the institution, Mr. Genet refused to take his son into his home. George's mother had run away with one of her paramours. Temporarily, George lived with his sister, who had become a prostitute. His counselor still kept in touch with the boy and when George reached the minimum age, arranged that the boy should enter the Army. After his release from the Army two years later, George was convicted once again for drunkenness.

By 1949, George appeared to have made a good adjustment to adulthood. The last counselor who saw him reported that he had secured a job which he liked and had been married. George was then twenty-one. He spoke glowingly of his counselor and of the services of the program: "I was just a little kid when we first used to see Mr. ———, and he was so helpful. I never thought I would get married. Gee, now I am going to have a family and be a father." Unfortunately, since his marriage, George has been convicted three times for drunkenness.

Traffic Violations

Traffic violations, unlike other crimes mentioned in this chapter, are frequently committed by people who are otherwise non-criminal. In the Cambridge-Somerville group, there were 27 boys whose only legal offense had been a relatively serious traffic violation. Forty-three boys who had been convicted for some major crime also had records for traffic offenses.

Analysis of the 70 traffic offenders uncovered some interesting and unexpected relationships. Characteristically, the traffic offenders had been raised by either overprotective or passive mothers and had lived in broken or quarrelsome-neglecting homes. Half of the traffic offenders, 51 percent, had been raised by either passive or overprotective mothers. Further analysis showed that 44 percent of those men raised by either overprotective or passive mothers, as compared to 20 percent of those raised by any other type of mother, had been convicted of traffic crimes (P < .001).[40] Overprotectiveness of the mother was most closely linked to traffic offenses in the background of criminals (P < .005) [41] (Table 71).

TABLE 71. RELATION OF MOTHER'S PERSONALITY TO TRAFFIC VIOLATIONS

Mother		Percent of Criminals Convicted of Traffic Violations
Loving-anxious	(N: 33)	17
Loving-neurotic	(N: 11)	18
Neglecting	(N: 18)	22
Absent	(N: 4)	25
Cruel	(N: 11)	55
Loving-normal	(N: 25)	64
Passive	(N: 16)	69
Overprotective	(N: 33)	76

A high proportion of traffic offenders came from either quarrelsome-neglecting or broken homes. Thirty-six percent of men raised in such family atmospheres, compared to 24 percent of other men, committed traffic offenses (P < .05).[42] Table 72 shows that men reared in broken or cohesive homes—if they become criminal at all—more frequently violated traffic laws (P < .01).[43]

TABLE 72. RELATION OF HOME ATMOSPHERE TO TRAFFIC VIOLATIONS

Home Atmosphere		Percent of Criminals Convicted of Traffic Violations
Quarrelsome-affectionate	(N: 26)	38
Quarrelsome-neglecting	(N: 27)	44
Cohesive	(N: 50)	62
Broken	(N: 27)	63

We have noted that either consistent or non-punitive discipline generally produced non-criminal boys. Nevertheless, if a child was among that small proportion which was disciplined consistently or non-punitively and became criminal, he was most prone to commit traffic offenses (P < .025) [44] (Table 73).

[40] X^2 16.3; d.f. 1.
[41] X^2 8.54; d.f. 1 (overprotective compared to all others).
[42] X^2 4.0; d.f. 1.
[43] X^2 7.32; d.f. 1 (comparison of cohesive and broken homes to others).
[44] Significantly more criminals disciplined consistently or erratically without punitiveness were convicted for traffic offenses: X^2 5.25; d.f. 1.

Although one might expect a higher rate of convictions for traffic crimes in better neighborhoods where more families could, presumably, afford cars, we found no such relationship. In fact, 24 percent of the men from good neighborhoods, as compared to 29 percent of the men from the worst neighborhoods, had records of traffic violations. These figures indicate that traffic offenses cannot be explained as a simple reflection of the availability of automobiles.

TABLE 73. RELATION OF PARENTAL DISCIPLINE TO TRAFFIC VIOLATIONS

Type of Discipline		Percent of Criminals Convicted of Traffic Violations
Love-punitive-lax	(N: 23)	39
Lax	(N: 30)	43
Punitive-lax	(N: 25)	52
Love-lax	(N: 19)	63
Love-oriented	(N: 26)	65
Punitive	(N: 7)	71

A short description of the case of a boy whom we will call Ralph Gonzales reveals the typical background of traffic offenders—a broken home and an overprotective mother.

Ralph Gonzales, at the end of his treatment, was regarded by his counselor as one of the outstanding successes of the Cambridge-Somerville program. Gonzales had first been visited by the staff in 1938, when he was eleven years old. His school had suggested Ralph's inclusion in the project because he was a "cheating, cowardly, cocksure, impulsive boy." In school he was known for stealing, refusing to obey authority, and abnormal sexual interests.

Gonzales' father had died when Ralph was a small boy. His family was composed of one brother and three sisters, ruled by a restrictive and anxious mother. The boy's counselor described the mother as "high-strung," superstitious, and intensely religious (she attended a Portuguese church every night of the week). The mother possessed immense and abnormal fears about the future of her children. She guarded them closely, defending them against the influences of their slum society. When her son got into trouble at school, the mother berated the principal; when the boy wanted to go to camp, she refused to let him leave her; when the boy committed a minor delinquency, she punished him for days. Ralph idolized his mother (at least verbally) and followed each of her whims.

At home, he was meek and obedient. At school, he was loud, aggressive, and exhibitionistic. The boy's counselor smoothed over his troubles at school, tutored him, arranged camp placements, and as he grew up, discussed sexual problems with him. By the time he was fifteen, the boy idolized his counselor (a woman) as much as he did his mother.

In 1944, Gonzales entered the Navy, where he made a creditable record. He wrote his mother constantly and his counselor at least once a week. During his war service, Gonzales' eardrums were broken by gunfire. He was discharged and pensioned. Upon his return home, he lived a quiet, unemployed life, associating with the neighborhood gang of discharged veterans. In 1949 he secured a steady job in a laundry, married, and settled down to family life. He had extraordinary difficulties in sexual relations with his wife (for a year and a half she refused to have any relations), but eventually this problem was overcome.

Today, Ralph has not committed any major crime. His counselor gives credit to the Cambridge-Somerville treatment. Nevertheless, Gonzales, now twenty-nine, has been arrested five times for traffic violations: once for a serious accident, once for using his brother's car "without permission," and three times for excessive speeding.

Summary

In our study we have attempted to establish links between specific types of crimes and the backgrounds of a large number of individuals (a summary of these causal syndromes appears in Table 74). This analysis has brought to light two facts.

First, certain early influences are broadly criminogenic. Parental neglect, quarrelsome-neglecting homes, and erratically punitive discipline figure prominently in the background of almost every variety of crime. *These factors are the common denominators of criminality.*

Second, these influences alone do not sufficiently explain the genesis of *particular* kinds of crime. They are combined with a

TABLE 74. SUMMARY OF CAUSAL SYNDROMES

	Property Crimes	Crimes Against the Person	Sex Crimes	Drunkenness	Traffic Violations
Maternal background	neglect (P < .001)	overprotection, neglect (P < .005)	passivity, neglect (P < .001)	neglect (P < .001)	overprotection, passivity (P < .001)
Paternal background	neglect (P < .005); criminal role model (P < .01)	cruelty, neglect (P < .005); criminal role model (P < .02)	neglect (P < .05)	absence, neglect (P < .025)	—
Disciplinary background	absence of consistency; erratic-punitiveness, laxity (P < .005)	absence of love; erratic-punitiveness, laxity (P < .02)	absence of consistency; erratic-punitiveness, laxity (P < .05)	absence of consistency and love; erratic-punitiveness (P < .01)	—
Home atmosphere	quarrelsome-neglecting (P < .001)	broken, quarrelsome-neglecting (P < .005)	quarrelsome-neglecting (P < .001)	broken, quarrelsome-neglecting (P < .001)	broken, quarrelsome-neglecting (P < .05)
Intelligence	average (P < .05)	—	—	—	—
Neighborhood	—	—	—	—	—

CHOICE OF THE CRIMINAL ACT

variety of other influences in producing different constellations of factors for each type of crime. Furthermore, certain environmental influences strongly *promote* one type of crime and *deter* other types of crime. Two examples illustrate this point: (a) passive mothers produced high proportions of sexual criminals and traffic offenders, yet their sons did not commit crimes of violence; (b) overprotective mothers had high proportions of "violent criminals" and traffic offenders among their sons but a very low proportion of sexual criminals.

With this empirical foundation, it is possible to make certain theoretical speculations concerning the motivation for each of the five types of crime.

Property crimes seem to be motivated primarily by a desire for attention and, to some extent, for material welfare. Property criminals had been emotionally and materially neglected by both their fathers and mothers. In addition, they had experienced lax or punitively erratic discipline. Consequently, one can argue that the development of property criminals occurs in the following manner: early family neglect gives rise to deep feelings of rejection and deprivation; the lack of consistent discipline leads to a rebelliousness unchecked by internalized inhibitions. These two elements in the child's background, particularly if supplemented by a delinquent sub-culture or criminal example, eventuate in participation in property crimes.

Crimes against the person appear to be a reaction against either maternal domination or paternal rejection. Retaliation against the cruelty or neglect of their fathers and the overprotectiveness of their mothers seems to be the primary motivation of these criminals. Once again, inconsistent punitiveness or laxity in discipline resulted in low inhibition. Love-oriented discipline seemed to be a strong preventive for this type of crime. The process generating violent crime might be described in this way: severe rejection or maternal domination causes feelings of frustration and rage, which are not inhibited by internalized controls. Because these children have aggressive models, they may in later life identify with the aggressor and express this aggression toward others.

Sexual crimes apparently stem from thwarted desires for maternal affection. Most of the sexual criminals had been raised by either passive or neglecting mothers. They also had neglecting or rejecting fathers. The process generating sexual offenses might follow this pattern: early family rejection increases the son's desire for affection. This desire is rebuffed by the parents and, consequently, the socially accepted modes of expressing affection are inhibited in the child. He then turns to deviant ways of expressing affection, because these patterns of behavior have not been forbidden in early life by the parents.

Drunkenness apparently occurred as an attempt to assuage feelings of rejection. The drunkards had been neglected by their mothers and fathers. Furthermore, inconsistently punitive discipline and quarrelsome or broken homes added to their feelings of rejection and anxiety. By drinking, we might hypothesize, these men were able to "forget" their insecurity.

The motivation for *traffic crimes* appears to be a search for mastery or power. On the one hand, the traffic criminal may be seeking an escape from the domination of an overprotective mother. On the other hand, he may be seeking recognition to compensate for the emotional passivity of his mother. By "controlling" a car at high speed or disregarding traffic regulations, the offender probably feels a sense of mastery and self-importance denied him in the home.

The differential effect of each environmental influence is summarized in the following pages.

1. MOTHER AND TYPES OF CRIME (Table 75)

The loving-normal mothers produced very few criminal sons. At no point did we find a significant relationship between this type of maternal background and the choice of a specific anti-social act. Apparently, factors other than maternal personality determine the motivation behind the choice of crime in children raised by a loving-normal woman.

A relatively small proportion of the sons of loving-anxious mothers were convicted for major crimes. If the son of a loving-anxious woman became criminal, he was more likely to commit property crimes than were the sons of loving-normal or overprotective women.

Although most of the sons of overprotective mothers did not become criminal, those who did had significantly greater tendencies to commit traffic violations and crimes of violence.

The sons of loving-neurotic mothers became criminal more often than did the sons of other types of loving mothers. Slightly more often, they tended to become drunkards.

The sons of cruel mothers had a relatively high rate of conviction, yet maternal cruelty was not related to any specific type of crime.

Passive mothers had many criminal children and, in particular, they contributed disproportionately to sex crimes and traffic crimes.

Children who had experienced maternal neglect were extremely likely to become criminal. Their anti-social acts were apt to be major crimes, and they had a tendency to commit crimes of more than one variety. Traffic crimes were the only type which these persons were not apt to commit. The neglected child becomes, apparently, an "across-the-board" criminal.

TABLE 75. PERCENT OF SONS OF EACH TYPE OF MOTHER CONVICTED OF EACH TYPE OF CRIME

Mother		Property Crimes	Crimes Against the Person	Sex Crimes	Drunkenness	Traffic Violations
Loving-normal	(N: 59)	22	0	2	15	27 [15]
Loving-anxious	(N: 33)	30	6	3	9	15 [3]
Overprotective	(N: 59)	31	10	5	17	42 [18]
Loving-neurotic	(N: 23)	35	0	0	22	9 [4]
Absent	(N: 8)	38	13	0	13	13 [0]
Cruel	(N: 22)	32	5	0	14	27 [5]
Passive	(N: 22)	45	0	14	14	50 [16]
Neglecting	(N: 25)	64	16	16	48	16 [0]

Note: The percentage in brackets represents the percent of sons of each type of mother who were convicted solely for traffic crimes. Boldface numerals indicate the existence of a statistically significant relationship between a particular type of background and a particular crime.

Although the mother's role model was discovered to be generally an important factor in the causation of crime, we found no significant relationships between her deviance and a particular type of crime.

2. FATHER AND TYPES OF CRIME (Table 76)

Paternal personality, although important in the causation of crime, seems to have only a slight relationship to the specific choice of a criminal act.

Boys raised by cruel fathers had a greater predilection to crimes of violence.

Boys whose fathers were absent from the home more often became drunkards.

Boys raised by neglecting fathers acted out their aggression through criminal behavior of every type.

TABLE 76. PERCENT OF SONS OF EACH TYPE OF FATHER CONVICTED OF EACH TYPE OF CRIME

Father		Property Crimes	Crimes Against the Person	Sex Crimes	Drunkenness	Traffic Violations
Passive	(N: 37)	30	0	5	16	21 [11]
Warm	(N: 95)	25	3	4	14	24 [12]
Absent	(N: 45)	40	4	2	27	36 [13]
Cruel	(N: 34)	35	**12**	3	15	35 [12]
Neglecting	(N: 34)	**56**	**15**	**12**	26	29 [3]

Note: The percentage in brackets represents the percent of sons of each type of father who were convicted solely for traffic crimes. Boldface numerals indicate the existence of a statistically significant relationship between a particular type of background and a particular crime.

Paternal role models, on the other hand, were related significantly to both property crimes and crimes against the person. Criminal fathers evidently established a pattern of aggression which the sons tended to follow.

3. DISCIPLINE AND TYPES OF CRIME (Table 77)

Two variables—consistency and the use of love-oriented measures—influenced the choice of crime.

Relatively few boys who had been disciplined consistently in a love-oriented manner became criminal. Relatively few boys who had been disciplined in a consistently punitive manner became criminal.

Boys disciplined in an erratic manner, which varied between

laxity and being love-oriented, had a higher rate of crime but no predilection to a particular type of crime.

Laxity in discipline led to an even higher rate of crime and, specifically, to property crimes, crimes of violence, and sexual offenses, but not to drunkenness.

Erratic discipline involving punitiveness was highly conducive to criminality. Boys disciplined in this manner had the highest conviction rates for every type of crime except traffic violations.

TABLE 77. PERCENT OF BOYS DISCIPLINED IN EACH MANNER CONVICTED OF EACH TYPE OF CRIME

Type of Discipline		Property Crimes	Crimes Against the Person	Sex Crimes	Drunkenness	Traffic Violations
Love-oriented	(N: 60)	22	0	0	15	28 [17]
Punitive	(N: 14)	14	7	0	0	36 [29]
Love-lax	(N: 40)	30	3	5	10	30 [13]
Lax	(N: 52)	42	**8**	6	19	25 [8]
Erratic-punitive	(N: 84)	**44**	**10**	**8**	**27**	26 [4]

Note: The percentage in brackets represents the percent of boys disciplined in each way who were convicted only for traffic crimes. Boldface numerals indicate the existence of a statistically significant relationship between a particular type of background and a particular crime.

4. HOME ATMOSPHERE AND TYPES OF CRIME (Table 78)

Cohesive homes, like consistent love-oriented discipline, tended to prevent criminality.

Quarrelsome but affectionate homes produced a higher number of criminals but did not relate significantly to particular kinds of crime.

Broken homes resulted in a particularly high incidence of violent crimes and drunkenness.

Quarrelsome-neglecting homes produced high rates of conviction for every type of crime.

Clearly, certain early influences are more important than others in molding the choice of crime. Of all factors, the mother's personality appears to be most significant; the statistical relationship between this variable and types of crime was most highly significant. Neighborhood and intelligence have practically no bearing on the choice of crime.

In sum, this section has demonstrated that the choice of crime is, to a large extent, determined by factors outside the criminal's control: his parents' personalities, their methods of discipline, and the nature of his family life. These relations indicate that the "symptoms" of criminality, like those of a particular disease, warrant close scrutiny in the analysis of causation.

TABLE 78. PERCENT OF BOYS FROM EACH TYPE OF HOME CONVICTED OF EACH TYPE OF CRIME

Home Atmosphere		Property Crimes	Crimes Against the Person	Sex Crimes	Drunkenness	Traffic Violations	
Cohesive	(N: 114)	24	3	3	12	27	[14]
Quarrelsome-affectionate	(N: 56)	32	2	4	13	18	[9]
Broken	(N: 43)	40	12	2	28	40	[12]
Quarrelsome-neglecting	(N: 37)	65	14	16	32	32	[3]

Note: The percentage in brackets represents the percent of boys from each type of home who were convicted only for traffic crimes. Boldface numerals indicate the existence of a statistically significant relationship between a particular type of background and a particular crime.

Up to this point, we have been concerned with the origins of criminality and with the prevention of crime. Our attention has been focused on why a man became a criminal and on why he committed a specific type of crime. In the next chapter, we will examine the complicated question of the age, duration, and cessation of deviant behavior.

CHAPTER VII

THE AGE OF CRIMINALITY

THE MAJORITY OF THE BOYS IN THE CAMBRIDGE-SOMERVILLE PROgram, both in the treatment group and in the control group, had stopped committing crimes by the time they reached their middle twenties. This general phenomenon of "reformation" has attracted the attention of Sheldon and Eleanor Glueck.

In their various research projects, the Gluecks studied the lives of convicts released from prison and of juveniles who appeared before Boston courts. For those who reformed, the Gluecks detected an approximate eight-year span as the duration of their criminal careers, regardless of the age at which criminality began. The Gluecks were unable to trace reformation either to the early experiences of the men or to the effects of penal institutions. Consequently, they postulated that reformation came about because of biological and emotional maturation.[1]

The Glueck research gave rise to two questions: Does criminality run in a cyclical pattern? And is there a cause-and-effect relationship between childhood experiences and later reformation?

Court records containing the age at which each crime was committed supplied the starting point for our investigation of the duration of criminality. Dividing the 104 criminals[2] into the age at which they committed their first offenses showed that "official" criminality generally begins during adolescence (Table 79). Sixty-

TABLE 79. AGE OF CRIMINALS AT FIRST CONVICTION

Age	Percent of Criminals (N: 104)
Under 13	18
13–17	48
18–22	24
Over 22	10

---

[1] Sheldon and Eleanor T. Glueck, *After-Conduct of Discharged Offenders*.
[2] Since we were concerned with major crimes, boys who committed only traffic violations were excluded.

six percent of the criminals had been juvenile delinquents according to the law, which considers a criminal "juvenile" through the age of seventeen.

Next, we divided each of the groups according to the age at which these criminals were last convicted. Of the 19 boys first convicted under the age of twelve, 32 percent had not been convicted for any major crime since passing their thirteenth birthday; an additional 21 percent had no court record after the age of eighteen; 26 percent more had not been convicted after their twenty-third birthday; yet 21 percent were still criminal.

Of the 50 boys first convicted between the ages of thirteen and seventeen, 48 percent ceased criminal activity before they reached the age of eighteen; an additional 30 percent had not been convicted after their twenty-second birthday; and 22 percent were still criminal.

Of the 25 boys first convicted between the ages of eighteen and twenty-two, 68 percent had no criminal records after the age of twenty-three and 32 percent were still criminal.

The Gluecks' findings led us to expect that a larger proportion of those who began criminal activities in early childhood would have ended them by adulthood. Nevertheless, approximately equal proportions of the boys who began their criminal activities in childhood and those who began in adolescence still were committing crimes after they had passed their nineteenth birthday (47%:52%) and after they had passed their twenty-third birthdays (21%:22%).

According to the cyclical theory, a larger proportion of those who began criminality in youth should have reformed at an earlier age. Although 78 percent of the boys first convicted before the age of eighteen had no records after the age of twenty-three, 68 percent of the boys first convicted between the ages of eighteen and twenty-three had no records after that age. The difference between these two proportions is not statistically significant. Thus, the court records of our sample do not support a cyclical interpretation of criminality.

Why, then, did the juvenile delinquents "reform"? Are there reasons stemming from the early life of an individual for his later reformation? Our findings indicate that there are. In the hope of finding those factors which are relevant to reformation, we divided the juvenile delinquents (i.e., those who had committed their first crimes before the age of eighteen) into two groups: the "reformed" delinquents and the "repeating" delinquents. We considered the 34 boys who had been convicted for their first crime as juveniles, but had no record for adult offenses, as "reformed" delinquents. The 35 boys who had committed crimes in youth and also after the age of eighteen were considered "repeaters."

Four factors—the mother's personality, the father's example, disciplinary methods, and neighborhood—differentiated the reformed delinquents from the repeaters.

Those delinquents who had been raised by loving mothers were most likely to reform; on the other hand, delinquents raised by overprotective or non-loving mothers were not likely to reform. Sixty-eight percent of the juvenile delinquents with loving mothers reformed, as compared to 45 percent of those with non-loving mothers, and 31 percent of those with overprotective mothers ($P < .05$).[3] It appears that a child who has been loved by his mother is not only relatively immune to criminal tendencies but that, if he does become criminal, he is likely to reform before he reaches manhood.

The mother's influence on reformation depended on her personality, not her role model, for we found no significant relation between maternal deviance and the son's reformation. The father's influence on reformation, however, proved to be through his role model and not through his personality. Only 30 percent of the delinquents raised by criminal fathers reformed, whereas 63 percent of those with alcoholic or sexually unfaithful fathers and 53 percent of those raised by non-deviant fathers reformed ($P < .05$).[4] We hypothesize that once a child has accepted his father's criminally deviant values these become so deeply ingrained that he will probably continue his anti-social behavior.

We found that delinquents who had been disciplined erratically without punitiveness or who had been undisciplined were most likely to reform. Sixty-four percent of the delinquents who had lax or erratically love-oriented discipline reformed, as compared to 40 percent of those who had been disciplined consistently (in

[3] X^2 4.4; d.f. 1.   [4] X^2 4.2; d.f. 1.

either a love-oriented or punitive manner) and 39 percent of those who had been disciplined in an erratic fashion involving punitiveness ($P < .05$).[5]

This finding lends credence to the theory that some children become delinquent because of a lack of guidance in the home; as they mature, however, they apparently come to accept societal standards of behavior. We suggest that those delinquents who had been controlled by consistent discipline rebelled for other, more complex, reasons than a simple lack of guidance; consequently, they were less apt to reform. Delinquents who had been disciplined by erratic punitiveness perhaps resented authority figures too much to accept authority later in life.

Children who came from the very worst urban areas were least likely to reform. Only 33 percent of the delinquents from the worst neighborhoods, but 63 percent of those from poor neighborhoods and 60 percent of those from good or fair neighborhoods, reformed as they entered adult life ($P < .05$).[6] Reasonably, we believe, one can assume that boys from the worst neighborhoods were the least socially mobile. That is, neighborhood conditions would remain relatively constant for these boys and there would be fewer new satisfactions deriving from maturation and independence. In addition, we know that these neighborhoods contain fewer effective social influences which might lead to reformation.

Other factors in the boys' early experiences did not, apparently, affect reformation. Once a child had become delinquent, his general home atmosphere seemed to have no direct influence on his reformation. Forty-two percent of those who came from cohesive homes, 50 percent of those from quarrelsome homes, and 60 percent of those from broken homes had no record for adult criminality. The difference in proportions is not statistically significant.

Intelligence had no significant relation to reformation. Forty-six percent of the juvenile delinquents with I.Q. scores above 90, compared to 56 percent of those with intelligence scores below this point, had no criminal records after the age of nineteen.

Whether or not a delinquent reforms can be partly explained in terms of his mother's personality, his father as a role model, his discipline, and his neighborhood. Nevertheless, experiences during

[5] X^2 4.2; d.f. 1.   [6] X^2 4.6; d.f. 1.

manhood, contemporaneous with reformation, probably play a critical part. As a boy enters adulthood, providing that he does not have a seriously underdeveloped conscience or has not been inculcated with a fundamental resentment of authority, many of the causes for his deviant behavior are eradicated. By leaving his childhood home, the frustrations of family life—so important in the background of delinquents—are avoided. Marriage, his career, or children may provide him with the emotional satisfaction he has sought in the past. As he leaves the adolescent gang, the status he gained as a participant in the delinquent sub-culture may be replaced by new sources of prestige as a member of the adult world.

Closely related to the analysis of factors contributing to reformation is the search for conditions which lead to an early beginning of delinquent behavior. One would expect to find that family life was strongly related to the age at which criminality began.

As a first step in the examination of this problem, we divided the criminals into two groups: the "early starters," those who began committing crimes before the age of eighteen; and the "late starters," those who had not been juvenile delinquents but had criminal records only after the age of seventeen. Sixty-nine men were early starters and 35 were late starters.

There is a tendency for the criminal who has received maternal love to be a late starter. Although the difference is not statistically significant, a higher proportion of the criminals with loving mothers had first been convicted only after the age of seventeen. Forty-one percent of the criminals with loving mothers, as compared to only 25 percent of the criminals with non-loving mothers, were late starters. Thus, during the period of life when the mother's influence is strongest, a low proportion of maternally loved boys became criminal. Of the 174 boys who had been raised by loving or overprotective mothers, only 20 percent were early starters, or juvenile delinquents.

More important than the presence or absence of a loving relationship between mother and boy was the particular personality of the mother. A significantly higher proportion of criminals who had passive or neglecting mothers were early starters. Eighty-three percent of the criminals with passive or neglecting mothers as compared to only 59 percent of the criminals with any other type of mother had committed their first crime before the age of eighteen ($P < .02$).[7]

The father's personality bore an interesting relation to the age at which criminality began. Ninety-one percent of the criminals who had passive fathers and 75 percent of those who had neglecting fathers were early starters. Sixty-two percent of the criminals with cruel fathers and 56 percent of those with warm fathers had committed their first crime in youth. Sixty-seven percent of the criminals with absent fathers were juvenile delinquents. A significantly higher proportion of the criminals with passive or neglecting fathers than of criminals with warm or cruel fathers had been convicted for juvenile offenses ($P < .05$).[8] This finding hints that even negative attention can deter criminality. Although a very small number of men with passive fathers became criminal, those who did seem either to have viewed paternal passivity as neglect or to have acted during adolescence because of dissatisfaction with the father as a male ideal.

Although the paternal role model had an important influence in the causation of crime, it was not significantly related to the age at which criminality began: 75 percent of the criminals with deviant fathers and 58 percent of the criminals with non-deviant fathers had been early starters.

Home atmosphere, too, seemed to be closely linked to the age at which criminality began. Forty-five percent of the criminals who had lived in broken homes, 56 percent of those from cohesive homes, 81 percent of those from quarrelsome but affectionate homes, and 88 percent of those who had lived in quarrelsome and neglecting homes were early starters in their criminal careers. A significantly higher proportion of the criminals from quarrelsome homes (with or without affection) had court records before the age of eighteen ($P < .001$).[9] Apparently, if a child from these homes becomes criminal, he has found the tensions so great that he reacts through anti-social behavior early in his life.

Neighborhood was of secondary importance in the etiology of

[7] X^2 5.8; d.f. 1.
[8] X^2 4.92; d.f. 1. Comparison of criminals with passive fathers to those with non-passive fathers almost reaches a significant level: X^2 3.13; d.f. 1.
[9] X^2 12.8; d.f. 1.

crime; nevertheless, it had a significant relation to the age at which criminality began. Only 52 percent of the criminals reared in good or fair neighborhoods as opposed to 74 percent of the criminals brought up in the poor or worst areas were early starters ($P < .05$).[10] Boys living in poor neighborhoods apparently find satisfactions, through delinquent gang membership, which are unavailable to children living in better neighborhoods. Children who live in the better neighborhoods become criminal later in life, in response to pressures other than the neighborhood.

We found no relationship between discipline and the age at which criminality began. Sixty percent of the criminals with nonpunitive discipline, 69 percent with punitive discipline, and 69 percent with lax discipline had been convicted at an early age.

One might expect that children with low intelligence would become criminal at an early age. They would experience their greatest frustration during the school years and would tend to express this frustration through criminality at that time. Seventy-five percent of the criminals with sub-normal intelligence, compared to 65 percent of the criminals with I.Q. scores over 81, were delinquents during school age. This difference, however, is not statistically significant.

These, then, are the factors which seem to prompt an early beginning of criminality: passive or neglecting mothers, passive or neglecting fathers, quarrelsome homes, and poor neighborhoods. As compared with late starters, juvenile criminals appear to be escaping from conflict in the home and from parents who fail to gratify emotional needs. Perhaps boys who would otherwise have become criminal at an early age "store up" their antagonisms if they live in areas not conductive to participation in delinquent acts.

We have shown how early starters differ from late ones. The former were typified by greater maternal rejection, paternal rejection or passivity, quarrelsome homes, and highly disorganized neighborhoods. Since, apparently, experiences in adulthood are critical to reformation of delinquents, it seemed reasonable to assume that events occurring during adulthood might also be causally related to some adult criminality. To eliminate the influence of adult experiences, we turned our attention to juvenile

[10] X^2 4.3; d.f. 1.

delinquents. We counted as delinquents only boys who had been convicted of crimes before the age of eighteen.

Not surprisingly, the father's and the mother's personalities were reflected in crime rates for juvenile delinquency. Loving mothers and warm fathers produced the lowest proportion of juvenile delinquents. Consistent discipline, too, resulted in little early delinquency. A high number of boys disciplined in a lax or erratically punitive fashion turned to crime at an early age.[11]

The importance of a masculine model is emphasized by the analysis of juvenile delinquency. Although we found no significant relation between maternal deviant behavior and early delinquency, paternal role models were strongly related to juvenile crimes ($P < .005$) [12] (Table 80).

TABLE 80. RELATION OF FATHER'S ROLE MODEL TO RATE OF JUVENILE DELINQUENCY

Father's Role Model		Percent of Boys Convicted as Juvenile Delinquents
Criminal	(N: 45)	44
Alcoholic or sexually unfaithful	(N: 69)	28
Non-deviant	(N: 139)	28

When we computed the rates for juvenile delinquency according to home atmosphere, we found some interesting additional information (Table 81). Broken homes, the *bête noire* of many so-

TABLE 81. RELATION OF HOME ATMOSPHERE TO RATE OF JUVENILE DELINQUENCY

Home Atmosphere		Percent of Boys Convicted as Juvenile Delinquents
Cohesive	(N: 114)	17
Broken	(N: 43)	23
Quarrelsome-affectionate	(N: 56)	30
Quarrelsome-neglecting	(N: 37)	61

cial workers who deal with children, resulted in significantly less juvenile delinquency than did quarrelsome-neglecting homes ($P < .001$).[13]

The analysis of all criminals shows that men from broken homes had a greater inclination toward crime than those from cohesive or quarrelsome but affectionate homes. Yet the immediate result

---

[11] See Appendix A for statistics.   [12] X^2 8.0; d.f. 1.   [13] X^2 43.41; d.f. 1.

of a rupture in the family does not seem to be delinquency. The juvenile delinquency rates for cohesive and for broken homes were not significantly different.

In order to understand the interplay of childhood background and adult experience, we made a special analysis of men who had no criminal records prior to the age of eighteen. We hoped to answer the question: What childhood backgrounds predispose a person toward criminality, yet do not result in immediate anti-social behavior?

As we had expected, we found that absence of parental love led to adult criminality even among those who had no juvenile delinquency records. Forty-three percent of those with no loving parent, as compared to 15 percent of those with at least one loving parent, became adult criminals ($P < .005$).[14] We found, however, that neither discipline nor parental role model were related to adult criminality; apparently these factors either lead directly to juvenile delinquency or tend to dissipate in their influence.

On the other hand, we found that broken homes were related to adult criminality although they were not significantly related to juvenile delinquency. Whereas 36 percent of the men with no juvenile delinquency records who came from broken homes became adult criminals, only 16 percent of those from cohesive homes and 13 percent of those from quarrelsome homes turned to crime in adulthood ($P < .005$).[15] Thus we see that broken homes lay a foundation for, though they do not result directly in, criminality. Broken homes, we hypothesize, provide an insecure defense against later stresses which might lead a man to crime.

We have found that the duration of crime and the age at which it begins are closely connected to childhood environment. Yet reformation and late onset of criminality seem to result from interaction between personality conditioned by the home and the experiences of adulthood.

[14] X^2 9.3; d.f. 1.   [15] X^2 8.06; d.f. 1.

CHAPTER VIII

A SUMMARY OF THE CAUSES OF CRIME

HAVING COMPLETED OUR DETAILED EXAMINATION OF CRIMINALITY in the boys who participated in the Cambridge-Somerville Youth Study, we can now attempt to weave these strands of evidence together. A pattern of causation has emerged—a pattern drawn from the lives of 253 boys who have now become men. Although these men have a rather restricted social-class background, and although a higher proportion than would normally be expected became criminal, this group seems, in many ways, to represent those boys who grew to adulthood during the depression and Second World War. Despite the danger of undue generalization, we believe that knowledge of the forces which influenced the Cambridge-Somerville boys can be effectively applied to an understanding of American male children in general. (This belief is strengthened by the fact that patterns of causation among the 253 control boys—reported in Appendix B—closely resemble those among the treated boys.

Admittedly, this study of causation suffers from certain limitations. One of these is, of course, that our sole standard of criminality is official court convictions, which contain no evidence concerning "undetected crimes." This, we believe, is a fault which cannot adequately be corrected in any study of criminality. Yet in our opinion it is not a serious fault, for only the exceptional criminal could escape detection for a period of almost thirty years. A second limitation is that we did not have access to records other than those from Massachusetts and federal courts. As we mention in the first chapter, however, a check on the residence of the Cambridge-Somerville boys indicated that relatively few had left the state (probably too few to change the fundamental picture).

Our study possesses some unique features. "Retrospective bias"

SUMMARY OF CAUSES OF CRIME

has been eliminated. It is not possible to explain the relationships which we have discovered between crime and the family as being due to parental disapproval *after* a boy became criminal. Our information was gathered before criminality began, rather than after it. Another advantage of this study is the wealth of information gathered by the Cambridge-Somerville Youth Study staff. Because of this, we were able to examine the interacting influence of a variety of factors in the early life of these men.

A brief summary of our findings concerning the genesis of crime may be an aid to understanding.

1. *Intelligence* was not strongly related to the causation of crime, although high intelligence may have allowed some offenders to escape the penalties of their crimes. We did find, however, that those who committed crimes against property were, most often, of average intelligence.

2. Except in those cases of boys suffering from a distinct neurological disorder, *physical condition* did not significantly affect the incidence of crime.

3. *Social factors,* in our sample, were not strongly related to criminality. The fact that a child's neighborhood did not, by itself, exert an independently important influence may surprise social scientists. Undeniably, a slum neighborhood can mold a child's personality—but apparently only if other factors in his background make him susceptible to the sub-culture that surrounds him. Cohesiveness in the family, consistent discipline, and affection from his parents seem to insulate a boy from the influence of a gang culture. On the other hand, we found that children who lived in "good neighborhoods," even though they came from neglecting families, tended to channel their frustrations in a non-criminal way.

These are our major conclusions about the influence of neighborhoods.

Men who came from good neighborhoods were more likely to "reform" after the age of eighteen than were men raised in poorer areas.

Neighborhood appeared to have a more important causative influence (although statistically non-significant) on juvenile delinquency than it did on adult criminality.

Other social factors were variously related to crime.

If a child's basic reference group was a delinquent gang, his chance of becoming criminal was significantly increased.

Second-generation Americans were less likely to become criminal than were the sons of native-born Americans.

Criminals were more likely than non-criminals to have rejected their father's culture.

Although the father's religion was not related to crime, a significantly lower proportion of criminals were raised by Catholic mothers who attended church regularly.

Neither the education of the father nor that of the mother was significantly related to criminality.

We recognize, of course, that the larger social environment limits a person's choices of behavior by channeling his drives into specific areas. We do not by any means wish to assert that a child in a middle-class environment who undergoes the pathological family influences described previously will become criminal. The middle-class environment may furnish other ways for expressing the dissatisfactions and personal disturbances created by such a family structure; yet we would argue that the basic drives of the person remain the same.

4. A child's *home atmosphere* had an important effect on whether he became criminal; indeed, the importance of the home cannot be stressed too greatly.

Cohesive homes produced few criminals. If a boy from such a home became criminal, he was most likely to commit traffic violations.

Quarrelsome but affectionate homes produced a higher proportion of criminals.

Broken homes precipitated many men into criminality, particularly into crimes of violence and drunkenness. Yet only a small proportion had records for juvenile delinquency.

The influence of broken homes has been overstressed, for the extreme tension found in a quarrelsome and neglecting home is even more conducive to criminality. Such homes produce an extremely high number of all types of criminals.

SUMMARY OF CAUSES OF CRIME

A quarrelsome home, with or without affection, led to delinquency which began at a relatively early age.

5. The effect of *discipline* in the genesis of criminality is a complicated problem, for the influence of discipline was dependent upon other factors. These following facts, however, seem to be well established.

Consistent discipline, whether of a punitive or love-oriented nature, tended to prevent criminality.

Lax discipline resulted in a relatively high proportion of criminals. In particular, laxity produced a large number of property, violent, and sexual criminals. Criminals who had been disciplined in a lax manner tended to begin criminal activity at an early age.

Nevertheless, criminals disciplined in a lax manner were more likely to reform than criminals disciplined in an erratically punitive way.

Erratically punitive discipline was closely related to criminality. Boys disciplined in this manner were most likely to commit every type of crime, except traffic violations. Such criminals were less likely to "reform" in later life than criminals disciplined in any other manner.

The effects of lax discipline and of erratically punitive discipline were dissipated, however, if the child's home was cohesive or if his parents were non-deviant in behavior. In other words, discipline affected criminality most strongly when other socializing factors were absent.

6. The *father's personality* had an important bearing on criminality. We established that warm fathers and passive fathers produced very few criminals. Paternal absence, cruelty, or neglect, however, tended to produce criminality in a majority of boys. More specific conclusions follow.

Paternal warmth tended to decrease crime among boys reared by non-loving mothers or by mothers who were deviant in behavior. Even if a father was criminal, paternal warmth militated against the development of criminality in his son.

Passive fathers seemed to be influential in lessening the crime rate among boys raised by non-loving mothers. If the mother's role model was deviant, on the other hand, paternal passivity did not reduce crime. Passive fathers, in general, produced few criminals; those sons who did turn to crime, however, had a tendency to do so during adolescence rather than adulthood.

Paternal absence resulted in a relatively high rate of crime, especially in drunkenness. Yet consistent discipline or maternal love militated against this effect.

The results of paternal cruelty depended completely upon the mother's attitude. Only if the mother was non-loving did high rates of crime appear. Consistently love-oriented discipline, in addition, reduced criminality among boys reared by cruel fathers.

Paternal neglect led to crime, except in those cases where maternal love or consistently love-oriented discipline were present. Neglected sons became criminal at an early age and were convicted in high proportions for every type of crime.

7. The *role model of the father*, we found, was also significantly related to criminality. Especially if the father rejected his son, the son tended to imitate the behavior of his father: if the father was criminal, the son tended to become criminal. Nevertheless, this relationship was dependent upon the attitude of the mother, upon her behavior, and upon discipline.

If the mother was loving, the son was less likely to imitate his father's role model.

If the mother was not loving, the son did not imitate the behavior of his father: the majority of such children became criminal, even though the father presented a non-deviant model.

If the mother as well as the father was a deviant role model, the son was extremely likely to become criminal.

Consistent discipline tended to interfere with a son's identification with a deviant paternal model.

The combination of paternal rejection and a deviant male model produced an extremely high proportion of criminals.

Boys raised by criminal fathers were especially prone to property crimes and crimes against the person, to early and to prolonged criminality.

8. Of all the influences which play a part in the genesis of criminality, the *mother's personality* appeared to be the most fundamental.

SUMMARY OF CAUSES OF CRIME

Maternal love, even though the love was complicated by an overprotective attitude, by anxiety, or by neurosis, *generally* led to low rates of crime.

Maternal passivity (in contrast to paternal passivity, which led to low rates of crime) was significantly related to a high crime rate and, specifically, to sexual crime and traffic violations.

Maternal cruelty and absence led to high criminality, but were not related to specific varieties of anti-social behavior.

Maternal neglect resulted in a high proportion of sons who committed a wide variety of crimes. Such children were likely to begin criminality early in life and were the least likely to "reform" as they entered adulthood.

The loving-normal and the loving-anxious mothers, with few exceptions, had non-criminal sons. Table 82 permits us to look

TABLE 82. RELATIONSHIP BETWEEN CERTAIN VARIABLES OF CRIMINALITY AND MOTHER'S PERSONALITY

	Loving-Neurotic Mothers (N: 23)	Overprotective Mothers (N: 59)	Cruel Mothers (N: 22)	Passive Mothers (N: 22)	Neglecting Mothers (N: 25)
Percent of sons convicted of crimes	43	37	45	57	72
Was this percent lower if the father was loving?	No	No	Yes	Yes	No
Was this percent increased if the father was criminal?	No	No	Yes	Yes	Yes
What type of crime was particularly related to this type of mother?	—	Crimes against the person, traffic violations	—	Sex crimes, traffic violations	Property crimes, sex crimes, crimes against the person, drunkenness
Did the role model of the mother affect the rate of crime?	No	No	Yes	—	Yes
Did significantly more of the sons begin their criminality early in life?	No	No	—	Yes	Yes
Did significantly more of the sons "reform" as they entered adulthood?	Yes	No	No	No	No

more closely at the relationship between criminality, maternal attitudes, and other important variables for the groups of mothers whose sons' crime rates were relatively high.

9. The son's *position in the family,* affected by family structure and attitude, in turn had an effect on crime. Specifically, those children who were viewed as "troublemakers" by their parents and those boys who fell in the middle range of the birth order were likely to become criminal.

Clearly, one cannot understand the origins of criminality by examining one factor alone; rather, one must understand the complex interaction of such determinants as the parents as individuals, the parents in relation to their child, and the family as it combines with neighborhood influences. As we have seen, if both parents are rejecting, or if both are deviant models, the son is very likely to become criminal at some point in his life. If inconsistent discipline, bad parental models, and the influences of a slum neighborhood are added to rejection, the boy is especially likely to become criminal.

This research has demonstrated—at least, for the boys in our sample—the falsity of several popular theories concerning the origins of criminality.

1. We did not find a strong, direct relationship between criminality and residence in a slum neighborhood.

2. We did not find a direct relationship between criminality and disciplinary methods except when a child is rejected by his parents or has deviant parental role models.

3. We did not find that punitive, harsh discipline (in whatever form administered) prevents criminality. Under certain conditions, consistently punitive discipline may deter criminality, but erratically punitive discipline promotes it.

4. We did not find that sons of passive males turn frequently to criminality to assert their "masculinity."

5. We did not find that broken homes constitute the type of atmosphere most conducive to criminality.

CHAPTER IX

IMPLICATIONS FOR THE FUTURE

THE PRECEDING CHAPTERS HAVE TRACED THE IMMEDIATE ENVIRONmental conditions that cause crime and the ineffectiveness of one attempt made to counteract these forces. We have hesitated to expand the practical and theoretical conclusions implicit in this study for fear that they would hinder the objective presentation of our findings. Now we develop some of these implications more fully, giving freer rein to speculation.

Implications for the Community

One of the authors of this study recently lectured before a group of psychologists and child guidance workers about the results of this research into the effectiveness of treatment. After the lecture, the head of a guidance department in one Massachusetts town came to the platform to discuss the research. He said, in a rather depressed manner: "Early next week, I have to go before my school board and request funds for the establishment of a counseling service in our town. One of the major aims of the new department is the prevention of delinquency. I came to this meeting expecting to get ammunition for my request, hoping to hear that psychological counseling *could* prevent crime. Instead, I find that the best-controlled experiment in this area has proved an almost total failure. I have to deal with practical businessmen; they want results for their money. How can I go back with a clear conscience and tell them that their money would be well spent if they invested it in psychological treatment for criminals?"

The speaker tried to reassure his questioner, telling him that there were hopeful indications about certain kinds of treatment and pleading that money would be well spent for further research into the results of different varieties of treatment. But it was of little avail. The guidance official replied with disgust: "That is all well and good for a researcher, but a request to businessmen for the 'advancement of science' will fall on deaf ears. The school board wants to *stop* crime, not study it."

The citizen who reads this book, whether he is in some way officially responsible for dealing with criminals or is simply disturbed by juvenile delinquency, gang warfare, youthful violence, and sexual "looseness," is concerned with curbing criminality. Yet knowledge of the causes of crime is essential to preventing and curing criminality.

For those new to the field of criminology, one of the most astonishing results of this research may be the finding that criminality is greatly determined by factors beyond the control of the individual. More than this, these determining factors can be analyzed. Under certain familial and social conditions, the child's choice about whether to conform to society's rules is, in very large measure, made for him.

For some, this may be a depressing conclusion. Its truth, however, is being demonstrated by the increasingly reliable way in which criminality can be predicted. A variety of research projects, particularly those conducted by Sheldon and Eleanor Glueck, are showing that it is possible to predict delinquency.[1] One such experiment in prediction was carried out by Richard Thompson on the Cambridge-Somerville boys.[2] Thompson selected 100 of the cases at random and presented descriptions of their family environment to Dr. Glueck, who then made a series of judgments based on home atmosphere, parental personality, and disciplinary practices, concerning whether or not particular children had become criminal. Using the court records of the boys as of 1948, Thompson compared Dr. Glueck's judgments with the records; the ratings proved correct in 91 percent of the cases. The Thompson experiment was an "after-the-fact" attempt at prediction; yet the results indicate great promise for future experiments. Currently, the New York Youth Board is applying the Gluecks' work

[1] Eleanor T. Glueck, "Status of Glueck Prediction Studies," *Journal of Criminal Law, Criminology, and Police Science*, Vol. 47, No. 1 (May–June, 1956).

[2] Richard E. Thompson, "A Validation of the Glueck Social Prediction Scale for Proneness to Delinquency," *Journal of Criminal Law, Criminology, and Police Science*, Vol. 43, No. 4 (November–December, 1952).

IMPLICATIONS FOR THE FUTURE

in a longitudinal study; the preliminary results confirm the expectation that accurate predictions can be made.

The staff of the Cambridge-Somerville program attempted, at the beginning of the study, to predict the future behavior of the boys. As each child entered the project, a committee of judges assigned him a "delinquency prognosis." In addition, the social workers and psychologists who investigated the child and his environment each made their predictions. Ratings ranged from plus 5 (least chance of becoming delinquent) to minus 5 (greatest chance of becoming delinquent). Slightly more boys were predicted as potential delinquents than as non-delinquents.

Approximately sixteen years after the judgments were made, we compared the predictions with the boys' actual court records. The predictions, particularly at the extreme ends of the scale, proved reasonably accurate (Table 83).

TABLE 83. PREDICTIONS OF CRIMINAL BEHAVIOR AND ACTUAL RESULTS

Prediction	Percent of Boys Convicted of Crimes	Percent of Boys Sentenced to Penal Institutions
Unlikely to become delinquent		
Plus 5, plus 4 (N: 18)	22	6
Plus 3, plus 2 (N: 43)	26	2
Even chance of delinquency		
Plus 1, 0, minus 1 (N: 75)	43	15
Likely to become delinquent		
Minus 2, minus 3 (N: 93)	43	11
Minus 4, minus 5 (N: 24)	75	50

Seventy-nine percent of the 101 children who were given ratings of plus 1 to plus 5 did not commit any crimes. Fifty-nine percent of the 129 children who were given ratings from minus 1 to minus 5 became criminal. Thus, for these 230 children, judged when they averaged ten years in age, the predictions proved to be correct in 68 percent of the cases.

The staff erred principally by overpredicting criminality. Apparently they were too alert for signs of misbehavior, but perhaps for this reason they correctly predicted as future delinquents a high proportion of those who committed certain serious crimes: 72 percent of those who became sex criminals and 92 percent of those who violently attacked other persons were correctly predicted by the judges as future criminals. They also correctly predicted delinquency for 71 percent of the men who served time in jail, reform school, or prison.

Our research into causation demonstrates that equally accurate and more specific predictions could have been made solely from certain factors in the child's environment, without any knowledge of the child himself. For example, if it had been predicted that all boys raised by neglecting fathers and none of the boys raised by other types of fathers would commit property crimes, the predictions would have been 69 percent accurate. If all the children with passive, neglecting, or cruel mothers had been predicted as future inmates of penal institutions, and if it had been predicted that none of the sons of other types of mothers would be committed to these institutions, the predictions would have been correct in 76 percent of the cases. If only the children raised by loving-neurotic or neglecting mothers had been predicted to be future drunkards, the judgments would have been accurate in 80 percent of the cases.

These predictions were not actually made; in 1935, insufficient knowledge of causation prevented their being made. Today, however, it is becoming increasingly clear not only that criminality can be predicted but that specific kinds of crime can be foreseen. Unfortunately, successful prediction does not guarantee successful prevention. The Cambridge-Somerville staff, although they based their judgments on partly irrelevant information, made relatively accurate predictions. These predictions did not, however, result in curing the children's problems.

In many respects, we have reached the same conclusions that Edwin Powers and Helen Witmer came to in their report on the program, *An Experiment in the Prevention of Delinquency*. At certain particular points, however, our conclusions differ from theirs.

Witmer and Powers implicitly maintained that shifts in counselors harmed the effectiveness of treatment. If this was so, it was not reflected in rates of crime.

Powers (but not Witmer) regarded the shortness of treatment as a handicap. We found that the length of treatment, within limits, bore no relation to rates of crime.

Witmer, more strongly than Powers, concluded that the type

of treatment advocated by Richard Clarke Cabot was ineffective in dealing with serious delinquency. We, on the other hand, have tentatively concluded, from those few cases where it was applied, that Cabot's plan of treatment was effective in preventing crime.

Our study of the over-all effects of Cambridge-Somerville treatment, however, offers grist for the mills of pessimists. Except in a small minority of cases (boys who had intensive treatment or were very young) the project failed to prevent crime.

Of course ministrations of the staff may have "succeeded" in ways which we did not measure. A boy might be criminal and yet have "matured" or "become better adjusted" as a result of the Cambridge-Somerville program. Some sociologists would even argue that, in certain social conditions, criminals are healthier than non-criminals. In *An Experiment in the Prevention of Delinquency*, Helen Witmer attempted to apply these other criteria of success, and the reader who wishes to know how the project promoted "growth of character" will find such an evaluation in that earlier volume. Nevertheless, since the original and major goal of the program was the prevention of crime, we believe that the most reasonable measure of the project's success is the criterion applied in this book: whether the boys who received treatment less often were convicted before a criminal court than the boys who did not receive treatment. In terms of this standard, the general program failed.

Although most delinquents had apparently stopped committing crimes by their middle twenties, this fact gives little succor to the schoolteacher who lives in a "blackboard jungle," to a police official looking at the rates of juvenile crime in his city, or to the mother worried about the "bad companions" of her adolescent son. Even the boy himself, caught in the unhappy consequences of his actions, cannot disregard his past behavior. The unfortunate aftereffects of a criminal career can continue to influence the personality indefinitely. Jean Evans' brilliant portrait of "Johnny Rocco," a reformed delinquent from the Cambridge-Somerville study, details the anxieties, the latent aggression, the memories of reform school which continued long after Johnny had stopped committing crimes.[3]

Our research shows, too, the inappropriateness of society's major

[3] Jean Evans, *Three Men*.

response to criminality: punishment of the offender. Incarceration in reform school is about as effective in curing delinquency as is whipping a stubborn donkey to make him carry a load. Of the 41 boys who were sentenced to Massachusetts reform schools, 22 percent went on to prison, an additional 56 percent committed serious crimes after release, and 7 percent more had records for such offenses as drunkenness. Surely there are more effective ways of helping these children.

We cannot argue, however, that the counseling approach of the Cambridge-Somerville study was more effective. The only indication that the treatment had a beneficial influence in preventing crime was that fewer treated boys spent time in prison or jail; yet even this fact, as we have mentioned, is open to several interpretations. Equal numbers in the treatment and control groups became criminals. Furthermore, they committed the same kinds of crimes and approximately the same number of crimes at each age period. Excluding traffic violations, the boys who received treatment had been convicted for 315 crimes and those in the control group had been convicted for 344.

Cambridge-Somerville treatment consisted primarily in the integration of community recreational and welfare resources for the aid of the children, with the addition of some individual and family counseling. Since the 1930s, the therapeutic philosophy of social workers has changed. Today, programs are in theory based on vastly more sophisticated psychological techniques. Unfortunately, the actual practices of many agencies have not, in our opinion, caught up with the new principles of social work. Many other agencies of social action utilize the approach of the Cambridge-Somerville staff, although few do so as intensively or for as long a period of time. It seems reasonable to suppose that when methods are generally similar, so are results. Knowing the disillusioning results of this program, we would advocate that similar agencies—whether they be child welfare programs, family casework bureaus, settlement houses, school guidance programs, probation offices, or child guidance clinics—objectively review the effectiveness of their programs. As delinquency preventives, strong evidence indicates that present public reform schools and social work programs fail. What approaches, then, can offer promise of greater success?

IMPLICATIONS FOR THE FUTURE

Any successful therapeutic program must be based on accurate knowledge of the causation of human action. The last chapter delineated the causes of criminality: on the one hand, the absence of parental affection made a child prone to criminality; on the other hand, family conflict, inconsistent discipline, and the influence of parents who themselves rebelled against the standards of society led to criminality. *It would seem, therefore, that a program of crime prevention must counteract these two conditions— the absence of affection and the inadequate internalization of socially acceptable values—first, by satisfying the primary emotional needs of the child and, second, by inculcating in the child a set of acceptable standards.*

If a child becomes criminal in response to frustration of his desire to be loved, to feel secure, and to have personal significance, then an important part of his rehabilitation must include satisfying these needs in a manner acceptable to society. In many cases, children turn to the prestige and recognition of a delinquent gang for the gratification of those needs which are frustrated in their homes. *A prevention program must replace the delinquent gang as the child's major source of satisfaction.*

Often, children who have not absorbed law-abiding parental standards become innoculated with the anti-social values of a criminal sub-culture. Other criminals have accepted the values of their parents, only to find that they are in conflict with the laws of society. *In order to prevent deviant behavior, the delinquent child must have an opportunity to internalize values consistent with those of society.*

Many psychologists would maintain that we have omitted an important element of successful treatment: the full analysis of unconscious motivations. Although deep analysis might be extremely beneficial, we believe that bringing these motivations to the delinquent's consciousness is both very difficult and unnecessary. Some of the work of the Cambridge-Somerville counselors took the form of psychotherapy, and, after reviewing our findings, psychiatrists at the Boston Psychopathic Hospital maintained that because frequent counseling based on a close relationship appeared to benefit the boys, "real" psychotherapy could work.

We do not deny the possibility of psychotherapeutic success; we do, however, question its practicality as a solution to criminality. Psychotherapy involves individual, intensive, and frequently expensive treatment. Sufficient personnel for carrying out such treatment is lacking. Furthermore, the extent to which individual therapy can change a delinquent remains questionable. Too often, psychotherapy allows the sources of deviance, particularly the family, to continue creating tensions. If there are methods which can redirect behavior without a full analysis of unconscious motivations, these surely deserve to be explored.

At almost the opposite extreme from the psychotherapists' approach is that propounded by many sociologists. Arguing that it is useless to try to change an individual in isolation from his subculture, sociologists have urged "group" or "gang" reorientation. The Chicago Area Project, the recent experiments with "detached" social workers in New York, the Roxbury, Massachusetts, Youth Program are practical applications of this proposal. These programs depend upon two methods: first, community leaders are called upon to exert their influence in curbing delinquency; second, social workers infiltrate delinquent gangs, gain leadership of them, and then attempt to guide the entire group into new and socially harmless activities.

Because of its newness, there have been no substantial measures of the effectiveness of group reorientation. In several ways, gang reorientation seems promising. It involves some alteration of the child's social environment and it may offer the boy new emotional satisfactions. Whether new values are internalized by the children, however, remains open to question. Our research has shown that the primary targets of these attempts, the slum neighborhoods with their delinquent traditions and groups, influence a child in only a secondary and temporary manner. The root of criminal behavior lies in the family.

When a delinquent spends most of his time in tension-producing circumstances, it seems reasonable to suppose that his aggression will continue. And even if delinquent groups could be "reoriented," we seriously question whether this approach by itself would provide sufficient emotional satisfaction or a sufficient opportunity for internalizing new values.

The most promising of current approaches, in our opinion, is milieu therapy. As practiced by August Aichhorn, Fritz Redl, Bruno Bettleheim, and Ernst Papanek, the purpose of milieu therapy is to mobilize the child's entire environment in an attempt to alter his behavior. The delinquent child is removed from his family and his neighborhood. He lives, plays, and studies in a new environment which is organized around the emotional needs of the child. Individual counseling, group therapy, and education are combined in the treatment. Characterized by permissiveness and absence of frustrating situations, the treatment center offers the delinquent security, prestige, and affection. Counselors attempt to establish warm relations with the child and then gradually begin putting limits on his behavior. Through identification with his counselors, the child, the therapists hope, will accept their values.

While psychotherapy concentrates on the individual in isolation from his group, and gang reorientation ignores many of the individual problems which have led boys to gang membership, milieu therapy acts in both directions simultaneously. Milieu therapy works toward building emotional security; it removes the child from an environment which encourages delinquency; and it provides an opportunity for the child to internalize values consistent with those of society. Perhaps most important, it furnishes a substitute "home" and thereby indirectly counteracts the unfortunate influence of the boys' original families.

Recent research indicates that several important changes in the child's behavior and character take place as a result of milieu therapy. In a series of studies at the Wiltwyck School, we discovered that the aggressive desires of delinquent children had decreased, their views of authority had become less punitive, and their acceptance of the expectations of society had increased markedly.[4] After several months at the school, the children had become distinctly more socialized. It is too soon, however, to know whether the changes are permanent.

These three approaches—psychotherapy, group reorientation, and milieu therapy—surely warrant further experimentation and investigation. The community would also be justified in searching out new techniques for combatting delinquency.

Unfortunately, the Cambridge-Somerville study failed as a large-

[4] William and Joan McCord, *Psychopathy and Delinquency*, Chapter VI.

scale attempt to prevent crime. Yet even in its failure it offers guidelines for new approaches. In our opinion, the Cambridge-Somerville project failed with so many cases primarily because it did not furnish satisfactions for deep emotional needs; nor did it eradicate the causes of delinquent behavior. Very few counselors saw their boys at regular and frequent intervals, and many of the conversations they had were directed toward superficial problems such as camp placement, health examination, and school progress. Seldom were close bonds established between counselor and boy; consequently, the counselor's efforts at guidance had little effect on the children.

Insufficiently equipped with knowledge concerning the causes of crime, the staff devoted much of its effort to symptoms rather than causes—the failure of the child to attend church, his inability to do adequate schoolwork, or his aloofness from "constructive" community organizations. By and large, the counselors failed to alert the boys' families concerning the emotional needs of their children, and they avoided making any radical changes in the family structure. Thus, many boys remained under the constant influence of parents who overtly or covertly encouraged delinquency.

Nevertheless, certain encouraging signs emerged from the experiment. Only 32 boys at any time during the study had frequent counseling, but these children had a lower rate of crime than did children who had only intermittent contact with their counselors. Also, the 12 boys who received the most consistent attention had better records than the 12 boys with similar environments who had only the usual services of the program. Frequent counseling over a long period of time may have tended to satisfy the child's emotional needs and to provide a better opportunity for internalizing new values.

Boys who were under ten at the beginning of treatment seemed to have received greater benefit from the program; significantly fewer became criminal. Again, we would attribute this to the greater pliability of children at this age.

There are some inconclusive indications that certain kinds of children benefited more from the treatment than did others. Although the difference was not significant, we found that the aggres-

IMPLICATIONS FOR THE FUTURE

sive and conformist children responded slightly more favorably to frequent counseling than did those children who were withdrawn.

Our research at the Wiltwyck School tentatively corroborates this: psychopathic children and those with behavior disorders exhibited greater changes in character than neurotic or psychotic children.[5] It seems reasonable to hypothesize that curative attempts will be more effective the more they are focused on aggressive rather than withdrawn children. Moreover, boys who had non-loving mothers responded more dramatically than did boys with loving mothers.

This study shows that several popular shibboleths are misconceptions. The aggressive child responded to treatment no less favorably than the conformist child. The length of treatment, by itself, had no relation to its effectiveness. A change in counselors did not necessarily rob treatment of whatever value it may have had. Male counselors were not superior to female counselors in preventing delinquency. And most important, treatment which concentrated on establishing a liaison between community agencies, without intensively treating the child himself, did not prevent criminality.

In addition to the suggestions which we have already made—suggestions which are certainly not new—we recommend that existing community agencies expend their energies in the following directions.

In the light of the material on causation discussed in this study, *intensive work with the family seems a prerequisite to successful treatment.* Even if families do not seek out such service, the experience of the Cambridge-Somerville staff indicates that families will respond to the approaches of social workers. An insistent approach to families where children seem destined for trouble can meet with the cooperation of the parents. Generally, parents who need guidance do not seek it; they must be sought out by the agencies themselves. Unfortunately, those counselors in the Cambridge-Somerville project who attempted to work with the parents were limited by time and training to a superficial approach.

Once accepted by a family, a community worker can accomplish a great deal. Ideally, if parents themselves would seek deep psychological counseling, the sources of criminality might be eradi-

[5] *Ibid.*

cated. If the parents could resolve their own problems, they would be able to give emotional support to their children. Since love from either parent tends to prevent criminality, intensive work with both parents might be unnecessary. Therapeutic efforts may wisely be concentrated upon the more amenable parent.

Although changing the structure of adult personalities may be too arduous a task for community agencies, one facet of family life, discipline, appears to be more open to change than the others. Consistently love-oriented discipline can overcome many of the harmful effects of otherwise unhealthy homes. Since inconsistent punitiveness has been shown to be definitely harmful, we would suggest that a valuable method of crime prevention is the education of parents in the use of non-punitive, yet consistent, methods of discipline. Education could change the attitudes of those parents who know no other means but physical violence to curb misbehavior.

Neighborhood influences, though relatively unimportant in crime causation, cannot be ignored. Some well-meaning parents are simply ignorant of techniques for keeping their sons away from gang membership. Through an aggressive P.T.A. program and discussion groups, well-intentioned parents might be taught the importance of recognition and affection in the home. Community or school programs aimed at increasing a feeling of status in the children might counter-balance neglect and rejection in the home.

Under certain conditions, we advocate removing a child from his home. Popular opinion to the contrary, a child is not always better off with his family. Quarrelsome and neglecting homes seem to be so damaging to a child that such environments warrant removing the boy from the home. Separation of a child from his parents (as occurs in broken homes) contributes less to criminality than do other factors. We realize, of course, that complicated family relationships and the scarcity of foster homes and other institutions can make this recommendation impractical for many cases. Yet *we urge reconsideration of the policy which keeps many boys with their families even when the parents do not wish to have them.*

Finally, the promise of success is so slight with spasmodic counseling that *we suggest that community resources for treatment be concentrated more intensively on fewer children.* Intermittent

IMPLICATIONS FOR THE FUTURE

treatment may actually be harmful to certain—particularly to withdrawn—types of children. There are indications that, if selection is necessary, children with rejecting mothers should be given priority.

These, then, are some of the implications for community action which emerged from our study of the Cambridge-Somerville experiment in the prevention of delinquency. The relative success of the Cambridge-Somerville predictions and the work of others in this area indicate that a new tool for the control of criminality is within our reach. Accurate prediction will mean that the community can apply its services for the prevention of criminality when the child is very young. Certain trends within the Cambridge-Somerville study and experiments with psychotherapy, group reorientation, and milieu therapy offer hope that an intelligent preventive program can meet with success.

Such a program must take cognizance of the different causal patterns which determine each type of criminal. *A treatment program tailored to the needs of each type of delinquent would, in all probability, meet with more success than a program which disregards the differences in causative background.* Specifically, we make the following suggestions.

Treatment of criminals who commit a wide range of anti-social acts should work toward total reorganization of the personality. A counselor must gain the confidence of these boys (perhaps through permissiveness), providing stable affection. Gradually, consistent punishment for misbehavior and praise for conformity should be added as ingredients of the relationship. These generally anti-social criminals appear to be the most difficult to treat; yet success would be the most rewarding for society.

Treatment of those who commit crimes against property should center on giving attention and recognition; in addition, it should provide consistent, non-punitive discipline.

Treatment of those who commit crimes against the person should attempt to counteract "identification with an aggressor." In certain cases, removal from the home may be necessary. In other cases, such as those of the sons of overprotective women, guidance given to the family may alleviate difficulties. Treatment should provide for a socially acceptable outlet for aggression. Furthermore, the counselor should avoid overdominance since many of these criminals have rebelled against too dominant parents.

Treatment of sex criminals should substitute affectionate warmth for the maternal passivity found in the backgrounds of these criminals. These delinquents need to be helped to discover socially acceptable means of gaining approval.

Treatment of drunkenness should aim at resolving the anxiety caused by rejection. Psychotherapy in some form would seem to be most appropriate for these delinquents.

Treatment of traffic offenders should aim at building self-confidence. Perhaps education which demonstrates the mastery entailed in "proper control" would be beneficial. Perhaps psychological counseling which exposes the underlying desire for power would be most helpful.

The prevention and cure of criminality depends upon knowledge of the sources of human behavior. The accumulation of this knowledge is the task of social science. Consequently, we regard the results of this study concerning the causation of human action as having equal importance with its consequences concerning the direct control of crime.

Implications for Social Science

A sharp distinction is often drawn between "pure" and "applied" social science. Pure research, dealing with broad and fundamental issues, has relevance to a variety of specific problems. Applied research, on the other hand, focuses on one specific problem, usually one connected with practical social policy. Yet the line between pure and applied science often becomes blurred: theories of human behavior depend on empirical studies for verification, and empirical research often generates fruitful theories. From Freud's research on the "applied" problem of neurosis, for example, have come fundamental discoveries concerning human nature.

Our research on the Cambridge-Somerville experiment falls

into the "applied" category in that it was confined to the problem of crime. In the process of this research, however, we have touched upon certain theories of human behavior. The results are particularly relevant to three branches of social science—sociology, psychoanalysis, and social psychology.

Sociological theory has been especially involved in the problems of criminality. The work of Albert Cohen in explaining the delinquent sub-culture, of Edwin Sutherland in delineating the features of "professional" and of "white-collar" crime, and of Clifford Shaw in outlining the values of gangdom are eminently worth while. These theories must, nevertheless, be placed in their proper context. Our research shows that only an understanding of the family environment can answer the central issue of deviant behavior: Why is one man influenced by a criminal sub-culture while another man, in the same general social environment, escapes it?

Perhaps the most widely accepted sociological explanation of crime is the theory of "differential association." As expounded by Edwin Sutherland and others, the theory asserts that criminal behavior is determined by association with those who commit crimes.[6] This theory calls attention to a basic similarity in the psychological adjustment of the criminal and of the non-criminal populations. It emphasizes that only the values learned are different; the motivation for, and techniques of, learning do not differ. The strongest piece of evidence in support of this theory is the fact that certain urban areas have a higher concentration of criminality than do other areas. Within these criminal centers, according to Sutherland, the young child learns and absorbs a set of antisocial values and attitudes. Gangs play the major rule in introducing the child into the deviant system.

No one can take issue with the general point of this position—that criminal behavior is learned. We pointed out earlier, for example, the strong connection between gang membership and crime. Yet the theory is very general: it omits consideration of the dynamics which lead a child within a delinquent area to chose the gang as his reference group. Nor does the theory explain the atypical middle-class child who suddenly commits a criminal

[6] Edwin H. Sutherland, *Principles of Criminology*.

act. The statements which follow about our findings concerning crime can be taken not as a denial of the importance of a delinquent sub-culture but as an explanation of the *genetic* process of crime.

First, we distinguished fundamental differences between the early familial backgrounds of criminals and non-criminals. A child is influenced by his family prior to association with a criminal sub-culture. Thus, membership in a delinquent gang, though important, plays only a secondary role in the causation of crime.

Second, a child who comes from a home of conflict and frustration, even if he lives in a relatively non-delinquent urban area, is likely to become criminal. Boys from cohesive homes in poor neighborhoods did not have higher delinquency rates than boys from cohesive homes in better neighborhoods.

Therefore, the great weight of our evidence points to the family as the crucible of deviant tendencies and to the neighborhood as the mold for the expression of these drives.

A second sociological theory assigns the major cause of crime to social disorganization. Some sociologists have maintained that differential association comes about because of social disorganization, but other theorists would go much further, maintaining that disorganization itself—a lack of common values, an absence of unifying forces, the decline of institutional social controls—directly causes crime. As evidence, sociologists such as Clifford Shaw and Henry McKay cite the relative permanence of high delinquency areas, regardless of shifts in the composition of the population.[7]

Undeniably, urban areas with high delinquency rates exist, but the fact that children from cohesive homes do not usually become criminal, regardless of where they live, indicates that social disorganization by itself influences causation only by establishing, in William James's terms, "live options" for the child.

Recently, sociological attention has been focused on the concept of roles—a third sociological explanation of human, and therefore, of criminal behavior. We believe that the use of this

[7] Clifford Shaw and Henry McKay, "Social Factors in Juvenile Delinquency," in National Commission on Law Observance and Enforcement, *Report on the Causes of Crime*, Vol. 11.

IMPLICATIONS FOR THE FUTURE 189

concept in explaining the causation of criminality could be of great value. For example, we found that maternal passivity had very different results from paternal passivity. This contrast can be theoretically explained (at least in part) through an examination of the roles of mother and father in our society. If we assume that the maternal role in American society is normally a dominant, directing role, then maternal passivity (if this is considered a "role") would cause frustration of the child's role expectations, and hence would often lead to greater aggression.

Using the concept of roles, some sociologists have pointed out that the mother in our society is the major agent in rearing and socializing the child. Consequently, sociologists like Talcott Parsons maintain that the mother becomes *the* emotionally significant adult. A child, whether boy or girl, would therefore tend to identify with the mother. Our evidence concerning this theoretical position is somewhat contradictory.

On the one hand, some of our evidence leads to the conclusion that the mother is emotionally more significant to the boy than is the father. Maternal neglect caused a more aggressive reaction than did paternal neglect; more boys with neglecting mothers than boys with neglecting fathers became criminal. If the mother was rejecting, paternal love did not significantly reduce criminality. Absence of maternal love led to high criminal rates regardless of the behavior or example of the father. Maternal personality bore a significant relation to all varieties of specific crimes, although the father's personality had a significant connection only to certain crimes.

On the other hand, some of our evidence indicates that the father is more significant than the mother; boys imitated the role model of their fathers to a much greater degree than they imitated their mothers'.

Our evidence, therefore, does not offer complete, but does offer partial, support to the opinion that the mother's position in the American kinship system makes her a more important figure for the child.

Going beyond this original contention, Talcott Parsons has hypothesized that one of the primary sources of aggression in American society is a boy's attempt to prove his masculinity through revolt against his mother. Parsons argues that the role of the mother in America incorporates an image of "goodness." Because of the mother's superior position as the socializer of the child, both boys and girls tend to identify with the mother. For girls, no harm is done, since later in life they will fulfill the feminine role. For boys, however, early identification with the mother causes concern over their masculinity. Because the mother represents "goodness," the child feels that he must prove his masculinity through being "bad." [8]

One might predict from Parsons' theory that the sons of passive fathers would more often become criminal. Such children, lacking forceful male figures for identification, would be more fully identified with the mother and, during latency or adolescence, more fearful concerning masculinity. Interestingly, if they became criminal, the sons of passive fathers did turn to crime during adolescence. In general, however, the sons of passive fathers had a very low rate of crime. This piece of evidence indicates that a boy does not necessarily equate the male role with assertion of "badness." The male role for boys reared by passive fathers was presented to them as being one of introversion, quietness, and withdrawal. By accepting this example, the sons may not have felt that aggressiveness was inherent in masculinity. Apparently, a child tends to connect "badness" with masculinity only if the father does so.

Sociologists themselves have criticized the two dominant theories of criminality—those of differential association and social disorganization. Walter Reckless, for example, has pointed out that the social disorganization theory does not explain why so many boys who come from these areas do not become delinquent, nor does it explain why boys who come from other areas become delinquent.[9] And Donald Taft, recognizing the importance of home conditions, has written: "Status in the family is a ticket for admission to status in other constructive social groups." [10] Unfortunately, these opinions have not been sufficiently absorbed into the fabric of sociological thought.

More promising has been the sociological investigation of role

---

[8] Talcott Parsons, *Essays in Sociological Theory*, Chapter XIV.
[9] Walter Reckless, *The Crime Problem*.   [10] Donald Taft, *Criminology*, p. 140.

structure. Through further analysis of family roles and role expectations, sociology can make substantial contributions to the understanding of criminal behavior.

From a different point of view, our study contains implications for psychoanalytic theory. In the most general, but also the most important, way, this research lends support to the basic psychoanalytic position that early experiences of the child within his family mold his adult attitudes, personality, and behavior. Not only did we find, during the course of this project, that significant relations link criminality to the early environment, but we also found direct connections between particular environments and particular kinds of crime.

Many of our specific findings could be used to support psychoanalytic theory. We have already, for example, given several general interpretations of the effects of paternal passivity. The strikingly low rate of crime for the sons of passive fathers could also be fitted into a psychoanalytic framework: in terms of the Oedipus situation, a passive father would offer little competition to his son for the mother's affection; the son would therefore not feel as great hostility toward his father or toward other symbols or authority. He would be less likely to become criminal.

If this interpretation is correct, we would then predict that the situation with girls would be reversed: passive mothers would cause low delinquency and passive fathers would cause high delinquency. If one considers the role expectations of girls, however, it seems more likely that maternal passivity would also cause a relatively higher rate of crime among girls.

In a similar fashion it would be possible to interpret other findings. We found, for example, that a boy tended to imitate his father if his mother rejected him. In psychoanalytic terms, this could be explained as a result of the Oedipus situation: the stronger the boy's desire for maternal love, heightened by frustration, the more he imitates his father in attempting to gain this love.

One of the greatest contributions of Freud to the understanding of human behavior is the concept of repression. In repressing a desire, the superego merely inhibits its actualization. Yet the desire remains and, under disguise, directs behavior. Repression of normal sexual life (caused by intense anxiety) may well be the cause of sexual crimes. Passive and neglecting mothers produced the highest proportion of sexual criminals. Probably the actions of these mothers led to severe repression of sexual desires. With normal expression blocked, the sexual desires exploded into abnormal paths.

Many of those who committed crimes of violence were raised by cruel fathers. Such fathers must have intensified the aggressive urges of their sons. At the same time, the aggression had to be repressed for fear of the father's retaliation. Later, the displaced aggression was expended in violent attacks upon other people (perhaps upon father figures).

While many of our conclusions could be explained by psychoanalytic theory, one result opposes the "ethos" of psychoanalysis, if not a specific theory. Traditional psychoanalysis maintains that an individual's character is molded during early childhood. Apparent changes in later life are not fundamental alterations in character but result from the development of new defense mechanisms. Unless a person undergoes psychoanalytic therapy, experiences subsequent to childhood have no basic effect upon the underlying sources of personality.

Yet our research shows that many criminals reform as they enter adult life, undergoing a radical change in their behavior. We could uncover only a few "causes" from the person's early childhood which explained why some men reformed and others did not. Conceivably, the "basic" personality of the reformed criminals may have remained the same. Perhaps, too, a deeper and more subtle analysis of childhood experiences could have disclosed the sources of reformation. Nevertheless, it seems more reasonable to assume that the change in behavior signified an important change in character, and that the causes of this change originated partly in adult, rather than childhood, experiences. More explicitly, it appears that criminality could be rather accurately predicted solely from a knowledge of a person's childhood experiences, but that prediction of reformation would have to be based partly upon a knowledge of the person's adult experiences.

Certain psychological theorists, such as Alfred Adler, Harry

Stack Sullivan, Karen Horney, A. H. Maslow, and Gordon Allport, have recognized the significance of this issue. Although they emphasize the importance of early interpersonal relations, these theorists argue that personality remains malleable. Gordon Allport, for example, has pointed out that pathological influences in childhood may totally form a personality by retarding its growth. He adds:

> But for the child who enjoys a normal affiliative groundwork, and who successfully enters the more advanced stages of socialization, the situation is different. In his case the foundations of character were established by the age of three or five, only in the sense that he is now *free to become;* he is not retarded; he is well launched on the course of continuous and unimpeded growth.[11]

Our findings regarding reformation support this position. We noted, for example, that those criminals who had been reared by loving mothers reformed more frequently than did criminals raised by overprotective or by non-loving mothers. Given a more stable basis early in life, they were more receptive to reformative influences as they matured.

Further support for the theory that personality does undergo a process of "becoming" comes from our analysis of the age at which criminality begins. We discovered that criminals who had been raised by loving mothers or who had lived in cohesive homes more often began to practice criminality only after they had entered adulthood. The later experiences of the individual tipped the balance toward criminality. It appears that family affection and cohesiveness is an extremely effective preventive of crime, but that it does not provide complete immunization to adverse influences occurring during adulthood.

In relation to psychoanalysis, then, our research supports the contention that early childhood experience is vitally important in the development of personality. In particular, maternal affection seems to be the necessary prerequisite for adequate socialization, and identification with the father is a prime determinant of behavior. Nevertheless, the research indirectly supports those critics of psychoanalysis who have maintained that Freudian theory fails to recognize the influence of adult experiences.

[11] Gordon Allport, *Becoming*, p. 33.

We believe that this research has relevance, too, in the investigation of issues of particular importance to social and personality psychology—issues such as "identification" and "conscience." Briefly, let us review the implications for each of these research problems.

Many social psychologists, modifying Freudian and learning theories, have been developing original hypotheses concerning those forces which lead to identification. Roughly, "identification" is the process by which an individual internalizes the attitudes and values of another person or of a group. Some empirical evidence points to identification as a function of discipline. Research at Harvard's Laboratory of Human Development has indicated that a child more often identifies with a parent if the parent uses "denial of love" as a primary technique.[12] Our research tends slightly to contradict this conclusion.

We found that consistent use of love-oriented techniques tends to result in low criminality, regardless of the role model of the parents. Perhaps because most studies of discipline are conducted with samples in which parental role models accord with societal values, discipline has been considered as the mediator between the parents' values and the child's behavior. We suggest that discipline operates directly on behavior, that it is not simply a mediator of parental values. As further evidence for this hypothesis, we found that consistently punitive discipline, as well as love-oriented discipline, tends to decrease criminality.

Another interpretation is possible. All the parents of the boys we studied, regardless of their own deviant behavior, condemned criminality in their sons. If one believes that a child identifies with the values, not the behavior, of his parents, then it can be argued that our data indicates that consistent discipline (either punitive or love-oriented) leads to identification, for it usually led to a lack of criminal behavior.

We also tested the link between identification and parental affection. If identification implies that the child imitates directly the behavior of the parents, our findings indicate that boys identify with the "aggressor" when the role model of the parent suggests a target (society) for the aggression. (Sons of criminals tended

[12] Robert Sears, Eleanor Maccoby, and Harry Levin, *Patterns of Child Rearing*.

IMPLICATIONS FOR THE FUTURE

to become criminal, especially if the sons were rejected.) Boys identified, with the help of love, when the role model was not aggressive. (Sons of non-deviants tended not to be criminal providing that their mothers were loving.)

One of the most complex issues facing social psychologists is the problem of conformity. How does a stable conscience develop? How do the attitudes connected with non-conformity develop? Since this research has been concerned with tracing the origins of consciences which either lack certain kinds of inner control or incorporate injunctions which are at variance with the demands of the dominant culture, our material bears directly upon this issue.

Before considering our findings, it should be pointed out that this research deals only with what might be called "the *basic* conscience"—those internalized inhibitions which prevent people from violating the most elementary injunctions of their cultures. Our research does not deal with the other aspects of conscience which Gordon Allport has recently outlined. Allport draws an important distinction between the "must" of conscience and the "ought" of conscience; between those moral inhibitions which are simply the "interiorized voice of the herd," and the "private codes of virtue and sin" which positively motivate an individual.[13]

By the dominant standards of American society, all the criminals were non-conformists. Each committed acts which were morally proscribed by the dominant culture. Yet in violating the standards of a larger society, these men may have been conforming to the standards of a deviant sub-culture. They may be, in actuality, conformists.

A fundamental question arises: Do criminals actually have "underdeveloped" consciences; are they truly rebels? Or have criminals simply internalized deviant standards; have they "sturdy" consciences, but ones which are in conflict with society's demands?

Although the evidence is cloudy, we believe three sets of facts indicate that criminals have underdeveloped, rather than simply deviant, consciences. First, the criminals underwent early pathological influences which were characterized both by inconsistency and by lack of affection. Failing to internalize the proscriptions

[13] Gordon Allport, *Becoming*, pp. 68–74.

of their parents, these children were free for the opportunistic expression of their impulses. In other words, rather than absorb a "value system" from the gang, it seems that delinquents use the gang for group expression of their primitive drives.

A second fact which supports this interpretation is the evidence showing lack of influence of a gang culture except under specifiable conditions. The values of the gang are not "absorbed" by the child simply through contact; there must be fertile ground within the child's personality before the gang can influence him.

Third, convincing evidence indicates that criminals are well aware of, and approve, the values of the dominant culture, rather than those of a deviant culture. A group of California researchers found that convicts in San Quentin prison gave even stronger support to the morality of society than did non-convicts.[14] A recent comparison which we made between delinquents incarcerated in a reform school and boys in a public school yielded the same results.[15] A study by Eleanor Maccoby of Harvard demonstrated that certain kinds of criminal deviance are equally condemned by people who live in slum areas and in middle-class neighborhoods.[16]

On the basis of the evidence that criminals have undergone pathological familial influences, that a deviant sub-culture affects an individual only if he has undergone these influences, and that criminals give strong verbal support to dominant values, *we would conclude that criminality is generally the result of a basic deficiency in conscience, a failure to internalize elementary inhibitions.*

This "deficiency of conscience" was not equally severe in all cases. Indeed, our research leads to the conclusion that there are two basic types of "deficiency," and therefore of criminality.

First, there were those criminals who could be called *limited non-conformists*. These were children who apparently violated the general mores in only one area of behavior. These children had insufficiently internalized inhibitions regarding the expression of aggression (violent criminals), or dependency (drunkards),

---

[14] T. W. Adorno and others, *The Authoritarian Personality*.
[15] William and Joan McCord, *Psychopathy and Delinquency*.
[16] Eleanor Maccoby, "Study of Values in Cambridge, Massachusetts," *Journal of Social Issues* (in preparation).

or sexual desires (sex criminals). We believe that this lack of inhibition in a particular area is a result of extremely strong anxiety concerning the normal mode of behavior or of heightened desires in that area.

David Walters, the boy whom we discussed in a previous chapter, typifies the limited nonconformist. He conformed to cultural restrictions about manners, traffic rules, property, and gang violence. Yet he deviated strikingly in his sexual activities. His sexual deviance was coupled with intense anxiety about conventional ways of satisfying sexual desire. He felt that heterosexual relations were "dirty" and that no woman would wish to marry him. Consequently, he turned to homosexual relationships. Anxiety about the normal mode of behavior was so intense that it overcame whatever anxiety he felt concerning the abnormal path. Walters had a cognitive awareness of the prohibition on homosexuality and, in all probability, he had a degree of fear about violating these norms. Nevertheless, his fear of, and disgust with, normal sexual expression proved to be stronger. Walters probably absorbed this fear from his mother.

The limited non-conformist appears to have a normally developed conscience except in one area of behavior. The overprotected child seems to be a general example of the limited non-conformist. As a group, overprotected children seem to have internalized sufficient controls to prevent the majority of them from becoming criminal. Few stole, truanted from school, or committed sexual offenses. Nevertheless, a number of them were nonconformist in two areas of behavior: they committed more than their share of crimes against other people and of serious traffic offenses. It should be noted in passing that the limited non-conformist is the type of deviant who most resembles the "compulsive conformist." Talcott Parsons has observed that there is a close similarity between the individual who, because of intense anxiety, must be a deviant, and the person who, again because of severe anxiety, feels that he can never transgress any of the prohibitions of his general culture.[17] Both types, we would suggest, have internalized a stern parental image which forbids "moral" flexibility.

[17] Talcott Parsons, *The Social System*, Chapter VII.

The *general non-conformist* is the type of person whose deviance is not limited to specific areas of behavior. In its extreme form, this generalized weakness of conscience can result in psychopathy. It is the psychopath who commits the whole gamut of crimes. He feels little, if any, guilt and cannot form close relationships with other people. His aggression and impulsivity are unhampered by "moral anxiety."

The prototype of the general non-conformist is, in our study, the individual who has been severely neglected as a child. The great majority of neglected children became criminal, and a high proportion of them were convicted for crimes of violence, sexual offenses, and drunkenness. In addition, they became criminal earlier in life and were unlikely to reform. Many of these neglected children probably became true psychopaths.[18]

If there are two different types of conscience deficiency leading to criminality, then it follows that conscience is not a unitary trait. There may be a weakness in one area of conscience and strength in the others. We believe that it is valid to picture the basic conscience as a combination of inhibitions which control specific types of behavior. Much criminality is of a highly specific nature, stemming from particular antecedents. Even those general nonconformists who violate laws of almost every kind have inhibitions regarding certain forms of behavior. A theory of the development of conscience must account for relatively isolated areas of conformity as well as for nonconformity.

In summary, our findings lead to the conclusion that three major variables determine the development of conformity: the mode of affectional relationships, the nature of the parental models, and the consistency with which a value is presented to the child.

The mode of affectional relationships is the underlying condition determining the development of conscience. Although our

---

[18] In *Psychopathy and Delinquency*, we proposed a "neuro-social" theory of psychopathy. One element of this theory was that severe parental rejection, by itself, can produce psychopathy. At that time, we pictured cruelty as being the strongest parental rejection. The present research, however, indicates that neglect rather than cruelty is the most severe form of rejection and the one most likely to lead to severe criminality. The behavior of criminals with neglecting parents hints at the existence of psychopathy among some of them.

research indicates that affection is not necessary for identification to take place, an affectionate bond between parents and child seems necessary for socialization. If a child is rejected by his parents, he will usually become rebellious, aggressive, and insecure—that is, a criminal. If neither parent loves the child, the incentive for socialized behavior is lacking; the child receives no reward for moderating his behavior to conform to societal demands. If even one parent is loving, the child can "strike a bargain," exchanging conformity in behavior for the parent's affection. Severe rejection in the form of parental cruelty or neglect frustrates the child and hence tends to heighten his aggressiveness. This aggression will be expressed through behavior unless social injunctions are internalized.

The nature of the parental model determines the content of the child's conscience. The larger social environment, the values of the greater society, are filtered through the child's parents. Since the child sees his parents' actions as appropriate objects for imitation, he tends to make their attitudes his own. Our research indicates that if a boy's father is punitive or cruel, the child becomes more aggressive. If the father is gentle and restrained, he provides an example of kindness. If the father is passive, the son tends to be introverted and withdrawn. And if the father himself rejects the standards of society, the son tends to disregard these standards.

The consistency with which a value is presented to the child determines the degree to which it becomes a part of his conscience. Consistency can, apparently, even be a substitute for affection. For the general nonconformist or the psychopath, it would seem that consistency of discipline accounts for the "islands" of conformity. In some areas of behavior, the psychopath has had only one model, a model which has consistently been impressed upon him. Providing conformity does not strongly oppose a basic drive, even the psychopath will accept this model.

Inconsistent discipline or total laxity results in a low degree of internalization; if either is coupled with punitiveness, strengthened aggressive drives result. The child of a quarrelsome family, in addition to lacking emotional security, is confronted with inconsistent models. The child of an "anti-social" father is presented with a model inconsistent with that of the general society. In all of these cases, the stable development of conscience is hindered.

Each of these influences is crucial in the development of conscience. Affection establishes the necessary base; the parents' model furnishes the content of conscience; and consistency insures the internalization of this content. If affection is missing, the child lacks rewards for conformity; if the parental model is antisocial, the child becomes confused with respect to values; if values are inconsistently enforced, he becomes uncertain as to their worth.

Knowing these regularities, the falsity of the view that a person simply chooses to be "wicked" from "perverse" desires becomes clear. This research demonstrates how a multitude of factors, all *independent* of the person's conscious choice, can restrict the individual's "will" to the point where criminality becomes the most available option. Naturally, some men escaped these general social pressures which led to crime. Yet when one considers that just one uncontrollable influence—the mother's attitude toward the child—may increase a boy's chances of crime by almost 300 percent, the public's condemnatory attitude toward criminals is vitiated.

This is our conclusion to research on the sources of crime in American society. More than twenty years ago, Richard Clarke Cabot conceived of the Cambridge-Somerville experiment. His primary goal, at its inception, was the prevention of delinquency; but he was also interested in the research which might result from his efforts. Unfortunately, his hopes for the success of treatment have gone largely unfulfilled. Part of this failure, we are convinced, must be attributed to the staff's inadequate knowledge of the origins of crime. This book, which has emerged directly from Cabot's pioneering efforts, will, we hope, aid in the solution of the perennial problem of crime—and thereby contribute to our society's knowledge of the genesis of human nature.

APPENDIX A

JUVENILE DELINQUENCY IN THE TREATMENT GROUP

IN THE TEXT WE DISCUSSED THE RELATIONSHIP BETWEEN SEVERAL VARIABLES and the age at which criminality began. Because the reader may be interested specifically in juvenile delinquency rather than in adult criminalty, we now present the causal patterns found in the backgrounds of only those boys who committed crimes before the age of eighteen. These patterns are fundamentally the same as those discovered in the backgrounds of all criminals.

APPENDIX TABLE 1. RELATION OF MOTHER'S PERSONALITY TO RATE OF JUVENILE DELINQUENCY

Mother		Percent of Boys Convicted of Crimes before the Age of Eighteen
Loving	(N: 115)	19
Overprotective	(N: 59)	22
Non-loving	(N: 77)	43

There is a highly significant relationship between maternal attitudes and juvenile delinquency ($P < .001$).[1] (Appendix Table 1). The relationship between paternal personality and juvenile delinquency is also significant ($P < .025$)[2] (Appendix Table 2), as is that between discipline and juvenile delinquency ($P < .03$)[3] (Appendix Table 3). Consistent discipline, whether punitive or love-oriented, led to lower delinquency. But there is no significant relationship between juvenile delinquency and intelligence (Appendix Table 4).

APPENDIX TABLE 2. RELATION OF FATHER'S PERSONALITY TO RATE OF JUVENILE DELINQUENCY

Father		Percent of Boys Convicted of Crimes before the Age of Eighteen
Warm	(N: 95)	19
Passive	(N: 37)	27
Non-loving	(N: 113)	36

[1] X^2 14.1; d.f. 2. [2] X^2 7.5; d.f. 2. [3] X^2 12.0; d.f. 4.

APPENDIX A

APPENDIX TABLE 3. RELATION OF PARENTAL DISCIPLINE TO RATE OF JUVENILE DELINQUENCY

Type of Discipline		Percent of Boys Convicted of Crimes before the Age of Eighteen
Love-oriented	(N: 60)	13
Punitive	(N: 14)	14
Love-lax	(N: 40)	23
Lax	(N: 52)	37
Erratically punitive	(N: 84)	37

APPENDIX TABLE 4. RELATION OF INTELLIGENCE LEVELS TO RATE OF JUVENILE DELINQUENCY

Intelligence Quotient		Percent of Boys Convicted of Crimes before the Age of Eighteen
111 and over	(N: 23)	13
91 to 110	(N: 111)	32
90 to 81	(N: 59)	25
80 and below	(N: 46)	26

APPENDIX B

ORIGINS OF CRIME IN THE CONTROL GROUP

WE HAVE CONCENTRATED IN THE TEXT UPON CASUAL PATTERNS IN THE background of the 253 boys who received treatment. Summarized below are the more important relationships we found concerning causation of crime among the 253 boys in the control group. Because of sparse information, the reliability of the ratings was considerably lower than for the treatment group. Even so, approximately the same patterns emerged as those we found among the boys who received treatment.

The pattern of crime in relation to intelligence in the control group (Appendix Table 5) resembles that found in the treatment group. The children of average or dull-average intelligence more often committed crimes. The differences within the control group were, however, statistically significant (P < .02).[1]

APPENDIX TABLE 5. RELATION OF INTELLIGENCE LEVELS TO CRIME IN THE CONTROL GROUP

Intelligence Quotient			Percent of Boys Convicted of Crimes	Percent of Boys Sentenced to Penal Institutions
111 and over	(N:	17)	24	6
91 to 110	(N:	168)	34	15
90 to 81	(N:	60)	50	17
80 and below	(N:	8)	25	0

One difference in intelligence appeared between the control group and the treatment group. Only 8 boys in the control group were rated as having an intelligence score below 80. In the treatment group, 46 children were so rated. This difference may be due to the fact that the two groups received different intelligence tests. Most of the control children were tested by the Kulhman-Anderson method, while most of the treatment group were tested by the Stanford-Binet method.

There is one difference in the rate of crime between the control boys and the treatment boys which approaches significance: of those children

[1] X^2 10.6; d.f. 1.

with average intelligence, 46 percent of the treatment group committed a crime compared to only 34 percent of the control group ($P < .10$).[2]

APPENDIX TABLE 6. RELATION OF TYPE OF NEIGHBORHOOD TO CRIME IN THE CONTROL GROUP

Type of Neighborhood	Percent of Boys Convicted of Crimes	Percent of Boys Sentenced to Penal Institutions
Good (N: 47)	26	4
Fair (N: 49)	33	13
Poor (N: 32)	44	22
Worst (N: 122)	49	16

The relationship between a particular neighborhood and the rate of crime was more pronounced among the control boys (Appendix Table 6) than among the treatment boys. The difference within the control group is significant ($P < .02$).[3] Yet, holding neighborhood constant, no significant differences in rate of crime appeared between the treatment group and the control group.

APPENDIX TABLE 7. RELATION OF HOME ATMOSPHERE TO CRIME IN THE CONTROL GROUP

Home Atmosphere	Percent of Boys Convicted of Crimes	Percent of Boys Sentenced to Penal Institutions
Cohesive (N: 79)	28	10
Quarrelsome-affectionate (N: 45)	47	18
Broken (N: 62)	42	13
Quarrelsome-neglecting (N: 33)	52	31

Although we used the same definitions for each category of home atmosphere, three judges agreed in their ratings of only 70 percent of the control cases chosen as a random sample. The reliability agreement for the treatment boys was 80 percent.

For both treatment and control groups, cohesive homes had the lowest proportion of criminals and quarrelsome-neglecting homes had the highest proportion. Within the control group, these differences were not significant. Holding home atmosphere constant (Appendix Table 7), no differences appeared between the treatment and control groups in the proportions of boys from cohesive, quarrelsome but affectionate, or broken homes who committed crimes. A significantly higher proportion of treatment boys were convicted whose homes were quarrelsome-neglecting ($P < .01$).[4]

When we held constant home atmosphere and type of neighborhood

[2] X^2 3.7; d.f. 1. [3] X^2 9.4; d.f. 3. [4] X^2 6.7; d.f. 1.

(Appendix Table 8), criminal rates corresponded to those of the treatment group. The pattern also was similar to that in the treatment group. If the home was cohesive, the neighborhood made little difference. If the home was not cohesive, a poor neighborhood increased the rate of crime (P < .01).[5] This trend was not statistically significant within the treatment group. If the neighborhood was good, the home made little difference. If the neighborhood was poor, a non-cohesive family significantly increased the rate of crime (P < .01).[6]

APPENDIX TABLE 8. RELATION OF HOME ATMOSPHERE AND TYPE OF NEIGHBORHOOD TO CRIME IN THE CONTROL GROUP

	PERCENT OF BOYS CONVICTED OF CRIMES	
Home Atmosphere	Good-Fair Neighborhood	Poor-Worst Neighborhood
Cohesive	(N: 38) 21	(N: 41) 34
Non-cohesive	(N: 50) 36	(N: 90) 48

A comparison of treatment and control groups, holding constant both neighborhood and home atmosphere, revealed no significant differences in the proportions of boys who became criminal.

When we considered the relation of father's personality to crime in the control group (Appendix Table 9), we maintained only the broadest distinctions between the fathers because of the slight amount of information available. Even when the fathers were rated in just three categories (loving, neglecting or cruel, and absent), three raters agreed on only 70 percent of cases. We believe that the unrealiability of judgments is at least largely responsible for the absence of significant differences. Nevertheless, the pattern is similar to that found among the treatment

APPENDIX TABLE 9. RELATION OF FATHER'S PERSONALITY TO CRIME IN THE CONTROL GROUP

Father		Percent of Boys Convicted of Crimes	Percent of Boys Sentenced to Penal Institutions
Loving	(N: 110)	35	11
Neglecting or cruel	(N: 47)	40	17
Absent	(N: 57)	42	16

boys. From the treatment group, divided into these same categories, significant differences did emerge (Appendix Table 10). A comparison of treatment and control groups, holding the father's personality constant, revealed no significant differences in the proportions of boys who became criminal.

[5] X^2 6.8; d.f. 1.   [6] X^2 7.0; d.f. 1.

APPENDIX TABLE 10. RELATION OF FATHER'S PERSONALITY TO CRIME IN THE TREATMENT GROUP

Father		Percent of Boys Convicted of Crimes	Percent of Boys Sentenced to Penal Institutions
Loving (warm or passive)	(N: 132)	33	6
Neglecting or cruel	(N: 68)	54	28
Absent	(N: 45)	47	9

We next examined the relation of mother's personality to crime in the control group (Appendix Table 11). As in the case of the fathers' personalities, the nature of the records prevented any distinctions but the broadest ones. Even when the control group mothers were divided into three large categories (loving, non-loving, and absent), three judges agreed on only 65 percent of the ratings. Nevertheless, a generally similar pattern to that of the treatment group emerged. Within the control group, there were no significant differences based on mother's personality in the proportions which became criminal or in the proportions sentenced to penal institutions. There were also no significant differences in rates of crime between the treatment and the control boys in any of the three maternal categories.

APPENDIX TABLE 11. RELATION OF MOTHER'S PERSONALITY TO CRIME IN THE CONTROL GROUP

Mother		Percent of Boys Convicted of Crimes	Percent of Boys Sentenced to Penal Institutions
Loving	(N: 182)	35	10
Absent	(N: 33)	34	11
Non-loving	(N: 29)	55	28

We wanted to discover the extent of joint parental influence on crime rates in the control group. Despite the low reliability in ratings of parental personality, we computed the rate of crime in families categorized as having two loving, one loving, and no loving parents (Appendix Table 12). In the control group as well as in the treatment group, a significantly higher proportion of children raised by two non-loving parents than children raised by two loving parents became

APPENDIX TABLE 12. RELATION OF PARENTAL AFFECTION TO CRIME IN THE CONTROL GROUP

Mother	PERCENT OF BOYS CONVICTED OF CRIMES	
	Loving Father	Non-loving Father
Loving	(N: 92) 32	(N: 62) 35
Non-loving	(N: 21) 57	(N: 40) 53

ORIGINS OF CRIME IN CONTROL GROUP

criminal (P < .005).[7] In families with loving fathers, a significantly lower proportion became criminal if the mother was loving (P < .05).[8] In the treatment group, we found no significant differences between these two groups. In families with non-loving mothers, the father's attitude apparently made no difference. Within the treatment group, however, we found that, under these circumstances, the father's attitude made a critical difference. In families with non-loving fathers, there was no statistically significant difference between the group with loving mothers and the group with non-loving mothers.

APPENDIX TABLE 13. RELATION OF FATHER'S ROLE MODEL TO CRIME IN THE CONTROL GROUP

Father's Role Model		Percent of Boys Convicted of Crimes
Criminal	(N: 36)	53
Alcoholic or sexually unfaithful	(N: 48)	45
Non-deviant	(N: 148)	25

When we examined the relation of parental role models to crime rates, we found that the role model of the father was significantly related to criminality among boys in the control group (P < .01)[9] (Appendix Table 13). The role model of the mother followed the same pattern, but did not reach a statistically significant level (Appendix Table 14).

APPENDIX TABLE 14. RELATION OF MOTHER'S ROLE MODEL TO CRIME IN THE CONTROL GROUP

Mother's Role Model		Percent of Boys Convicted of Crimes
Criminal	(N: 13)	57
Sexually unfaithful or alcoholic	(N: 13)	45
Non-deviant	(N: 185)	30

[7] X^2 10.5; d.f. 1.   [8] X^2 4.8; d.f. 1.   [9] X^2 13.1; d.f. 2.

WORKS CITED

Abrahamsen, David. "Study of 102 Sex Offenders at Sing Sing," *Federal Probation*, Vol. 14, No. 3 (September, 1950).
Adorno, T. W., and others. *The Authoritarian Personality*. New York, Harper, 1950.
Allport, Gordon. *Becoming*. New Haven, Yale University Press, 1955.
Breckinridge, Sophonisba S., and Edith Abbott. *The Delinquent Child and the Home*. New York, Russell Sage Foundation, 1912.
Bromberg, Walter. *Crime and the Mind*. Philadelphia, Lippincott, 1948.
Burt, Cyril. *The Young Delinquent*. New York, Appleton-Century-Crofts, 1925.
Cohen, Albert K. *Delinquent Boys*. Glencoe, Ill., Free Press, 1955.
Dawson, C. E., "A Study in Youthful Degeneracy," *Pedagogical Seminary* (December, 1896).
Evans, Jean. *Three Men*. New York, Knopf, 1954.
Glueck, Eleanor T. "Status of Glueck Prediction Studies," *Journal of Criminal Law, Criminology, and Police Science*, Vol. 47, No. 1 (May–June, 1956).
Glueck, Sheldon, and Eleanor T. Glueck. *After-Conduct of Discharged Offenders*. London and New York, Macmillan, 1944.
—— *Unraveling Juvenile Delinquency*. New York, Commonwealth Fund, 1950.
Goddard, Henry H. *Feeblemindedness*. New York, Macmillan, 1914.
Hamza, Mukhtar. "The Dynamic Forces in the Personality of Juvenile Delinquents in the Egyptian Environment," *British Journal of Psychology*, Vol. 44 (1953).
Healy, William, and Augusta Bronner. *Delinquents and Criminals*. New York, Macmillan, 1928.
Jenkins, Richard. "Motivation and Frustration in Delinquency," *American Journal of Orthopsychatry*, Vol. 27, No. 3 (July, 1957).
Karpman, Benjamin. *The Sexual Offender and His Offenses*. New York, Julian Press, 1954.
Levy, David. *Material Overprotection*. New York, Columbia University Press, 1943.
Lindner, Robert. *Rebel Without a Cause*. New York, Grune and Stratton, 1944.
Maccoby, Eleanor. "Study of Values in Cambridge, Massachusetts," *Journal of Social Issues* (in preparation).

McCord, William, and Joan McCord. *Psychopathy and Delinquency.* New York, Grune and Stratton, 1956.

Merril, Maud A. *Problems of Child Delinquency.* Boston, Houghton Mifflin, 1950.

Murchison, Carl. *Criminal Intelligence.* Spencer, Mass., Hefferman Press, 1926.

Parsons, Talcott. *Essays in Sociological Theory.* Glencoe, Ill., Free Press, 1954.

—— *The Social System.* Glencoe, Ill., Free Press, 1951.

Powers, Edwin, and Helen Witmer. *An Experiment in the Prevention of Delinquency.* New York, Columbia University Press, 1951.

Reckless, Walter. *The Crime Problem.* New York, Appleton-Century-Crofts, 1955.

Sears, Robert, Eleanor Maccoby, and Harry Levin. *Patterns of Child Rearing.* Evanston, Ill., Row Peterson, 1957.

Shaplin, Judson T. "Child Training and the Identification of Pre-Adolescent Boys with Their Parents." Unpublished Ph.D. dissertation, Harvard University, 1954.

Shaw, Clifford, and Henry McKay. "Social Factors in Juvenile Delinquency," in National Commission on Law Observance and Enforcement, *Report on the Causes of Crime,* Vol. 11. Washington, D.C., U.S. Government Printing Office, 1931.

Shideler, Ernst. "Family Disintegration and the Delinquent Boy in the United States," *Journal of the American Institute of Criminal Law and Criminology,* Vol. 8 (1918).

Slawson, John. *The Delinquent Boy.* Badger, Mass., Gorham Press, 1926.

Sutherland, Edwin H. *Principles of Criminology.* Philadelphia, Lippincott, 1947.

Taft, Donald. *Criminology.* New York, Macmillan, 1950.

Teuber, Hans Lucas, and Edwin Powers. "Evaluating Therapy in a Delinquency Prevention Program," *Psychiatric Treatment,* Vol. 21 (1955).

Thompson, Richard E. "A Validation of the Glueck Social Prediction Scale for Proneness to Delinquency," *Journal of Criminal Law, Criminology, and Police Science,* Vol. 43, No. 4 (November–December, 1952).

Thrasher, Frederick M. *The Gang.* Chicago, University of Chicago Press, 1936.

Tulchin, Simon H. *Intelligence and Crime.* Chicago, University of Chicago Press, 1939.

Weer, H. Asley. "Male and Female Broken Home Rates and Types of Delinquency," *American Sociological Review,* Vol. 5 (1940).

Weiss, H. R., and Richard Sampliner. "A Study of Adolescent Felony Violators," *Journal of Criminal Law, Criminology, and Police Science,* Vol. 34 (1944).

INDEX

Abbott, Edith, 80
Abrahamsen, David, 79, 81
Absent father: effect of, 24, 89, 90-92, 105-10, 205, 206; and property crimes, 128, 154; and crimes against persons, 134, 154; and sex crimes, 138-39, 154; and drunkenness, 143, 150, 154, 170; and traffic violations, 154
Absent mother: effect of, 24, 99, 104-10, 206; and property crimes, 128, 153, 171; and crimes against persons, 133, 153, 171; and sex crimes, 138, 153, 171; and drunkenness, 142, 153, 171; and traffic violations, 147, 153, 171
Acne, 67
Adustment, boy's, 2, 3n, 9-11, 25, 27-28, 177; *see also* Group reorientation
Adler, Alfred, 117-18, 192
Adolescence: types of crimes committed in, 22; relation of sex of counselor to success of treatment with boys in, 30-31; official criminality generally begins and ends during, 157-58, 177; *see also* Juvenile delinquency
Adult criminals, 8, 40, 163-65, 168
Affectionate relationships, 15, 95-103, 198-99; *see also* Cohesive home; Love-oriented discipline
Age: average, in group, 3; relationship between, and success of treatment, 12, 29-33, 37, 41; of boys convicted for crimes other than traffic violations, 21-23; of criminality, 157-65, 182, 193; and effect of discipline in relation to genesis of criminality, 159, 169; and parents' personality in relation to genesis of criminality, 159-60, 169-72
Agencies, *see specific types*, e.g., Family welfare agencies
Aggression, in father, 94
Aggressive behavior, 3, 25, 32-36, 38, 41; case studies of, 42-50, 56-60; and re-orientation, 180; response to treatment, 183, 186; as attempt to prove masculinity, 189-90; and cruel fathers, 192; and non-conformists, 196-98; rejection and, 199
Aichhorn, August, 181
Alcoholic father, 47, 87; and role model, 93-94, 111, 112, 119, 128, 131-32, 134, 136, 159, 164
Alcoholic mother, 102, 144, 207
Alcholics, and arrests for drunkenness, 141; *see also* Drunkenness
Allport, Gordon, cited, 15, 21, 37, 195; quoted, 8, 14, 193
Anthropologists, 62
Anxiety, among boys, 33, 38, 69, 78, 186, 197
Anxious mother, 96, 97; and property crimes, 128, 153; and crimes against persons, 133, 153; and sex crimes, 138, 153; and drunkenness, 142, 153; and traffic violations, 147, 148-49, 153; relationship between certain variables of criminality and, 171
Arson, 125
Assault, 126
Attitudes, 194, 195; *see also* Values
Authoritarian discipline, 74-75
Authority: acceptance of, 3n; attitude toward, 38, 58
Automobile, theft of, 125, 132

Baruch, Dorothy, 81
Behavior: genesis of criminal, 9; as factor in crime rate, 25; sexual deviant, 50-56; predictions of criminal, 174-76; theories of human, 186; family environment and deviant, 187; *see also specific types*, e.g., Aggressive behavior
Bender, Lauretta, 81
Bettleheim, Bruno, 181
Big Brother Association, 4

INDEX

Biological factors, 14
Birth order, and crime, 117-18
Bowlby, John, 81
Boys: importance of birth order of, 117-18, of position in family, 172; *see also* Cambridge-Somerville Youth Study
Boy Scouts, 19
Breckinridge, S. P., 80
Broken homes: effect of, 14, 17, 25, 79-86; as factor in crime rate, 25; and property crimes, 130, 156; and crimes against persons, 133, 134-35, 150, 155, 156, 168; and sex crimes, 139-40, 156; and drunkenness, 143-44, 146, 150, 152, 155, 156, 168; and traffic violations, 146, 147, 150-52, 156; and age of criminality, 162; relation to juvenile delinquency, 164-65, 168; as foundation of criminality, 165, 172; in control group, 204
Bromberg, Walter, 62, 79, 87, 125
Bronner, Augusta, 80, 124-25
Burgess, Ernst, 67
Burt, Cyril, 74, 75

Cabot, P. Sidney de Q., 3
Cabot, Richard Clarke, 1, 26, 37-38, 41, 200; death of, 3
Cambridge-Somerville Youth Study: as effort to prevent delinquency, 1-8; aims and methods of this follow-up study, 9-18; use of records of, for study of origin of crime, 62-123, for choice of particular types of crime, 124-56, for age of criminality, 157-65; implications of, for the future, 173-200
Camp, *see* Summer camps
Career, effect on reformation, 161
Car theft, 125, 132
Causation of crime, 9, 13-14, 17, 24, 62-103, 124, 150, 166-72; *see also specific causes*, e.g., Home atmosphere
Chicago, University of, research at, 67-68
Chicago Area Project, 180
Child guidance clinics, 95, 178
Children, maladjusted, 1, 2, 12; *see also specific types of maladjustment*, e.g., Aggressive behavior
Child welfare programs, 178
Chi-square 'test of significance, two-tailed, 13, 20n
Churches, 2, 31, 182; *see also* Religion
Class structure, and crime, 69-71
Clinical worker, 6

Cohen, Albert, 69, 124, 187
Cohesive homes, 25, 81-82, 83; types of discipline in, 84, 86, 162, 167, 168, 169, 193; type of neighborhood and, 85, 188; property crimes and, 129, 130, 155, 156; crimes against persons and, 135, 155, 156; sex crimes and, 139-40, 155, 156; and drunkenness, 144, 155, 156; and traffic violations, 147, 155, 156; in control group, 204, 205
Community, implications of study for, 173-86
Community services, 7, 19, 32, 33, 44, 70, 178, 182, 183
Conflict, in homes, 81-86, 179; *see also* Quarrelsome homes
Conformist behavior, 25, 33-36, 41, 183
Conformity, problem of, 194, 195-200
Conscience, 194, 195-200
Control group in Cambridge-Somerville Youth Study, 1-4, 5, 8, 11-18, 203-7; number and type of crimes in, 11, 20-27, 40; results in, 19-61
Counseling, 2, 3, 15, 16, 25-67 *passim*, 178, 181
Counselors of treatment group, 3-8 *passim*, 182-83; effect of change of, 4, 26-27, 40, 47-48, 57-59, 176-77; personality of, 12; relationship with boys, 19, 28-30, 38; sex of, 30-31, 37, 41; case study illustrations of, 41-61, 119, 121, 131-32, 136-37, 140-41, 145-46, 148-49
Court records, *see* Records, court
Crime: definitions of, 9, 18n; successful treatment of, 9; types of, 20-27, 125-27 (*see also specific types*, e.g., Crimes against property); after release from reform school, 40; origins of, 62-103; as group phenomenon, 67-68; societal influences and, 67-73; son's position in family and, 117-23; percent of sons of each type of mother convicted of each type of, 153; percent of sons of each type of father convicted of each type of, 154; percent of boys disciplined in each manner convicted of each type of, 154-55; percent of boys from each type of home convicted of each type of, 155-56; sociological explanation of, 187; origin of, in control group, 203-7; *see also specific topics*, e.g., Causation of crime
Crime rate: statistical comparison of, in control and treatment groups, 7; effect

INDEX

of treatment on, 19; relation of length of treatment to, 25-26; effect of changing counselors on, 26-27; relation of individual counselors to, 27-29; relation of counselors of predicted delinquents to, 28-29; relation of age of boy and sex of counselor to, 30-31; relation of treatment intensity to, 32; relation of treatment intensity and boy's personality to, 35; relation of treatment intensity and mother's personality to, 36-37; relation of intelligence levels to, 65-66; relation of type of neighborhood to, 67-72; relation of mother's religion to, 72-73; relation of father's religion to, 72-73; relation of parents' education to, 73; relation of parental discipline to, 73-79; relation of home atmosphere to, 79-83; relation of home atmosphere and parental discipline to, 84-85; relation of home atmosphere and type of neighborhood to, 85-86; relation of father's personality to, 88-91; relation of parental discipline and father's personality to, 91-92; relation of father's personality and role model to, 93; relation of parental discipline and father's role model to, 94; relation of mother's personality to, 95-100; relation of parental discipline and mother's personality to, 101-2; relation of mother's role model to, 102; relation of parental discipline and mother's role model to, 103; relation of parental passivity to, 106-7; relation of father's personality and maternal passivity to, 107; relation of mother's personality and paternal passivity to, 107; relation of parental affection to, 108; relation of father's and mother's personality to, 109; relation of mother's and father's personality to, 110; relation of parental discipline and role models to, 111; relation of parental role models to, 111; relation of mother's personality and father's role model to, 112; relation of father's personality and mother's role model to, 113; relation of parents' personalities and role models to, 114; relation of parental deviance and absence of love to, 115; relation of son's role in the family to, 117; relation of birth order to, 118; for juvenile delinquency, 164-65, 201-2; in control group, 203-7

Crimes, undetected, 10, 17, 166

Crimes against property, 20-27, 125-26, 127-32, 150-56 *passim*, 169, 170, 171, 185

Crimes against the person, 126, 132-37, 150, 151, 153-56, 170, 171, 175, 185-86, 197

Crimes of violence, 40, 168, 169, 192, 198

Criminal act, choice of, 124-56

Criminal father, influence of, 87, 93-94, 111-17 *passim*, 127, 133-34, 150, 159, 164, 169, 207

Criminality, 2; value of police records as measure of, 10-11; primary and secondary factors in, 15; definition of, 18n; decrease in, after adolescence, 22; physical condition and, 66-67; varieties of, 124-56; age of, 157-65; *see also* Crime

Criminal mother, 102, 207

Criminals, *see specific types of crimes committed by* (e.g., Crimes against property) *and specific types of behavior* (e.g., Aggressive behavior)

Criminal sub-culture, *see* Delinquent sub-culture

Criminology, field of, 1, 62, 69, 174

Cruel father, 89, 90-94 *passim*, 105-10 *passim;* and property crimes, 128, 154; and crimes against persons, 132, 135, 150-52 *passim*, 154, 192; and sex crimes, 138, 154; and drunkenness, 143, 154, 170; and traffic violations, 154; and age at which delinquency starts, 162; and crime in control group, 205, 206

Cruel mother, 99-100, 104-10 *passim;* and property crimes, 128, 153; and crimes against persons, 133, 153; and sex crimes, 138, 153; and drunkenness, 142, 143, 153; and traffic violations, 147, 153; relationship between certain variables of criminality and, 171; and prediction of criminality, 176

Cruelty, as evidence of aggressive behavior, 33

Culture patterns, influence of conflicting, 14, 68-73, 168

Dawson, C. E., 64
Deformities, 67

INDEX

Delinquency, *see* Crime; Deviant behavior; Juvenile delinquency; and *specific phases of*, e.g., Gangs
Delinquency prognosis, *see* Prediction of delinquency
Delinquent sub-culture, 14, 62, 69-72, 160, 167, 179, 187-88, 195, 196
Depression, effects of, 71
Desertion, 80, 82-83, 89
Deviant behavior: causes of, 62-123, 166-72; types of, 124-56; age, duration, and cessation of, 157-65
Differential association, 62, 68, 187, 190
Discipline, parental, 3*n*, 14-15, 16; relation of, to crime rate, 24, 73-79, 101-3, 129-55, 172; types of parents' personalities and, 39, 40, 63, 73-79, 92-103, 194; types of, 74-79, 184, 199-200; relation of home atmosphere and, to crime rate, 84-85; effect on reformation, 159-60; and age at which criminality starts, 163; effect of, in genesis of criminality, 169, 172; relation of, to rate of juvenile delinquency, 202; *see also specific types of parents' personalities*, e.g., Cruel father
Divorce, 80, 82-83, 89, 99
Drunkenness: number of cases of, in treatment and control groups, 20-27, 40; as choice of criminal act, 126, 127, 141-46, 150, 152, 153-56, 168, 170, 171, 176, 196-97, 198
Drunkenness, father's, 136, 145; *see also* Alcoholic father

Eczema, 140, 141
Education, relationship of parents', to son's crime, 73, 168
Educational problems, boys', 3, 38, 46, 56, 181
Embezzlement, 125
Emotional deprivation, 95; *see also* Love, withdrawal of
Emotional security, importance of, 25, 100
Endocrinologists, 67
England, research on relationship between discipline and crime in, 74
Enuresis, 67, 121
Environment, 15, 17-18, 42, 63, 67-73, 168; *see also* Home atmosphere; Neighborhood
Epilepsy, 66

Erratic punishment, 94, 101-2, 103, 111-17 *passim*, 172, 184, 202; and types of crimes committed, 150-56 *passim*; and reformation, 159-60
Ethnic maladjustment, 72; *see also* Culture patterns
Etiology of crime, *see* Causation of crime
Evans, Jean, 177
Ex-convicts, 1, 10, 158

Family: counselors and, 19, 31-32, 38; influence of, 62, 69-70, 79-86, 188; structure of, and crime, 104-23; son's position in, and crime, 117-23, 172, 190; effect of, on age of beginning of delinquent behavior, 161-63; need for intensive work with, 183-84; *see also* Home atmosphere; Parents
Family welfare agencies, 3, 4, 178
Faris, R. E. L., 68
Father: bearing of background of, on delinquent behavior of son, 72-73; and crime, 86-95; case study illustrations of types, 119, 120-23, 131-32; *see also* Parents; Personality, father's; Role model; and *specific types of*, e.g., Cruel father
Feeblemindedness, 64
Forgery, 125
Foster home care, 4, 45, 137, 141, 145, 184
Fraud, 125
Freud, Sigmund, 86, 186, 191-92
Friendship, value of, 1, 2, 3, 4, 36

Game laws, violation of, 125
Gang reorientation, 180, 181
Gangs: membership in, 14, 86, 91, 131, 163, 168, 184; values of, 67-72, 187; influence of, 70, 187-88, 196; *see also* Delinquent sub-culture
Glandular abnormalities, 67
Glueck, Sheldon and Eleanor: research on juvenile delinquency, 1, 10, 62, 69, 95-96; on relationship between delinquency and discipline, 74-75; on influence of home, 81; on backgrounds of delinquents, 87, 88; on reformation, 157-58; on prediction of criminality, 174
Goddard, H. H., 64
Group reorientation, 180, 181, 185

INDEX

Groups, influence of, in crime, 67; *see also specific types of groups*, e.g., Gangs
Guilt, feelings of, 38

Hamza, Mukhtar, 65
Harvard Laboratory of Human Development, 87, 194
Healy, William, 80, 124-25
Home atmosphere, 2, 3, 12-13, 15, 16, 188; as factor in crime, 25, 39, 63, 79-103; case illustrations of, 42-60; and property crimes, 129-32, 150, 155-56; and crimes against persons, 132-37, 150, 155-56; and sex crimes, 139-40, 150, 155-56; and drunkenness, 143-46, 150, 155-56; and traffic violations, 147-49, 150, 155-56; effect on reformation, 160; and age at which criminality starts, 162, 163; relation of, to rate of juvenile delinquency, 164; effect in genesis of criminality, 168-69; relation of, to crime in control group, 204-5; *see also* Foster home care; Parents
Homicide, 20-27, 126
Homosexuality, 53-54, 119, 126, 197
Hostility of son toward father, 56, 86, 87, 125
Husband-wife relationships, 87
Hypno-analysis, 125

Identification, 194-95
Illegal behavior, 18*n*
Illegitimacy, 126
Incarceration rate, *see* Penal institutions
Inhibitions, 198
Intelligence, boys', 2, 12, 14, 39, 40; and crime rate, 25, 63, 64-67, 202; and choice of crime, 129, 150, 155; relation of, to reformation, 160; and age at which criminality starts, 163; and causation of crime, 167; relation of, to rate of juvenile delinquency, 202; relation of, to crime in control group, 203-4
Intelligence tests, use of, 16, 39, 64, 65, 203

Jail, 23, 32, 37, 40, 178
James, William, 188
Jenkins, Richard, 79
Judge Baker Clinic, 80
Juvenile delinquency, 157-65, 168; relation of parental discipline to rate of, 202; relation of intelligence levels to rate of, 202; *see also* Crime; Deviant behavior; and *specific phases of*, e.g., Gangs

Karpman, Benjamin, 79, 87, 125
Kidnaping, 126
Kulhman-Anderson intelligence test, 203

Larceny, 125
Laxity in parental discipline, 75-79, 199-200; and crime rate, 92, 101-2, 103, 111-12; and property crimes, 129, 150, 155; and crimes against persons, 134, 150, 151, 155; and sex crimes, 139, 150, 155; and drunkenness, 143, 155; and traffic violations, 148, 155; and age at which delinquency starts, 162, 164, 202; and genesis of criminality, 169
Levy, David, 95
Lindner, Robert, 62, 79, 87, 125
Lombroso, Ceasare, 64
Love, withdrawal of, as disciplinary technique, 15, 75, 76-79, 194
Love-oriented discipline, 75-79 *passim*, 83-85, 101, 103, 111; and property crimes, 129, 154-55; and crimes against persons, 134, 154-55; and sex crimes, 139, 154-55; and drunkenness, 143, 154-55; and traffic violations, 148, 154-55; and reformation, 159-60; and prevention of criminality, 169, 170, 194; and juvenile delinquency, 202
Loving father, *see* Warm father
Loving mother, 15, 24, 34, 36-37, 95-100 *passim*, 112, 114-17 *passim*, 193, 206; and property crimes, 128, 153; and crimes against persons, 132-33, 153; and sex crimes, 138, 153; and drunkenness, 142, 153; and traffic violations, 147, 153; and likelihood of reformation, 159; and age at which delinquency starts, 161, 201; relationship between certain variables of criminality and, 171

Maccoby, Eleanor, 196
McCord, William and Joan, study of psychopathic personality, 81*n*
McKay, Henry, 68, 80, 188
Mailer, N., 68

INDEX

Maladjusted child, *see* Children, maladjusted
Malicious destruction, 125
Manslaughter, 20
Marriage, effect on reformation, 161
Masculinity, 172, 189-90
Maslow, A. H., 193
Massachusetts, 2, 11, 74-75, 166, 178
Medical aid, 3, 32, 38
Mental defectiveness, as cause of criminal behavior, 64-66
Mental disease of father, 87
Mental health, 3n
Mental health clinics, 4
Mental hospitals, 54
Merril, Maud, 74, 75
Milieu therapy, 34, 181, 185
Mother: classification of types of, 12-13, 96-103; relationship beween ethnic maladjustment and son's crime, 72n; case study illustrations of, 118-23, 130-31, 140-41, 144-46; *see also* Parents; Personality, mother's; Role model; and *specific types of*, e.g. Cruel mother
Mullins, Claude, 81
Murchison, Carl, 64

Neglected children, 17, 25, 47, 82, 198; and choice of crimes, 130, 134-35, 139-40, 147, 150-52, 155-56; and foster home care, 184; in control group, 204
Neglecting father, 89, 91-94 *passim*, 104-10 *passim*; and property crimes, 127, 128, 129, 150, 154, 176; and crimes against persons, 132, 135, 150-52 *passim*, 154; and sex crimes, 138-39, 150, 154; and drunkenness, 143, 150, 154; and traffic violations, 154; and age at which delinquency starts, 162, 163, 170; in control group, 205, 206
Neglecting mother, 96, 98-99, 100, 104-10 *passim*, 192; and crimes against property, 127, 128, 129, 150, 153; and crimes against persons, 132-33, 150, 153; and sex crimes, 138-39, 150, 153; and drunkenness, 142, 150, 153; and traffic violations, 147, 150, 153; and age at which delinquency starts, 161, 163; relationship between certain variables of criminality and, 171; and prediction of criminality, 176
Neighborhood, 2, 13; as factor in crime rate in control and treatment group, 24-25, 40; types of, 39, 70-71, 85-86;
influence upon delinquency, 63-72, 167-68, 184, 188; influence upon choice of crime, 130, 135, 150, 155; and reformation, 159-60; and age at which criminality starts, 162-63; relation of type of, to crime in the control group, 204, 205
Neurological handicaps, 66
Neurosis, 186
Neurotic mother, 96, 97, 99, 104-10 *passim;* and property crimes, 127-28, 153; and crimes against persons, 133, 153; and sex crimes, 138, 153; and drunkenness, 142, 153; and traffic violations, 147, 153; relationship between certain variables of criminality and, 171; and prediction of criminality, 176
New York Youth Board, 174-75
New York Youth Program, 180
Non-conformity, 195-98; *see also* Conformity, problem of
Non-deviant behavior: in father, 94, 104, 111-17, 128-29, 134, 159, 164, 169, 207; in mother, 102-3, 104, 111-17, 207
Non-loving father, 24, 87, 92-95 *passim*, 106-8 *passim*, 114, 201, 206; *see also* Rejection
Non-loving mother, 24, 34, 36-37, 95-110 *passim*, 161, 170, 171, 183, 201, 206; *see also* Rejection
Non-support, 125
Nye, F. Ivan, 18n

Oedipus complex, 86, 191-92
Official records, *see* Records, court
Overprotected children, 197
Overprotective mother, 95, 96, 99, 104-10 *passim*, 150-52; and property crimes, 127-28, 153; and crimes against persons, 132-33, 135, 150, 153; and sex crimes, 138, 153; and drunkenness, 142, 153; and traffic violations, 146, 147, 150, 153; and likelihood of reformation, 159; and age at which delinquency starts, 161, 201; relationship between certain variables of criminality and, 171; guidance for, 185-86

Papanek, Ernst, 181
Parents: attitude toward Cambridge-Somerville study, 3; personality of, 12-13 (*see also* Personality); influence of, 14-15, 100-3, 120-23, 172; son's re-

lation to, and crime, 38, 117-23; education of, 168; therapeutic treatment for, 183-84; relation of attitudes of, to crime in control group, 206; *see also* Discipline, parental; Father; Mother; Role model

Park, William, 67

Parole, violation of, 126

Parsons, Talcott, 189-90, 197

Passive father, 88-89, 90-92 *passim*, 93, 100, 104-10 *passim*, 113, 190, 191, 199; and property crimes, 128; and sex crimes, 138; and drunkenness, 143; and traffic violations, 154; and age at which delinquency starts, 162, 163, 170, 201

Passive mother, 98, 99, 100, 104-10 *passim*, 150-52, 192; and property crimes, 128, 153; and crimes against persons, 132, 133, 150, 153; and sex crimes, 137-38, 139, 150, 153, 186; and drunkenness, 142, 143, 153; and traffic violations, 146-47, 150, 153; and age at which delinquency starts, 161-62, 163; and prediction of criminality, 167; relationship between certain variables of criminality and, 171

Penal institutions, 11; relation of treatment intensity to percent of boys sentenced to, 32; comparison of number in control group and treatment group committed to, 40; intelligence level of boys sentenced to, 65-67; type of neighborhood in relation to number of boys sentenced to, 71; relation of parental discipline to number of boys sentenced to, 73-79; relation of home atmosphere to percent of boys sentenced to, 83; relation of father's personality to percent of boys sentenced to, 89-90; relation of mother's personality to percent of boys sentenced to, 99-100; *see also specific types of*, e.g., Jail

Permissiveness in discipline, 74-75, 181, 185

Personality, boy's, 12, 14, 16, 38, 39; effect of treatment on, 19; as factor in crime rate, 25; relationship between treatment intensity and, 33; reorganization of, 185, 192-93

—— father's, 16, 39, 189, 191-92; as factor in crime rate in control and treatment group, 24, 86-95, 104-23, 169-70, 205-6; relation of, to property crimes, 127, 128-32, 150, 151, 154, 176; and crimes against persons, 132, 135, 150-52, 154, 192; and sex crimes, 138-39, 150, 151, 154; and drunkenness, 142-43, 150, 152, 154, 170; and traffic violations, 154; and age at which criminality starts, 162, 164; and rate of juvenile delinquency, 201

—— mother's, 12-13, 16, 39, 189-90, 200; as factor in crime rate in control and treatment group, 24, 95-123 *passim*, 176, 206; relationship between treatment intensity and, 34, 36-37; case illustrations showing, 41-61 *passim*; relation of, to property crimes, 127-28, 129-32, 150, 151, 153; and crimes against persons, 132-33, 150, 151, 153; and sex crimes, 137-38, 150, 151-52, 153; and drunkenness, 142, 150, 152, 153; and traffic violations, 146-49, 150, 152, 153; effect on reformation, 159-60; and age at which delinquency starts, 161-62, 164; influence in genesis of criminality, 170-71; relation of, to rate of juvenile delinquency, 201

Physical condition of child, 2, 14, 63, 64-67, 167

Physically handicapped fathers, 87

Physical punishment, 75-79; *see also* Discipline, parental; Punitive discipline

Police, 2, 4, 5, 10, 11, 71; *see also* Records, court

Powers, Edwin: analysis of Cambridge-Somerville project with Witmer, 5-6, 7-8, 14, 22n, 176; hypothesis concerning treatment, 21; article with Teuber, 38n

Prediction of delinquency, 2-3; accuracy of, 15, 27-29, 185; relation of age at start of treatment of boys predicted on borderline of, to crime rate, 29-30

Preference table, 39n

Prevention of delinquency, 1-8, 10, 200; relationship of causation and, 13-14; supportive counseling and, 39-40; and cure of criminality, 173-186 *passim*

Prison, 8; age of criminals in, 22; sentences, 23, 32, 40, 178; *see also* Penal institutions

Probation, violation of, 126

Probation officers, 4, 11, 126

Prognosis, *see* Prediction of delinquency

Property crimes, *see* Crimes against property

Psychiatrists, 14, 62, 63, 69, 95, 124
Psychoanalysis, 179-80, 181, 187, 191, 192-93
Psychoanalysts, 62, 79, 87, 129
Psychological theorists, 192-94
Psychologists, 14, 15, 16, 62, 63, 69, 175, 179-80
Psychology, 125, 194
Psychopaths, 81n, 198, 199
Psychotherapy, 19, 179-80, 181, 185, 186
P.T.A. program, 184
Punishment, 178, 185; see also Discipline, parental; Penal institutions; Punitive discipline
Punitive discipline, 15, 24, 75-79, 172, 184; and crime rate, 92, 101-2, 103, 111-12, 164, 169; and property crimes, 127, 129, 150, 155; and crimes against persons, 133, 134, 150, 155; and sex crimes, 139, 150, 155; and drunkenness, 143, 150, 152, 155; and traffic violations, 148, 149, 150, 155; and reformation, 160; and age at which delinquency starts, 162, 202

Quarrelsome homes, 25, 82, 83, 84, 85-86, 184, 194-95; and property crimes, 129, 130, 150, 155-56; and crimes against persons, 134-35, 150, 155-56; and sex crimes, 139-40, 150, 155-56; and drunkenness, 143-44, 150, 152, 155-56; and traffic violations, 147-49, 150, 155-56; and age at which delinquency starts, 162, 163-65 *passim;* and reformation, 167-70 *passim;* in control group, 204

Rape, 126
Reckless, Walter, 68, 190
Records, from Cambridge-Somerville Youth Study, 5, 13-14, 15-16, 17; on control group, 16, 203-7
Records, court, 5, 7, 10-11, 125, 166, 174; relationship to case records, 17, 63; and age of first conviction, 157-58; prediction of criminal behavior and results as shown in, 175
Redl, Fritz, 181
Reformation, factors in, 1, 22-24, 157-65 *passim*, 167, 169, 171, 192-93
Reform schools, 22-23, 32, 40, 178, 196; case histories of boys committed to, 54, 132, 140-41, 144-46
Rejection: of child by parents, 15, 18n, 42-43, 100, 103, 104-10 *passim*, 112-13, 170, 172, 189, 199; of parents by boys, 18n; case histories of, 42-60; and treatment, 185, 186
Religion, influence of, 3-4, 14, 42, 51, 52; relationship between parental, and crime, 72-73, 168
Repression, concept of, 191-92
Robbery, 20-27, 125, 126
Role, concept of, 188-89; father's, 86-95, 189-90; mother's, 95-103, 189-90; son's, 117-23
Role model: parental, 15, 86-117, 165, 194-95, 198, 199-200, 207; mother's, 102-3, 153; father's, 128-29, 133-34, 154, 159-60, 162, 163-64, 170
Roxbury, Massachusetts, Youth Program, 180

Sampliner, Richard, 65
School guidance programs, 178
Schools, 2, 31, 52, 58, 182; see also Educational problems
Second World War: effect on Cambridge-Somerville study, 4, 166; effect of, on counselors, 26
Self-report techniques, 10, 18n
Separation of parents, 80, 82-83, 99
Settlement houses, 178
Sex crimes: number of, in treatment and control groups, 20-27, 40; choice of, 126, 137-41, 150-56 *passim*, 169; cause of, 171, 191-92, 197, 198; and prediction, 175; treatment of, 186
Sex deviants, case history of, 50-56; see also Homosexuality
Sex problems of boys, 38
Sexually unfaithful father, 93, 94, 111, 112, 164, 207; and choice of criminal act, 128-29, 134
Sexually unfaithful mother, 102, 144, 207
Shaplin, Judson, 87-88
Shaw, Clifford, 67-68, 80, 187, 188
Sheen, Fulton, 74
Shideler, Ernst, 79-80
Slawson, John, 80
Slum areas, relationship of crime to, 67-69, 70, 172; family disorganization in, 85; see also Neighborhood
Social agencies, 2, 4, 32
Social disorganization, criminality and, 67-73, 85, 188, 190
Social factor, 167; see also specific factor, e.g., Neighborhood
Social living, elements of, 1

INDEX

Social policy, 8, 62
Social psychologists, 194, 195
Social psychology, 187
Social roles, 22; *see also* Role
Social science, implications of research on delinquency for, 8, 62-64, 69-70, 186-200
Social welfare assistance, 3, 32, 178
Social work agencies, 13-14, 15, 16, 60-61, 63
Social workers, 2, 19, 175, 178, 180
Societal influences, and delinquency, 67-73
Sociologists, 10; research in causation of crime, 62, 67-69, 71, 79-80, 125, 180, 187-91
Sodomy, 126
Somerville, *see* Cambridge-Somerville Youth Study
Sons, *see* Boys; Father; Mother
Spock, Benjamin, 74
Stanford-Binet intelligence tests, 39, 65, 203
Stanford University, research at, 74
Status anxiety, 69
Sub-culture, *see* Delinquent sub-culture
Sullivan, Harry Stack, 193
Summer camps, 3, 32, 53, 131
Sutherland, Edwin, 62, 68, 187

Taft, Donald, 190
Teuber, Hans Lucas, 38n
Thompson, Richard, 174
Thrasher, Frederick, 67-68
Traffic violations, 20; number of, in treatment and control groups, 20-27, 197; as choice of crime, 126, 146-69, 150-56 *passim*; relationship of, to mother's personality, 171; treatment for, 186
Treatment: method used in, 12, 16, 176-77; duration of, 12, 25-26, 40, 176, 183; evaluation of effects of, 14, 19-37, 40, 183-85; intensity of, 31-61; case study illustrations of, 41-61

Treatment group in Cambridge-Somerville Youth Study, 1-4, 5, 11-18; factors in selection, 1-4; methods used with, 3-5, 12, 16, 176-77; subjective evaluation by the boys in, 5-6; number of crimes committed by members of, 11; results in, 14, 19-61, 183-85; records on, 16; number and type of crimes in, 20-27; effectiveness in prevention, 176-86; juvenile delinquency in, 201-2
Trespassing, 125
Truancy, 126
Tulchin, Simon, 64-65

Understanding, as factor in crime prevention, 1
Undisciplined children, 24; *see also* Neglected children
Urban areas, 62, 188; *see also* Neighborhood; Slum areas

Vagrancy, 125
Values: of delinquent sub-culture, 62, 67-72, 187, 195; of family, 72-73, 85, 92-95, 190, 194; and crime prevention, 179-81 *passim*, 187, 194-200 *passim*

Warm father, 88, 89-92 *passim*, 104, 105, 107, 113, 169-70, 199; and property crimes, 128; and sex crimes, 138; and drunkenness, 143; and traffic violations, 154; and age at which delinquency starts, 162, 164, 201; in control group, 205, 206
Weer, Ashley, 80
Weiss, H. R., 65
Wilcox, Annie, 81
Wiltwyck School, 32-33, 34, 181, 183
Withdrawn children, 25, 32-36, 40, 41, 50-56, 183, 185
Witmer, Helen, analysis of Cambridge-Somerville project with Powers, 5, 6-7, 9, 12, 14, 22n, 25, 27, 176, 177

Y.M.C.A., 3, 19

PATTERSON SMITH REPRINT SERIES IN CRIMINOLOGY, LAW ENFORCEMENT, AND SOCIAL PROBLEMS

1. *Lewis: *The Development of American Prisons and Prison Customs, 1776–1845*
2. Carpenter: *Reformatory Prison Discipline*
3. Brace: *The Dangerous Classes of New York*
4. *Dix: *Remarks on Prisons and Prison Discipline in the United States*
5. Bruce et al.: *The Workings of the Indeterminate-Sentence Law and the Parole System in Illinois*
6. *Wickersham Commission: *Complete Reports, Including the Mooney-Billings Report.* 14 vols.
7. Livingston: *Complete Works on Criminal Jurisprudence.* 2 vols.
8. Cleveland Foundation: *Criminal Justice in Cleveland*
9. Illinois Association for Criminal Justice: *The Illinois Crime Survey*
10. Missouri Association for Criminal Justice: *The Missouri Crime Survey*
11. Aschaffenburg: *Crime and Its Repression*
12. Garofalo: *Criminology*
13. Gross: *Criminal Psychology*
14. Lombroso: *Crime, Its Causes and Remedies*
15. Saleilles: *The Individualization of Punishment*
16. Tarde: *Penal Philosophy*
17. McKelvey: *American Prisons*
18. Sanders: *Negro Child Welfare in North Carolina*
19. Pike: *A History of Crime in England.* 2 vols.
20. Herring: *Welfare Work in Mill Villages*
21. Barnes: *The Evolution of Penology in Pennsylvania*
22. Puckett: *Folk Beliefs of the Southern Negro*
23. Fernald et al.: *A Study of Women Delinquents in New York State*
24. Wines: *The State of Prisons and of Child-Saving Institutions*
25. *Raper: *The Tragedy of Lynching*
26. Thomas: *The Unadjusted Girl*
27. Jorns: *The Quakers as Pioneers in Social Work*
28. Owings: *Women Police*
29. Woolston: *Prostitution in the United States*
30. Flexner: *Prostitution in Europe*
31. Kelso: *The History of Public Poor Relief in Massachusetts, 1820–1920*
32. Spivak: *Georgia Nigger*
33. Earle: *Curious Punishments of Bygone Days*
34. Bonger: *Race and Crime*
35. Fishman: *Crucibles of Crime*
36. Brearley: *Homicide in the United States*
37. *Graper: *American Police Administration*
38. Hichborn: *"The System"*
39. Steiner & Brown: *The North Carolina Chain Gang*
40. Cherrington: *The Evolution of Prohibition in the United States of America*
41. Colquhoun: *A Treatise on the Commerce and Police of the River Thames*
42. Colquhoun: *A Treatise on the Police of the Metropolis*
43. Abrahamsen: *Crime and the Human Mind*
44. Schneider: *The History of Public Welfare in New York State, 1609–1866*
45. Schneider & Deutsch: *The History of Public Welfare in New York State, 1867–1940*
46. Crapsey: *The Nether Side of New York*
47. Young: *Social Treatment in Probation and Delinquency*
48. Quinn: *Gambling and Gambling Devices*
49. McCord & McCord: *Origins of Crime*
50. Worthington & Topping: *Specialized Courts Dealing with Sex Delinquency*
51. Asbury: *Sucker's Progress*
52. Kneeland: *Commercialized Prostitution in New York City*
53. *Fosdick: *American Police Systems*
54. *Fosdick: *European Police Systems*
55. *Shay: *Judge Lynch: His First Hundred Years*
56. Barnes: *The Repression of Crime*
57. †Cable: *The Silent South*
58. Kammerer: *The Unmarried Mother*
59. Doshay: *The Boy Sex Offender and His Later Career*
60. Spaulding: *An Experimental Study of Psychopathic Delinquent Women*
61. Brockway: *Fifty Years of Prison Service*
62. Lawes: *Man's Judgment of Death*
63. Healy & Healy: *Pathological Lying, Accusation, and Swindling*
64. Smith: *The State Police*
65. Adams: *Interracial Marriage in Hawaii*
66. *Halpern: *A Decade of Probation*
67. Tappan: *Delinquent Girls in Court*
68. Alexander & Healy: *Roots of Crime*
69. *Healy & Bronner: *Delinquents and Criminals*
70. Cutler: *Lynch-Law*
71. Gillin: *Taming the Criminal*

* new material added † new edition, revised or enlarged

PATTERSON SMITH REPRINT SERIES IN CRIMINOLOGY, LAW ENFORCEMENT, AND SOCIAL PROBLEMS

72. Osborne: *Within Prison Walls*
73. Ashton: *The History of Gambling in England*
74. Whitlock: *On the Enforcement of Law in Cities*
75. Goldberg: *Child Offenders*
76. *Cressey: *The Taxi-Dance Hall*
77. Riis: *The Battle with the Slum*
78. Larson: *Lying and Its Detection*
79. Comstock: *Frauds Exposed*
80. Carpenter: *Our Convicts.* 2 vols. in one
81. †Horn: *Invisible Empire: The Story of the Ku Klux Klan, 1866–1871*
82. Faris et al.: *Intelligent Philanthropy*
83. Robinson: *History and Organization of Criminal Statistics in the U. S.*
84. Reckless: *Vice in Chicago*
85. Healy: *The Individual Delinquent*
86. *Bogen: *Jewish Philanthropy*
87. *Clinard: *The Black Market: A Study of White Collar Crime*
88. Healy: *Mental Conflicts and Misconduct*
89. Citizens' Police Committee: *Chicago Police Problems*
90. *Clay: *The Prison Chaplain*
91. *Peirce: *A Half Century with Juvenile Delinquents*
92. *Richmond: *Friendly Visiting Among the Poor*
93. Brasol: *Elements of Crime*
94. Strong: *Public Welfare Administration in Canada*
95. Beard: *Juvenile Probation*
96. Steinmetz: *The Gaming Table.* 2 vols.
97. *Crawford: *Report on the Penitentiaries of the United States*
98. *Kuhlman: *A Guide to Material on Crime and Criminal Justice*
99. Culver: *Bibliography of Crime and Criminal Justice, 1927–1931*
100. Culver: *Bibliography of Crime and Criminal Justice, 1932–1937*
101. Tompkins: *Administration of Criminal Justice, 1938–1948*
102. Tompkins: *Administration of Criminal Justice, 1949–1956*
103. Cumming: *Bibliography Dealing with Crime and Cognate Subjects*
104. *Addams et al.: *Philanthropy and Social Progress*
105. *Powell: *The American Siberia*
106. *Carpenter: *Reformatory Schools*
107. *Carpenter: *Juvenile Delinquents*
108. *Montague: *Sixty Years in Waifdom*
109. *Mannheim: *Juvenile Delinquency in an English Middletown*
110. Semmes: *Crime and Punishment in Early Maryland*
111. *National Conference of Charities & Correction: *History of Child Saving in the United States*
112. †Barnes: *The Story of Punishment*
113. Phillipson: *Three Criminal Law Reformers*
114. *Drähms: *The Criminal*
115. *Terry & Pellens: *The Opium Problem*
116. *Ewing: *The Morality of Punishment*
117. †Mannheim: *Group Problems in Crime and Punishment*
118. *Michael & Adler: *Crime, Law and Social Science*
119. *Lee: *A History of Police in England*
120. †Schafer: *Compensation and Restitution to Victims of Crime*
121. †Mannheim: *Pioneers in Criminology*
122. Goebel & Naughton: *Law Enforcement in Colonial New York*
123. *Savage: *Police Records and Recollections*
124. Ives: *A History of Penal Methods*
125. *Bernard (ed.): *Americanization Studies.* 10 vols.:
    Thompson: *Schooling of the Immigrant*
    Daniels: *America via the Neighborhood*
    Thomas: *Old World Traits Transplanted*
    Speek: *A Stake in the Land*
    Davis: *Immigrant Health and the Community*
    Breckinridge: *New Homes for Old*
    Park: *The Immigrant Press and Its Control*
    Gavit: *Americans by Choice*
    Claghorn: *The Immigrant's Day in Court*
    Leiserson: *Adjusting Immigrant and Industry*
126. *Dai: *Opium Addiction in Chicago*
127. *Costello: *Our Police Protectors*
128. *Wade: *A Treatise on the Police and Crimes of the Metropolis*
129. *Robison: *Can Delinquency Be Measured?*
130. *Augustus: *John Augustus, First Probation Officer*
131. *Vollmer: *The Police and Modern Society*
132. Jessel & Horr: *Bibliographies of Works on Playing Cards and Gaming*
133. *Walling: *Recollections of a New York Chief of Police;* & Kaufmann: *Supplement on the Denver Police*
134. *Lombroso-Ferrero: *Criminal Man*

* new material added   † new edition, revised or enlarged

PATTERSON SMITH REPRINT SERIES IN CRIMINOLOGY, LAW ENFORCEMENT, AND SOCIAL PROBLEMS

135. *Howard: *Prisons and Lazarettos.* 2 vols.:
     The State of the Prisons in England and Wales
     An Account of the Principal Lazarettos in Europe
136. *Fitzgerald: *Chronicles of Bow Street Police-Office.* 2 vols. in one
137. *Goring: *The English Convict*
138. Ribton-Turner: *A History of Vagrants and Vagrancy*
139. *Smith: *Justice and the Poor*
140. *Willard: *Tramping with Tramps*
141. *Fuld: *Police Administration*
142. *Booth: *In Darkest England and the Way Out*
143. *Darrow: *Crime, Its Cause and Treatment*
144. *Henderson (ed.): *Correction and Prevention.* 4 vols.:
     Henderson (ed.): *Prison Reform;* & Smith: *Criminal Law in the U. S.*
     Henderson (ed.): *Penal and Reformatory Institutions*
     Henderson: *Preventive Agencies and Methods*
     Hart: *Preventive Treatment of Neglected Children*
145. *Carpenter: *The Life and Work of Mary Carpenter*
146. *Proal: *Political Crime*
147. *von Hentig: *Punishment*
148. *Darrow: *Resist Not Evil*
149. Grünhut: *Penal Reform*
150. *Guthrie: *Seed-Time and Harvest of Ragged Schools*
151. *Sprogle: *The Philadelphia Police*
152. †Blumer & Hauser: *Movies, Delinquency, and Crime*
153. *Calvert: *Capital Punishment in the Twentieth Century* & *The Death Penalty Enquiry*
154. *Pinkerton: *Thirty Years a Detective*
155. *Prison Discipline Society [Boston] Reports 1826–1854.* 6 vols.
156. *Woods (ed.): *The City Wilderness*
157. *Woods (ed.): *Americans in Process*
158. *Woods: *The Neighborhood in Nation-Building*
159. Powers & Witmer: *An Experiment in the Prevention of Delinquency*
160. *Andrews: *Bygone Punishments*
161. *Debs: *Walls and Bars*
162. *Hill: *Children of the State*
163. Stewart: *The Philanthropic Work of Josephine Shaw Lowell*
164. *Flinn: *History of the Chicago Police*
165. *Constabulary Force Commissioners: *First Report*
166. *Eldridge & Watts: *Our Rival the Rascal*
167. *Oppenheimer: *The Rationale of Punishment*
168. *Fenner: *Raising the Veil*
169. *Hill: *Suggestions for the Repression of Crime*
170. *Bleackley: *The Hangmen of England*
171. *Altgeld: *Complete Works*
172. *Watson: *The Charity Organization Movement in the United States*
173. *Woods et al.: *The Poor in Great Cities*
174. *Sampson: *Rationale of Crime*
175. *Folsom: *Our Police [Baltimore]*
176. Schmidt: *A Hangman's Diary*
177. *Osborne: *Society and Prisons*
178. *Sutton: *The New York Tombs*
179. *Morrison: *Juvenile Offenders*
180. *Parry: *The History of Torture in England*
181. Henderson: *Modern Methods of Charity*
182. Larned: *The Life and Work of William Pryor Letchworth*
183. *Coleman: *Humane Society Leaders in America*
184. *Duke: *Celebrated Criminal Cases of America*
185. *George: *The Junior Republic*
186. *Hackwood: *The Good Old Times*
187. *Fry & Cresswell: *Memoir of the Life of Elizabeth Fry.* 2 vols. in one
188. *McAdoo: *Guarding a Great City*
189. *Gray: *Prison Discipline in America*
190. *Robinson: *Should Prisoners Work?*
191. *Mayo: *Justice to All*
192. *Winter: *The New York State Reformatory in Elmira*
193. *Green: *Gambling Exposed*
194. *Woods: *Policeman and Public*
195. *Johnson: *Adventures in Social Welfare*
196. *Wines & Dwight: *Report on the Prisons and Reformatories of the United States and Canada*
197. *Salt: *The Flogging Craze*
198. *MacDonald: *Abnormal Man*
199. *Shalloo: *Private Police*
200. *Ellis: *The Criminal*

* new material added † new edition, revised or enlarged